FROM CINCINNATI TO THE COLORADO RANGER

THE HORSEMANSHIP OF ULYSSES S. GRANT

DENISE M. DOWDALL

HISTORYEYE
Dublin

Copyright © Denise M. Dowdall, 2012

Published by HISTORYEYE
94 Merrion Park ,
Blackrock,
County Dublin,
Ireland

All rights reserved, including the right to reproduce or store this book or portions thereof in any form or by any means, electronic , mechanical, photocopying, recording or otherwise ,without prior permission from the publisher.

Printed in Ireland

FIRST EDITION

ISBN 978-0-9574021-2-6

To Cliff and Lilly

Contents

Acknowledgements   *vii*

Introduction   *viii*

Chapter 1	Farmer Ralston's Colt	1
Chapter 2	Dave	9
Chapter 3	York	13
Chapter 4	Fashion and Psyche	24
Chapter 5	Nelly	30
Chapter 6	The Cicotte Mare	45
Chapter 7	Eclipse	52
Chapter 8	Tom and Bill	55
Chapter 9	Rondy	63
Chapter 10	Jack	68

Chapter 11	Kangaroo	81
Chapter 12	Charlie	89
Chapter 13	Egypt	96
Chapter 14	Son of Lexington	100
Chapter 15	Traveller and Cincinnati	107
Chapter 16	Jeff Davis	113
Chapter 17	Little Rebel	126
Chapter 18	Butcher Boy	135
Chapter 19	Dexter	149
Chapter 20	Young Hambletonian	161
Chapter 21	Logan	169
Chapter 22	Leopard and Linden Tree	177
Chapter 23	St. Julien	184
Chapter 24	Silver	193
Chapter 25	The Colorado Ranger	200
Bibliography		*206*
Index		*216*

Acknowledgements

I am indebted to the many eyewitness accounts of Grant's skill with horses and the inclusion of these references by several of his biographers. Of particular use was Grant's own correspondence, painstakingly edited by the late Professor John Y. Simon. It is through his own words that Grant's passion for horses becomes especially real. I would like to thank Cheryl Snyder for information provided about her grandfather, Mike Ruby, and the breed forever associated with his name, the Colorado Ranger . Many thanks to Lola and Mike Storck for showing me parts of St. Louis that would have been totally out of bounds without a car. A special mention of gratitude to Pam Sanfilippo, site historian with the U.S. Grant National Historic site in St Louis, and to Marc Kollbaum, curator of Jefferson Barracks. Also the kind assistance of the men and women of the Missouri Historical Society Library and the St. Louis Public Library is gratefully acknowledged.

Introduction

Ulysses Grant was the first of only three United States presidents to be granted the freedom of the city of Dublin. But he is very much the odd man out among the other two recipients, Presidents Kennedy and Clinton , belonging as he did to an earlier era and political tradition. In the winter of 1879, Grant paid a short visit to the city to acknowledge the honour in person. His spontaneous decision sent Dublin's new lord mayor, Sir John Barrington, into a panic, as he was only a few days in the job himself . Barrington recognised that the visit was likely to be the highlight of his time in office, so there followed a flurry of activity to come up with a fittingly "grave" and "dignified" itinerary. In the space of a dreary morning and afternoon, Sir John brought Grant to a dizzying number of venues including the Stock Exchange, the Bank of Ireland, the Royal Academy, Trinity College, City Hall , the Viceroy's Lodge and the Zoological Gardens. In the evening, a banquet was held in the general's honour, during which he made what he described as "his longest speech ever" (over a thousand words). Professor Samuel Haughton of Trinity College caught something of its flavour when he said that, to paraphrase the Vicar of Wakefield, there were things in Grant's speech which he had often thought of but had never heard said before. [1]

During his visit to Trinity College earlier in the day, Grant had been invited to view the Ninth Century *Book of Kells*. The general wasn't one to feign interest in things that bored him . According to one of the professors present he spent a lot of time examining the floor, showing no more interest in the monks' illustrations than

---

[1] *The Irish Times*, Jan 4th, 1879.

in " a row of old boots in a pantry ". [2] The Lord Mayor might have saved himself a good deal of bother if he had simply brought Grant to the many stud farms on the outskirts of the city, where he could have viewed the fine thoroughbreds for which the area was renowned. Had he done so, it is almost certain those famous eyes would have lit up under the grey January sky.

Because horses were always Grant's passion. Virtually his whole life story could be told through their eyes. They were his outstanding interest in childhood and arguably his sole source of glory as a cadet at West Point. In the saddle, Grant was very nearly dashing. It was about the only place where he didn't slouch. Wisely he courted the love of his life, Julia Boggs Dent, on horseback. During the Mexican War, perhaps his chief act of bravery was a daring ride to secure ammunition for his regiment. Like many good horsemen, Grant depended on a horse for a living at one time, and the brief periods when he was without one seemed to coincide with the low points in his life. A devoted family man, he took pains to nurture a love of horses in his children, but with mixed results. As he spent virtually the entire Civil War in the saddle, his horsemanship became inseparable from his effectiveness in the field. Horsemanship made him into a man of action : a commander who went forward when other generals might theorise or dither. He lived a charmed life on the battle ground, emerging from all his many campaigns virtually without a scratch. If anything his love of fast horses was his downfall in terms of physical injury. It was a risk he obviously considered worth taking. And anyone who rode with Grant usually did so at their peril.

In a way horses are the key to understanding this enigmatic figure since they were such an integral part of his culture and character. Loyal to a fault to comrades and friends, he was no less inclined to stick by his horses long after they had ceased to be useful . Like the horses he rode, he was also just a little mysterious, with many qualities and talents that defied easy definition: "A mystery, even to himself", said his staunch war-time ally, William Tecumseh Sherman. [3] And like them also he was largely unconscious of his powers. Grant's passion for horses helped to illustrate some of the complexities of his character, showing how he had a unique way of living with contradictions. Here was a man who could hardly bear to go horse racing because he thought it cruel. Yet his enthusiasm for the role of the cavalry during the Civil War consigned thousands of horses to certain injury, neglect and death.

---

[2] *New York Times*, Jan 26th, 1879.

[3] John Y. Simon ed., *General Grant by Matthew Arnold with a rejoinder by Mark Twain*. Page IX. Preface to 2nd Edition. Kent State Univ. Press, 1995.

Today it is doubtful whether anyone first thinks of Ulysses Grant as a gifted horseman whose ideas about handling horses predated today's well- known horse whisperers by over a century. But in his day he appeared to enjoy great fame as a rider. Scores of equestrian books published in the Nineteenth Century were dedicated to him. During the war, the northern public queued up to donate horses to him. After it, pamphlets and lithographs celebrated his most obscure boyhood accomplishments. In the years after Appomattox , the public had an insatiable appetite for these seemingly trivial details. It was as if people wanted to divine the seeds of greatness in his early equestrian feats.

After the war , Grant found an outlet for his energies in the driving of fast trotters. It became his favourite recreation . He was a man in love with speed and, given the times he lived in, horses were the means of conducting that love affair. Appropriately the pinnacle of Grant's fame and fortune coincided with the golden age of the trotter. He took the opportunity to drive many of the most celebrated of his era - horses that were household names. Virtually all his horses were connected to the greatest trio of Nineteenth-Century stallions foaled in the United States - "Lexington ", "Rysdyk's Hambletonian" and "Ethan Allen". Grant took a boyish delight in the pedigree of his bloodstock and the increasingly handsome price tags associated with it. Yet during his presidency his innocent weakness for horseflesh sometimes left him vulnerable to less than innocent forms of patronage, not to mention criticism from the press. Whoever shared his equestrian passions had a peculiar hold on him. It could be a short cut to his affections. Many of Grant's friends in later life - a curious mix of the great and the greedy - also enjoyed the thrill and exhilaration of the trotting culture. It went a good way toward forging many an unlikely alliance.

In times of extreme pressure during the Civil War, Grant sought refuge in the notion of being free some day to retire to a farm and train young colts. His cherished aim seemed to have been the production of fast, quality carriage horses of his own pedigree: something that would leave a lasting impression on the American horse. After the war, he planned to spend several months a year at the farm in this very pursuit. [4] In the late 1860's and early 1870's,Grant did undertake a surprisingly intensive horse breeding programme, both at the White House grounds and at his farm near St. Louis. But with no let up in his executive duties, he pursued his dream from a distance. The tone of his letters in this period often betrayed his frustration at

---

[4] John Y. Simon, ed., Letter to Charles Ford, March 24th 1867, *Papers of U.S. Grant,* Vol. 17. Southern Illinois Univ. Press.

having to postpone visits to the farm again and again. Characteristically he trusted the people he hired to oversee his agricultural interests a little too much. The enterprise was neither profitable nor professional, draining his limited resources relentlessly.

Horses taught Grant much about the world. He would use his simple observations of them to illustrate his views on wider matters. Hence, the various Federal armies at the beginning of the war moved "like horses in a balky team, no two ever pulling together."[5] Of the highly strung General Sherman, Grant made the hilarious observation: "I always find it the best way to turn Sherman out like a young colt, and let him kick up his heels. I have great confidence that he will come in all right in due time."[6] He was also wise enough to realise that some of his generals, like some of his horses, went better on a loose rein.

Through the years, many individuals featured in Grant's story because of a common equestrian passion. The Sultan of Turkey. The wealthy elite of the "Gilded Age". The most dedicated horse breeder of the east coast who lost everything to a man he trusted. One of the greatest horsemen of Colorado who faced the challenges of the dust bowl era, and triumphed over adversity. This book attempts to bring many of these strands together. It also touches on the role that Grant's favourite wing of the army, the cavalry, played in the War between the States, and how he deployed the mounted regiments to carry out his major plans. Most decision makers of the War dismissed the role of the cavalry, believing it had had its day. Grant didn't share this view. When Ulysses was a young cadet at West Point, the height of his ambition was to be an officer of cavalry, since he reasoned that his fondness for horses would make him particularly comfortable in the job.[7] This simple ambition was never realised. Yet he clung to it tenaciously, even when he had attained the heights of Lieutenant General with an army of over half a million men under his command.

Perhaps Grant's affinity for these animals from an early age helped to develop those traits which made his name. The first principle of horsemanship - to always go forward - seems also to have been the golden rule of his generalship. The qualities needed in a good horseman would have proved invaluable in a military career of Grant's calibre and were much in evidence throughout his campaigns.

---

[5] Horace Porter, *Campaigning with Grant*. Page 241. Nebraska University Press.

[6] Albert D. Richardson, *Personal History of Ulysses S. Grant*. Page 451. American Publishing Co. 1868.

[7] Ulysses S. Grant, *The Memoirs of Ulysses S. Grant*. Page 249. Penguin Classics. 1999.

Swift reaction to a shifting situation. The ability to get inside the mind of another being with a dramatically different perception of the world. Above all his experiences as a young teamster, driving his father's horses great distances through the Ohio countryside, tested those reserves of independence, bravery and knowledge of topography that made him unique from a young age.

Today, while virtually every trace of Grant's time in St Louis has been obliterated by a parking lot or a tall building, it is the places associated with his rural world that survive - White Haven, Hardscrabble , above all the barn that housed his mares and foals - now the focus for modern day tourists. Horses continue to be bred on the Gravois pastures : the deliberate-moving Clydesdale now instead of the fleet, highly strung roadsters that fascinated Grant .

Though a taciturn man, Grant liked nothing better than "talking horse". For him it was the ultimate ice breaker in company, for friend and foe alike. Ferdinand Ward, the man responsible for Grant's financial shipwreck in the 1880s, noted that the general never tired of discussing horses, even with people of "low station", while at the same time he could show a stony reserve to visiting dignitaries. Luckily, Grant didn't just speak about his horses . He also wrote about them. In letters to close friends, penned from the Executive Mansion, Grant's "horse talk" sits along side his thoughts on affairs of state. There were many facets to Grant's equestrianism. The sheer numbers of horses that he owned or rode - particularly during and after the war - told a surprisingly rich tale. Indeed by the end of his eventful life, Grant had either owned, ridden or driven well over a hundred horses, and one of the most interesting collections at that.

When that other leading passion in Grant's life - travel - lead to the arrival of two fine eastern stallions of his choosing on the shores of America in 1879, a lasting equestrian legacy unfolded. The emergence of the Colorado Ranger breed in the Twentieth Century was a fitting post-script to his equestrian interests, which no doubt he would have relished.

Chapter 1

Farmer Ralston's Colt

Appropriately, the future general who liked nothing better than using "blinds" to deceive the enemy, was named after the Greek warrior who fooled the Trojans with a wooden horse. The choice of name had been his maternal grandmother's, a well read woman with a romantic turn of mind, who was Grant's favourite relation. She had been given a loan of Fenelon's *Telemachus* by Grant's father, Jesse, an avid self-taught reader who considered the saga of the Greek general a particular favourite. The child was eventually christened Hiram Ulysses out of consideration for his grandfather, who favoured the name Hiram.[8] But he was always known as Ulysses, or Lyss for short - an unusual name in the district.

Grant's father was a self-made man - industrious, driven and thrifty. Hard work had made him prosperous . He had married Hannah Simpson - a pious and withdrawn Pennsylvanian whose ancestors had farmed the red marshy ground on the hilly fields of Ulster's South Tyrone since the early Seventeenth Century. The couple set up a

---

[8] Lloyd Lewis, *Captain Sam Grant*. page 17. Little, Brown and Co.

home and a tannery business on the Ohio frontier, and Ulysses was the first of six children, coming into the world on April 27th 1822.

Horses were indispensable to Jesse's tannery business. They pulled the wagons that constantly went back and forth to Cincinnati. Piled high on the wagons were the grisly buffalo hides that came from there to Jesse's yard in Georgetown . They made the return journey three years later as vast rolls of leather. Around Jesse's place every available fence and gate was draped with pungent-smelling skins as they dried slowly in the sun.[9]

Ulysses' first public encounter with a horse was a happy one. And it was all thanks to the circus. The youngster was only two years of age when the travelling troupe paid a visit to Georgetown . Ulysses asked his parents if he could sit on the back of a pony for a few circuits of the ring. For the first time in his life the unusually placid child shrieked with delight and didn't want to get off. It was a lucky discovery of an unusual affinity . It was also to be the first of many triumphant encounters with circus horses.[10]

His gift seems to have been recognised early. Though he had little time for dogs, Ulysses enjoyed being in the company of horses to a rare degree. Even as a toddler he was able to weave in and out of the legs of customers' teams at his father's yard, occasionally swinging out of their tails. It was from these lengthy encounters, often with unfamiliar horses, that he developed an instinctive understanding of their ways. The sight was known to cause consternation among onlookers. But his unflappable mother thought otherwise . " Horses seem to understand Ulysses", was her typically laconic response. How was Ulysses able to get away with it ? Perhaps the answer lies in the fact that he was unusually still from an early age. There is an anecdote told about when he was a toddler and someone let a gun fire off just at his head. He never flinched. Grant was showing signs of a peculiar nervous system where he could stand in the midst of exploding shells or horses' hooves without blinking, yet the sound of music was an unbearable ordeal to his ears.

Ulysses was a robust and healthy child, apart from suffering intermittently from the scourge of the frontier - malaria and its accompanying ague. He was a busy child too , even by the standards of the day , working long hours both before and after school. By the tender age of five or six he was helping to ride the tannery work

---

[9] *Ohio Arch. and Hist . Society* Publications. Vol. 31. page 242.

[10] Lloyd Lewis,*Captain Sam Grant*. page 21. Little, Brown and Co.

horses down to the river for water twice a day. Perhaps in imitation of some of the circus stunts he had seen, he taught himself to stand on the horses' backs as they trotted along, balancing himself with the reins. In time he could achieve the stunt when the animals were going at full tilt. For the beam room tannery horses, working the bark grinder in a monotonous circle, it would surely have been a refreshing experience to let rip on the way down to the river, in the company of a small, adventurous child who had no nerves.

At that time Ulysses would tease the neighbours' children about how slow and poor their ponies were compared to his father's . Tragedy struck one day when the son of Grant's nearest neighbours, the Baileys, was killed in a riding accident. He had been trying to keep up with young Grant, perhaps attempting to carry out one of his fast stunts, when his pony tripped and fell on him. The incident was the first in a recurring theme in Grant's life. Those that rode with him always did so at their peril, as his approach to equestrian pursuits was one of extreme bravery bordering on recklessness.

Aside from the tannery business, Jesse Grant held a fifty acre tract of woods not far from the village. From there fire wood and bark for the tannery was cut . Although he was still too young to do the chopping, Ulysses often drove the team of horses that hauled the wood back into the village. Such was the trust he fostered in the horses he handled that at the age of six he could hitch an untrained three year old colt to a sled without help , and haul firewood for the day. By standing on the manger of the stable, he was able to reach the higher parts of the animal's head.

Ulysses was soon a familiar figure in Georgetown , driving his wagon on the roads and over the notorious steep ridge to the west of the village that the locals dubbed "Judgement." "Judgement" routinely stalled many a teamster's wagon but never little Grant's. When asked to identify the secret of his success, his terse reply was "because I don't stall myself." [11] Jesse Grant, who was anything but terse, began to take immense pride in his eldest son's precocity, losing no time in boasting to friends on the subject. But it was much to the son's discomfort. It made him coy about his gifts, particularly since his mother , Hannah , disapproved of the smallest word of praise .

By the time he was old enough to hold a plough, Ulysses did what needed to be done at his parent's farm in addition to his school work. He loved the farm work as much as he detested helping in the tannery. And his enthusiasm naturally stemmed from the fact that he was free to work with the horses as he helped turn the

---

[11] *The Herald and Torchlight*, Wed Oct 18th 1865, page 1.

soil, sow the crops, bring in the harvest and care for the farm animals.[12] This would have included the important jobs of grooming and feeding the horses, and cleaning, polishing and repairing the tack: tasks which required considerable attention to detail. At the plough he would have learned the importance of consistent vocal commands as he followed the horses forward to make straight drills. What little leisure time he had was largely taken up with horses also. From an early age, Ulysses had been everywhere on a horse within a fifty mile radius of Georgetown, riding out to visit relations or hitching a horse for sleigh rides when the snow came. It made him the best travelled boy in the neighbourhood.[13]

Ulysses Grant would swap and trade horses like other children swapped toys and fruit . On account of his industry he was able to purchase his own horse for seventeen dollars at the age of nine. From that day on he was seldom without a pony of his own. [14]A year earlier he had acquired the famous Farmer Ralston's colt for his father , and with it the reputation as the most artlessly honest child in the village. Perhaps the story surrounding this colt illustrates Grant's character better than any other horse. Ulysses spotted a fine colt of the sought-after "Printer" stock , owned by his father's neighbour. Already a fine judge of a horse, the boy insisted that his father should buy it. Jesse wouldn't hear of it at first. But he eventually changed his mind and sent Ulysses off with the money, together with instructions on how he was to negotiate the deal. Ulysses was to offer Farmer Ralston $20 first; if he would not take that, it was to be $22; and if he would not take that, the final offer was to be $25. The first thing the young horse trader did when he arrived at the farm was to let Ralston in on the plan. "It would not require a Connecticut man to guess the price finally agreed upon. " said Grant. [15]

When word got out around the neighbourhood, the children of the village didn't let their friend forget about it for a long time. In spite of the harmlessness of the episode, it appeared to haunt him all his life, revealing a surprising sensitivity to ridicule. Years later Grant told the story against himself in his memoirs, saying how it caused him much "heart burning" . The ridicule that accompanied the transaction appeared to make him unusually sensitive to criticism about his business acumen in

---

[12] Ulysses S. Grant, *The Memoirs of Ulysses S. Grant*, pages 10-11. Penguin Classics.

[13] Ibid, pages 10-11.

[14] Albert D. Richardson, *The Personal History of U. S. Grant,* page 55. American Publishing Co. Connecticut. 1868.

[15] Ulysses S. Grant, *The Memoirs of Ulysses S. Grant*, page 13 . Penguin Classics.

particular. For ever more there appeared to be a stubborn determination on his part to prove the detractors wrong.

But there was another version of the incident , told by the White brothers in the village, which showed him in a much more clever light. According to this version, Ulysses knew the colt was worth far more than that, even more than $25. He thought he might risk losing the colt if he only offered the farmer $20, as Jesse suggested. In offering the farmer $25, Ulysses knew he would be securing the deal while still getting a bargain. His judgement was vindicated by subsequent events. When the horse went blind a few years later he was sold on for only $5 less than the original price. But there was a poignant postscript to the story . Many years later Ulysses was to experience more "heart burning" when he recognised the fine colt he once prized working the tread wheel of the ferry boat in Maysville in an endless circle.

Young Ulysses would show a unique talent for breaking in colts throughout his childhood in rural Ohio. It was the same area that produced Queen Victoria's horse trainer, the extraordinary John Rarey, who lived less than eighty miles from Jesse's door at Groveport. Jesse Grant stated that he never knew a single horse to baulk at Ulysses. Jesse too had been knowledgeable with farm horses from a surprisingly tender age and evidently had to work so hard with them that he sometimes fell asleep in the saddle. There was a story told in the Grant family of the six year old Jesse carrying home a large bag of barley on the back of his horse. During the long ride the exhausted boy nodded off and fell to the ground. When he awoke he found that the huge sack was now on the ground also, and he had no means of lifting it on the horse again. The tiny boy hatched a plan. He rolled the sack onto fallen branches and maneuvered the horse underneath so that he could lower it down onto the animal's back.

Economic demands of the time left little room for sentiment in the treatment of animals, and rough handling was the norm. Horses were a source of commerce for hard-nosed Jesse Grant. But for Ulysses they were far more. He found a majesty in their presence that never left him. He appeared to possess several traits that would have given him unrivaled supremacy in his field : a unique balance of firmness and patience in his personality, an ability to stay on the horse's back no matter what, an unswerving self-belief, and a passion for his subject amounting almost to obsession.

However he came by these skills at such a young age, it is certain that his reputation as a horseman among the local farmers and townspeople was well established by the tender age of eight or nine. Indeed many of the local farmers would take their troublesome colts to young Ulysses to be broken to harness or saddle. His encounters with these animals were often a crowd puller in the town square, just five minutes from Grant's house . He would seldom disappoint the spectators. Yet he couldn't be induced to train a horse for money, unlike John Rarey who was willing to cash in on his gift from the age of twelve and even advertised in the local newspapers.

At that time there was a particular incident in his life which soured his willingness to train other people's horses, and revealed a deep-seated distaste for trickery. A neighbouring farmer arrived at Jesse Grant's door with a young horse, and asked if his son would deliver a letter for him some twenty miles away. Ulysses agreed and prepared to set off on the farmer's horse . Just then the man mentioned his true intention: "Oh, and could you make that colt pace for me while you're at it !". The pace - faster than a trot in which the near fore and near hind legs move together - was much sought after for a saddle horse but was not always easily attained, particularly if the horse wasn't short-backed. A well timed tug of the rein or a subtle application of knee pressure or body weight was the usual way in which a rider could induce the horse to start pacing.[16] When Ulysses returned from his mission the horse was reported to be pacing perfectly. But its rider vowed that he was finished with training horses for people. Sadly years later, a letter written by Jesse Grant on the subject seemed to reveal that he had put the neighbour up to the ruse . This wasn't to be the last of Jesse's strokes to backfire.

When horses were suffering from "distemper" ,Ulysses was often called on to carry out the favourite method of treatment at that time, which involved a long gallop at top speed until the disease had been "burned out" of the animal. The practice was as much a panacea for rider as for horse ,with Grant retaining the habit throughout much of his life . It became his favourite method of banishing the headaches that plagued him from time to time. It was a common sight to see Ulysses riding furiously through the streets of the village with only a bridle on the horse. According to his childhood friend, Dan Ammen, Grant " rode usually without a saddle, a blanket being strapped on the back of the horse, and without stirrups." [17] Another of Grant's school friends in Georgetown , James Sanderson, would borrow books from Jesse Grant's thirty-five volume library - the largest in town - in return

---

[16] Robert West Howard, *The Horse in America*, page 141. Follett Publishing Co. Chicago.

[17] Adm. Daniel Ammen, "Recollections and Letters of Grant" , *North American Review*, Vol. CXLI, No. 347. Oct. 1885, page 362.

for letting Lyss ride his father's four year old colt while his parents were out of town. The arrangement suited both boys well as Sanderson liked to read while Ulysses was delighted with the idea of having a free ride on a horse he admired from a distance. Eager to increase the challenge, he pleaded with Sanderson to be allowed to jump the young horse over hurdles. But his friend refused to let him in case there was an accident and the deal was revealed. Sanderson also noted that Ulysses went bare-back virtually at all times but achieved tremendous speeds in spite of this, scaring virtually "every female in the village" that he came across.

In Georgetown it was known that Ulysses could not be thrown! In the days before rampant litigation, the visiting circus would have a pony that was trained to buck off any dare-devil child brave enough to stay on its back. The prize on offer was the princely sum of a dollar but the circus invariably kept its money. But many a trick pony would meet its match in young Grant. During one show, Ulysses did several circuits of the ring without being bucked off. In desperation, the ring master chucked a monkey on the boy's head, certain that this would dislodge him. The audience screamed with laughter as the tiny, chattering creature began pulling the rider's hair and scratching his face. But Ulysses could not be budged. His face never moved a muscle either. Needless to say, Ulysses claimed the prize money. [18]

On another occasion at the circus, he sat in the audience with his cousin Jimmy Marshall. The trick pony entered the ring - a creature "slick and round as an apple": his mane hogged and his back greased to make staying on his back even more impossible. Ulysses bided his time, studying the pony's technique as every child was dislodged one after another. Eventually he told Jimmy that he had worked out how he could stay on. When it was Ulysses' turn to ride the pony the little creature started up again, bucking and careering around the ring. His rider calmly embraced the animal's fat neck in a bear hug, and the two became inseparable. No doubt the ring master thought he was safe in offering the enormous prize of $5 to any boy in the crowd who could stay on. Instead he had to part with his money to the determined little figure who had made a science out of staying on fractious mounts.

Horses had become an easy source of income as well as a way of gaining certain privileges at home. Ulysses detested the monotonous, foul-smelling tannery work. He often paid his pals to substitute for him there while he busied himself instead with ploughing the fields or handling the wagon teams. As a result, there

---

[18] *The Ohio Democrat*, June 26th 1868, page 1.

was never any objections at home to pastimes such as swimming, taking a horse to visit relations, or impressing the girls with horse drawn sleds in the Winter snow. Grant emphasised this in his memoirs, saying that he was never once scolded or punished at home, mainly because of his industry with the horses. [19]

---

[19] Ulysses S. Grant, *The Memoirs of Ulysses S. Grant*, page 11. Penguin Classics

Chapter 2

*D*ave

Always with an eye for a business opportunity, Jesse Grant won the contract to build a new county jail in the spring of 1834. It would be a long job of some seven or eight months, and would involve hauling enormous amounts of logs by horse for the construction. Ulysses took an enthusiastic interest in the project and volunteered to do all the hauling. His only condition was that he must have "Dave" for the job. A huge hulking animal owned by a nearby farmer, this unlikely named horse had long been coveted by Ulysses from a distance. Now the perfect opportunity had come to persuade his father to purchase "Dave". As usual Jesse took his son's advice in all matters relating to horses. But he took a more sceptical view of his son's involvement in the project. The seven year old was tiny for his age and would a liability in the arduous job ahead. Wisely Jesse did not discourage Ulysses but instead appointed a man to look out for him and then take over when he had thrown in the towel, as he was sure to do, perhaps after a week or so.

But when the week was up the man came to Jesse and said that he wasn't needed . Ulysses could control a team of horses better than any man and could do the work. The boy stayed on the project for the entire Summer and Autumn, reputedly loading the huge logs in the woods with "Dave" when there was nobody to help him .He achieved this by lashing them to a chain so that "Dave" could haul them onto a half felled tree, where they could be rolled onto the wagon positioned underneath. Jesse's boasts about his "genius" son became even more overblown . Yet it is debatable whether the story of the wagon loading is authentic. It bears too much similarity to Jesse's own adventure with his horse and the sack of barley at the age of six. Perhaps Jesse was projecting his own equestrian feats onto Ulysses. The fact that he spent a good part of his life providing his son with a procession of highly desirable horses to ride would seem to bear this out.

Jesse Root Grant was now one of the town's most prosperous citizens. He diversified his interests - expanding into a casual livery business, picking people up at the stage coach, and delivering them to their homes and further afield. Ulysses was to become a key player in Jesse's new enterprise, selecting and training the horses for the job, and using his well-honed stable management skills. He was well acquainted with training horses on a lunge line, as he made reference to the practice to some of his Civil War aides.[20] But for Grant this was recreation rather than work.

Indeed Jesse's new enterprise was an absolute boon to his eldest son, who saw his work with horses being greatly augmented and with the exciting prospect of travel into the bargain. In time Jesse would give the boy a real challenge : that of conveying goods and customers by coach to far off exotic destinations like Cincinnati, Louisville , Maysville and even Toledo which was some two hundred and fifty miles away. From the age of fourteen or so, Ulysses often made these journeys entirely on his own, developing a confidence and self-reliance that was to see him through later life. Many of the trips undertaken by the youngster would read like something out of Mark Twain, although Grant himself would describe these times as "uneventful" .

While journeying back home alone from his destinations, mostly through the dense oak forests of southern Ohio, he was to develop one of his most celebrated superstitions - namely an aversion to turning back on the road. If he ever took a wrong path, he would never retrace his steps. Instead he found a way of coming out at the familiar route by pressing ahead parallel to it. Undoubtedly this behaviour was partly learned at the plough. But perhaps it also stemmed from an innate sense of adventure. The net result was that he seldom ever got lost or disorientated in the countryside.

Many of young Grant's travelling companions were alarmed at the idea of being conveyed to their destinations by so small a driver. Although the forests were free of wolves by now , they were not free of highwaymen. Jesse had unswerving

---

[20] Horace Porter, *Campaigning with Grant,* page 167. Nebraska University Press.

faith in his son however, and refused to listen to any objections. When he arrived in Cincinnati , Lyss would put himself up in one of the finest hotels of the town, the Dennison, where he struck up a friendship with the owner's son, William .(Later mayor of the city) . Often he would scout for passengers in town for the return journey.

When Ulysses was eleven or so he was hired to bring some passengers to Augusta in Kentucky ,about twelve miles away. By now he was a veteran teamster - silent and serious on top of the coach. On the way back he picked up a fare from two finely dressed young ladies, bound for Georgetown . When they arrived at the White River Ford, it was heavily flooded and impassable. But Ulysses didn't think so. Without consulting anyone, he plunged the two-horse buggy into the swollen waters, to the utter consternation of his well dressed passengers. Soon everything was swimming - horses, buggy , suitcases, probably petticoats as well. The women shrieked in terror. Surely this spelled the end for them all now. Suddenly the little hunched up driver at the front said : "Do not speak ! I will get you through safely !." With some skill, he steered the horses to the other side of the ford and up the bank.[21] It is not reported what the young ladies paid Ulysses for their amphibious journey or indeed whether they paid him at all. But they had made it to Georgetown that day, albeit in a bedraggled state ,while other travellers with less ambitious drivers had not.

In a tone of wonderful understatement, Grant referred in his memoirs to another incident on the road .[22] By now he was the ripe old age of fifteen and could drive a neighbour to Flatrock Kentucky ,a journey of some seventy miles. At his destination he eyed a young horse belonging to a relation of his passenger , Mr Payne. He took a great fancy to the animal and felt he simply had to have him. So he traded him on the spot for one of his own team, turning a profit of ten dollars. Payne himself had reassured his brother regarding the transaction, saying that the boy's father usually allowed him to do what he liked with horses. The only snag was that the newcomer had never been trained to harness. But this seemed only minor detail to the confident young teamster.

All went well on the road until the team was attacked by a vicious dog. This completely unnerved the new horse who bolted off, taking the rest of the team with

---

[21] Lloyd Lewis, *Captain Sam Grant* , page 39. Little, Brown and Co.

[22] Ulysses S. Grant, *The Memoirs of Ulysses S. Grant*, pages 11-12. Penguin Classics.

him. After a considerable struggle, Grant was able to get the horses under control. But the drama was far from over. Ulysses decided to rest the horses for a while in order to calm them down. When he started up again, however, the rookie horse began his antics once more, "kicking at virtually every stride".

Now they were in deep trouble - hurtling headlong towards the Maysville turnpike where a steep embankment and a twenty foot drop awaited them. The passenger was out of his wits with terror. He must have asked himself why he had agreed to take a lift from this wild youngster who had seemed so quiet on the outside, or indeed why his kinsman had agreed to sell him the horse in the first place.

The young driver needed all his skill and experience to avert disaster. He pulled up the horses just at the brink of the drop. With that, Mr. Payne decided he'd had enough excitement for one day. He fled from the vehicle and hitched a lift with a passing freight wagon - an uncomfortable but infinitely safer form of transport.

Ulysses was now on his own. He knew he had to come up with a plan. His uncle Roswell lived in nearby Maysville. If he could get himself there, then at least he'd be able to borrow another horse and continue homeward. He took off his bandanna and put it over the eyes of the new horse. Blindfolded, the animal was biddable enough to travel with the team to his uncle's place. On reaching the town the next day Ulysses swapped the horse for an experienced one and started for home. Remarkably, he met up with Mr. Payne in Maysville and persuaded him to climb aboard once more, which says much for his powers of persuasion. Ulysses had won out in the end. He had also demonstrated an incredible recklessness with other people's safety. Twenty five years on, many of his boyhood passengers, including Mr. Payne, would have been amused to recognise the Lieutenant General of the Federal army as the quaint little driver who terrified them out of their wits in the Ohio countryside.

Before Grant ever saw the inside of a military academy, he was an expert on the topography of his native countryside, knew how to negotiate a team through difficult terrain on long journeys, and could think on his feet in a crisis. He had also learned the importance of attention to detail, and had tested fully his own reserves of bravery and self-reliance. And it was largely his early work with horses that had enabled him to do these things. In addition, the opportunity for travel that horses gave him, expanded his horizons and made him outward-looking. In years to come, formal military training would refine these well-established tendencies.

Chapter 3

*Y*ork

Jesse Grant lobbied enthusiastically for his eldest son to go to the military academy at West Point. Although Ulysses was an unlikely candidate for army life, his father reasoned it was the best opportunity for him to get a good, free education. Besides, West Point graduates were very much in demand as engineers and surveyors in business and were generally "made up for life". Many of Georgetown's citizens laughed at the idea of small, unremarkable Grant heading off to the jewel of America's military schools. One villager showed his mirth to Jesse Grant's face on the street one day, but it was said that this man's spite stemmed from the fact that Ulysses had named his hulking draught horse, "Dave", after him some time back.[23] Ulysses was sent reluctantly east to begin his life as a military cadet in May 1839, dreading everything about the move except the opportunity to visit New York.[24]

Standing just five feet one inches tall, with homespun clothes and an accent steeped in the tones of rural Ohio, Grant cut an unimpressive figure as he entered

---

[23] Albert D. Richardson, *The Personal History of U. S. Grant*, page 63. American Publishing Co. 1868.

[24] Ulysses S. Grant, *The Memoirs of Ulysses S. Grant*, page 15. Penguin Classics.

the academy. His walk was shuffling and unmilitary, remaining so throughout his life in spite of West Point's best efforts to smarten it up. Even on foot he gave away the fact that had spent most of his time on a horse since the age of five. [25] To make matters worse officials got his name wrong. His sponsor, congressman Thomas Hamer , had written "U. S. " instead of "U. H." Grant on his application and it couldn't be changed. But that was the least of his irritations in his new home.

The U. S. military academy of 1839 was a forbidding, isolated place. Although picturesque in the Summer, the academy was freezing cold in Wintertime, and its air was heavy with the fish oil used to light the lamps. The cadets' day was marked out by two constants: drumbeat and drill. For the first few months the freshmen lived in tents on the plain and then moved into spartan barracks with hard beds. (At the end of his life Grant's doctor urged him to curl himself up on his side in bed to help him sleep. Grant remarked that he hadn't laid in bed that way since entering West Point.[26])

The freshmen or plebes were subjected to callous treatment at the hands of more senior cadets. This treatment was denoted by innumerable terms - "deviling ", "hazing" , "plebe jumping" to name but a few. Black marks or demerits were meted out for the smallest infringement of the rules. Two hundred of those in a year and the cadet was sent home. Grant received his fair share of penalties, usually for being late to church or reveille or some infringement of the rigid dress code. Third year was his worst for demerits - ninety eight in total. [27] At mealtime the staple diet was meat of dubious origin consumed with the aid of crumbling, foul-smelling cutlery.

More senior cadets, including William Tecumseh Sherman, had great sport with Grant's new initials and took to calling him Sam . The name stuck . Although not a failure, the man from Ohio with a frontier education didn't exactly distinguish himself in the classroom. Interestingly Grant's standing in mathematics was always high, showing a natural aptitude for the subject. The West Point library had a large selection of novels on its shelves and these were of most interest to the indifferent student, one his favourites being Charles Lever's *Charles O'Malley, Irish Dragoon* . Another word in the West Point slang lexicon was "fessing" : making a poor recitation in class. There seemed to have been a lot of "fessing" going on at the

---

[25] Lloyd Lewis, *Captain Sam Grant,* page 63. Little, Brown and Co.

[26] Richard Goldhurst , *Many are the Hearts* , page 151. Reader's Digest Press.

[27] *The New York Times* 1885. May 3rd , pages 2-4.

academy. But in the riding hall the term took on another layer, usually that the cadet had reached the limit of his endurance from saddle-pounding or chafing. [28]

Grant's small, lumbering frame ruled him out of any honours on the sports field. Instead it was his horsemanship that made him known among his peers. And perhaps it played a large part in sustaining him through those tough years. Given Ulysses' particular passion, he was entering West Point at just the right time. Because the forty- nine horses of the academy were starting out on their careers there also. A decision had been made by the college superintendent, Richard Delafield, to revitalise equitation in the curriculum. The presence of dragoons in the United States army had waned in the preceding years and it was hoped to re-establish a regiment before long. In 1839, Delafield arranged for the Secretary of War to supply a sergeant, five dragoons and twelve horses to the academy so that the cavalry school could get under way. [29] The rest of the horses arrived the following year.

Though proper cavalry tactics were not introduced into the curriculum until the 1850s, the course that Ulysses attended would have included bridling, saddling, mounting and dismounting, riding in all the gaits (including bare-back), and jumping low obstacles - pretty basic stuff to a young man born in the saddle. In fact Grant's stable management was so far ahead of everybody else that even the cavalry staff were in awe of him. [30] In the more advanced classes, cadets rode out across country and learned the basics of horse care. And if there were ladies looking on, the cadets indulged in what was pleasantly called "tearing rides". [31]

The academy riding hall was a rather low- key building in those days. (The enormous riding pavilion of 1855 had yet to be built). It was not a comfortable arena to ride in, being dark, dusty and cramped, with a tanbark floor that muffled the sound of the hooves and cushioned the numerous falls of the cadets. The corners came up very quickly, particularly if the rider had a hurdle to negotiate. Horses could fall on their noses if they took the corners too sharply, which many of them did since the cadets were encouraged to perform everything at top speed. To make matters worse, these activities were often conducted under the gaze of picnic parties in the

---

[28] Merlin Sumner, Ed. *The Diary of Cyrus B. Comstock*, pages 94, 98 & 103. Morningside House Inc.

[29] Stephen E. Ambrose, *Duty, Honour, Country*, page 135. John Hopkin's Univ. Press.

[30] W. E. Woodward, *Meet General Grant*, page 51. Garden City Publishing Co. 1928.

[31] Merlin Sumner, ed. *The Diary of Cyrus B. Comstock*, page 190. Morningside House Inc.

gallery who came to be entertained. (By the 1890s onlookers were banned by the instructors as they were thought to put off the cadets. [32])

Inside the academy riding hall, Grant's natural talent was refined by some classical training in the saddle . Initially the cadets were under the watchful eye of James McAuley, the first instructor to be employed by the academy. He was soon followed by a Pennsylvanian of Prussian origin called Henry Hershberger - a dashing veteran of the Black Hawk War, whose superb riding skills and near hypnotic influence on the horses made him a formidable figure among the cadets. [33] His training methods were a little on the ruthless side for the uninitiated, with cadets spending their first months on horseback without a saddle. The next phase was no less painful - sitting astride the hard West Point dragoon saddle without stirrups, to help the student establish a good independent seat, which Hershberger considered indispensable to the art of riding . Usually the entire hour and a quarter long session was performed at a trot, causing much grumbling, discomfort and perhaps permanent back trouble among the less athletic cadets.

During this time Grant got to know the individual horses of the academy . Now he had a chance to gain prominence in a field where he had a natural advantage. Just as horses afforded him many privileges in Georgetown, so they could make his passage through the academy a little more bearable, sustaining his spirit just enough to see out his cadetship.

But other cadets had a different opinion . To many of the students, particularly the northerners, the time spent in the saddle was more of an ordeal than the dreaded optics class or even parade drill. Until the 1850s the majority of the riding animals doubled up as artillery horses. As a result they could be sour. William Dutton of the class of '46, declared that some of the horses were "the hardest I ever rode". Another cadet, George Horatio Derby, spoke of "the hardest of all possible saddles, strapped on the backs of the hardest of all possible horses, and without any stirrups". It is evident from the diaries of cadets such as Cyrus Comstock that not even the thickest trousers could rescue a novice rider from severe chafing injuries. [34]

The horses themselves fell into two distinct categories: immovable lumps or runaway trains. The latter were especially known to take off in front of the riding

---

[32] The *New York Times*, Mar 4th 1893, page 6.

[33] Lieut. Oliver E. Wood, *West Point Scrap Book* , pages 289-90 . D. Van Nostrand. 1871.

[34] Merlin Sumner, ed., *The Diary of Cyrus B. Comstock*, page 96. Morningside House Inc.

hall bar. Getting kicked was a constant danger too, particularly in the confines of the hall. The internal pillars of the arena were unwanted obstacles to the riders. There was often no room to fit a galloping horse between the other riders and a looming pillar. Comstock described how his friend, Ebenezer Gay, broke his leg badly as he crashed between a pillar and somebody else's saddle when his horse bolted on him. [35] Tasting the tanbark floor was a regular occurrence. Darius Couch (later divisional commander with the Army of the Potomac), spent several days in the academy infirmary in a semi-conscious state after being badly thrown by a horse called "Pink".[36]

Next to horses, Hershberger's second love was sword play . (He founded a fencing school in Chambersburg in 1861, which was soon disrupted by the outbreak of war .[37]) And so the cadets had to spend long periods wielding their sabers on horse back - slashing at straw-filled dummies or wooden posts at a flat out gallop. (These props were replaced by leather pads in later years.) Apart from endangering the ears of the horses, this exercise had other unwanted consequences. The saber could get stuck fast in the wood and would be either left behind or manage to drag an already insecure rider off his mount . It was one of the few tasks on horseback that Grant disliked. A variation on the theme was an exercise called "running at the rings" in which a small ring , no more than five inches in diameter, was attached to a strap suspended from a post, five and a half feet tall. The cadet had to take the ring from the post with his saber either at a gallop or while leaping a bar at the same time. [38] (A few years later these same maneuvers were to strike terror into the hearts of T.J Jackson's classmates as they watched him lurch precariously in the saddle . [39] In spite of being a son of the Shenandoah valley, Jackson was never comfortable on a horse. During the Civil War he chose the less than dazzling "Little Sorrel" as his charger, a horse that his men sarcastically dubbed "Fancy". Sorrel would have won no prizes at a show, but he suited Jackson well and had amazing stamina. The

---

[35] Merlin Sumner, ed.,*The Diary of Cyrus B. Comstock*, page 176. Morningside House Inc.

[36] John C. Waugh, *The Class of 1846*, page 59. Ballantine Books New York.

[37] *Valley Spirit Newspaper*, April 3rd 1861, page 5.

[38] H. R. Hershberger, *The Horseman. A Work on Horsemanship*, pages 82-87. Henry G. Langley, 1844.

[39] Dabney Maury, *Recollections of a Virginian* , page 23. Charles Scribner's Sons.1894.

horse carried him on his final mission at Chancellorsville in 1862. (Ironically Jackson's image is permanently fixed in the saddle thanks to the poetry of John Greenleaf Whittier and the paintings of E. B. F. Julio.)

Riding out in platoon formation on the half mile square West Point plain was often no less eventful. It was difficult to hold a horse there. In the dust clouds, cadets often misinterpreted the bolting of one or two classmates as an order to charge and would raise their sabers without the authorisation to do so, much to the displeasure of the drill sergeant. In one such drill, described by Cyrus Comstock, the horse of cadet George McGunnigle Dick tripped and fell, and the men behind had no option but to jump over him. A picture emerges of the horses at West Point being hard-bitten and challenging mounts from the beginning - always one step ahead of their riders and apt to throw them off with nearly military precision. This makes Grant's sheer joy in working with these horses all the more extraordinary and puts his equestrian achievements in context.

These achievements came quickly. Soon it was discovered that the horsemanship of the man from Ohio could not be rivaled, much to the chagrin of the plantation- reared cadets from south of the Mason Dixon Line. One such cadet was James Longstreet - a tall, athletic Georgian one year ahead of Grant - who was to witness many of Grant's exploits both then and in years to come. According to Longstreet, himself an accomplished rider, there was no more daring horseman in the academy than Sam Grant, for horse and rider were like the fabled centaur. Longstreet recalled Ulysses striding purposefully towards the riding hall in his old dusty clothes for the exercises that he enjoyed so much. At that time cadets tended not to wear their uniforms for riding, but instead put on the oldest clothes they owned. According to a fellow cadet, Grant usually wore loose fitting pantaloons (over which his spurs were always buckled), a torn coat and leather gig-top hat. [40]

Noting his proficiency, the riding master allowed Grant to undertake the training of some of the green or troublesome horses that had been purchased by the academy. As his roommate Rufus Ingalls observed, he would go about this work with great patience and consistency, displaying an uncanny ability to make the animal understand exactly what he wanted. Ingalls remembered that he had a particular aptitude for jumping. When they were tackling hurdles in class, Grant

---

[40] Henry Coppee, *The Life of Grant*, page 22. Richardson and Co. New York. 1868.

habitually had the bar raised a foot higher than everyone else and would usually clear it. [41]

Like most riding instructors the world over, both then and now, Hershberger could be described as "an amusing sort of tyrant "with a voice that was " both strident and cynical". [42] He emphasised loudly to his pupils the importance of being seated over the horse's centre of motion at all times. He demanded precision and delicacy in application of the aids and kindness in the treatment of the horse. "In all corrections. . . . . the rider should endeavour rather to work on the mind than the body of the horse", he wrote in his short, practical riding manual published in 1844. [43] One of his golden rules was "never trust to your horse". It followed from this that if any mishap occurred in the saddle it was always the rider's fault. Luckily for Grant the riding master had a particular interest in the science of jumping a horse.

Exasperated by cadet Grant's unflappability one day, Hershberger decided to take his star pupil down a peg or two. Grant was mounted on a particularly wild horse that everyone else refused to ride. Hershberger kept putting the bar up higher and higher. Grant kept on clearing it and showed no signs of quitting. The jumping only came to an end when the horse's gigantic effort caused the saddle girth to burst and the rider tumbled to the floor. "Cadet Grant, six demerits for dismounting without leave!", shrieked Hershberger. In spite of this Ulysses retained some affection for the gruff instructor. Years later when the Pennsylvanian had fallen on hard times, Grant found a position for him as mail agent on the railway between Harrisburg and Hagerstown. [44]

After the examinations in June of the third year, each cadet received a furlough until the end of August. By this time, the Grants had moved from Georgetown to nearby Bethel. Always the indulgent father, Jesse bought Ulysses a beautiful bay colt called "Agua Nova" to train. With it he rode, as one witness said, like a "pursued Sioux Indian" to either visit his old school pals or ride out in the company of one of the local Morris girls, an accomplished horsewoman.

As with the onlookers in the town square of Georgetown or the audiences at his boyhood circuses, Sam Grant began to attract spectators at West Point when he

---

[41] Horace Porter, *Campaigning with Grant,* page 342. Univ. of Nebraska Press.

[42] Col. Nicholas Smith, *Grant the Man of Mystery,* page 27. The Young Churchman Co.1909.

[43] H.R. Hershberger, *The Horseman etc.* page 48. Henry G. Langley 1844.

[44] *Herald and Torch Light Newspaper.* 27 March 1884, page 2.

sat on a horse. Indeed many cadets would visit the riding hall just to watch him. Egbert Viele, a plebe in 1842, said it was better than any circus to watch Grant ride. Even cadet Alfred Pleasonton in the class below noted that there was something mysterious about Grant's way with the horses, although he thought the Ohio man an ungraceful rider. [45] At the time the academy had acquired a horse with a particularly difficult temperament. But it had proved so dangerous to ride that the riding faculty was considering having it shot. Only two people in the academy could ride the horse - the tall, dashing Tennesseean,Cave Couts, (later destined for a career in the cavalry), and Sam Grant. But it was said that only one of those two could claim to ride it well. Grant made a point of using this horse every time he went on parade. Viele observed that it was a joy to observe the stylish control he enjoyed over the intractable animal .

The jewel in the crown of the West Point stables was "York" , a three-quarter bred chestnut stallion, seventeen hands high with tremendous gathering power. He needed tactful riding. It was on this horse that Sam set the academy high jump record. "York" was a horse that could jump for fun but he didn't suffer fools gladly. He had a talent for dumping any rider he considered unworthy of him, after which he'd fall into line with the other horses and complete the drill on his own.[46] Samuel G. French , also of the class of '43, described "York's" peculiar jumping technique, one that made it almost impossible for the rider to stay on. Approaching the fence in a slow collected canter, he would dwell in front of the obstacle before launching himself over it through the sheer power of his hindquarters. Then he would land steeply on the other side with his hind heels almost facing the ceiling. [47] "It was a perilous feat and none of us cared to try it ", French added.

Just on the verge of entering West Point, June 1843, cadet James B. Fry wandered into the riding hall and in the process stumbled upon a priceless spectacle . A large audience of staff and spectators, including Superintendent Delafield , had assembled to see the graduation exercises of the class of '43. To the accompaniment of a regimental band squeezed into the corner of the hall, the show began with various formation maneuvers on horseback carried out by several riders. As with most graduations, the onlookers grew bored and became more interested in their own chat and banter than in what was going on in the hall. The climax of the show

---

[45] *New York Times*, Aug 17th 1880. "Cavalry Men and Horses". Interview with Gen. Pleasonton.

[46] Stephen E. Ambrose, *Duty, Honour, Country,* page 135. Johns Hopkins Univ. Press.

[47] James Grant Wilson, *General Grant*, page 33. D. Appleton and Co. 1897.

soon got their attention again. All the riders fell into line at the side of the arena. There was an air of excitement as Sgt. Hershberger ordered one of his dragoons to place a bar at arms length over his head, the other end of the bar resting on the wall. Could one of the riders be planning to jump this ? Surely not!

Cadet Grant's name was called out. Fry observed a slight figure on a huge sorrel horse break free from the ranks and come bounding down the cramped hall towards the enormous jump. Everybody held their breath as "York" approached the bar. Few believed he would jump it. Many expected the rider to break his neck. To their relief, horse and rider just sailed over the bar and landed with a loud thud. To prove it wasn't a fluke, the exercise was repeated four more times for the delighted crowd, each repetition as good as the first, except for one attempt during which the horse caught the bar with his knees. [48] "Very well done sir! Class dismissed!", roared Hershberger . After what he saw in that riding hall, Cadet Fry's first reflection was that the young man who performed such a feat of horsemanship could do anything if he wore a sword. [49]

There was some disagreement about the height of the jump achieved. Some witnesses swore it was five and a half feet , others said over six feet. [50] Dabney Maury maintained in his recollections of West Point that it was all of six feet. Grant himself was a poor historian on the subject of his equestrian feats and never mentioned the height of the jump. But assuming the dragoon who held the bar wasn't below average height, then by raising the bar well over his head ,the jump was likely to have been at least five and a half feet .

What testifies to the quality of the jump is that the record stood for most of the Nineteenth Century. Decades later while visiting the Spanish riding school in Vienna , Ulysses Grant III was proud to see the name of his famous grandfather posted up on the wall in honour of his achievement on "York". [51]

Grant rode the horses of West Point long before show jumping had been invented. Yet in his own way he was an early practitioner of the art. The forward jumping seat, taken so much for granted today, was only invented by the Italian cavalry officer, Federico Caprilli , in the early 1900s. It was Caprilli's revolutionary concept that freed the horse's back and neck, enabling the horse to jump higher

---

[48] Lieut. Oliver E. Wood, *West Point Scrap Book*, page 289. D. Van Nostrand, 1871.

[49] James B. Fr *North American Review.* Vol . CXLI . No. 349, page 540.

[50] Col. Nicholas Smith, *Grant, the Man of Mystery* , page 29. The Young Churchman Co. 1909.

[51] Ishbel Ross, *The General's Wife*, page 17 . Dodd ,Mead and Co. 1959.

obstacles without rider interference. Before then cavalry riders sat back in the saddle while jumping, leading to the horse hollowing over the fence with its head in the air and with a tendency to land after the jump with the hind feet first. Is this how Grant made his high jump on "York" ?

This technique might have sufficed for a small jump or ditch but would hardly have allowed the numerous adjustments to the horse's centre of motion that a vertical jump of almost six feet involved. Grant would probably not have cleared the jump if he had sat in this way. He must have had a system of his own for jumping such heights, in which he was able to remain over his horse's centre of gravity, perhaps sitting only slightly upright with a light seat, then slipping the reins to allow freedom for the horse's mouth and neck . With no bar on the floor to give him a ground line, it would have been difficult for the horse to judge his take off point. "York" would have had to rely on his rider to tell him when to take off.

It was with good reason that Grant treasured the memory of his high jump achievement on "York" , reminiscing about it with General Fry and others a few months before his death in New York. Characteristically he gave all the credit to his horse when he remarked: " York was a wonderful horse. I could feel him gathering under me for the effort as he approached the bar" .

Yet his association with the horses of West Point wasn't always steeped in glory. In his second year Grant was punished with two extra tours of duty for "kicking a horse". Then later in march 1843, two month's before his graduation triumph on "York", the academy order book recorded that cadet Grant was to be confined to his room for a week for "maltreating his horse". [52] Was it a misunderstanding on the part of the officer who penalised him, as Lloyd Lewis suggests in his book, *Captain Sam Grant* ? Many of the horses acquired by the academy were fractious and difficult, Grant often riding the worst of them because of his experience. Perhaps a swift and timely schooling of the horse had been called for which the prosecuting officer disagreed with. It seemed an uncharacteristic breach of conduct from one renowned for his harmony with horses. Sometimes Grant dealt with a rearing horse by tapping it between the ears with a pistol butt - a technique that would have brought him into conflict with Hershberger. [53] Perhaps Grant's answer to the charge is to be heard much later on during the Civil War, when

---

[52] Lloyd Lewis, *Captain Sam Grant*, page 93. Little, Brown and Co.

[53] H.R. Hershberger, *The Horseman* etc , page 48. Henry G. Langley 1844.

a brutal teamster came on the receiving end of one of the general's few recorded outbursts of anger.

Grant showed an aptitude for something else while at West Point. Benefiting from the inspired teaching of Robert Walter Weir, who subsequently taught James Whistler at the academy, he demonstrated a flair for art. He produced several paintings as a cadet. In one of these Grant chose the subject that was close to his heart :a horse with his nose in a feed bag. The subject was not the spirited, highly strung type that Grant liked to ride . Instead the painting depicts a stocky, hairy cart horse, full of character, tucking into a well-earned feed. The horse is lovingly drawn with some nice detail. The large ears flop down in a state of relaxed contentment while one of the feathered back legs rests slightly up off the ground ,as many a horse would stand. Although captured in a state of ease, the horse appears laden down by the heavy equipment harnessed to it : an easygoing soul oppressed by the yoke of military life perhaps ?

In the 1850's, James Hawes , the head of the cavalry school, initiated a very useful practice. Each year the cavalry instructor drew up a list of seniors who were considered to be particularly cut out for cavalry service on the basis of their horsemanship. This was then forwarded to the academic board on their graduation. [54] Although the list wasn't definitive, it nonetheless read like a roll call of cavalry officers in the Civil War - Jeb Stuart, Fitzhugh Lee, Kenner Garrard, McGregg and Averill. Undoubtedly Grant's name would have featured prominently had the initiative been around in his day .

---

[54] James L. Morrison, *The Best School: West Point 1833-1866*, page 100.

Chapter 4

*F*ashion and Psyche

Grant graduated from West Point without much distinction in 1843, but he had done enough. Although completely unmilitary, he had survived his four long years and had forged some good friendships. He had done well in mathematics and had gained a reputation as the bravest horseman in the academy, bringing out the best in a difficult but talented horse that everyone else preferred not to ride.

Naturally Sam's first choice of regiment on leaving West Point was the dragoons. And he must have been bitterly disappointed when he was given his second choice instead, the infantry. There were no vacancies in the mounted regiments that year. The excitement of getting fitted for his fine new uniform, and showing it off to his friends in Ohio served as a distraction from the disappointment. In his memoirs Grant set the scene for his debut on the streets of the big city, Cincinnati - a brevet lieutenant in full military dress. Feeling every bit as impressive as "old fuss and feathers", General Winfield Scott, whom he had once marveled at on the parade ground of West Point, he rode forth to greet the world. To add to the splendour he was mounted on the handsome new horse his father had recently given him as he rode proudly down the road.

Just then a filthy little street urchin ran up to him, hollering: " Soldier! will you work? No Sirree! I'll sell my shirt first!". On reaching home he found a drunken stable hand had put a white stripe down the side of his trousers, and was marching barefoot around the yard in exaggerated military fashion. The new soldier couldn't wait to get the uniform off. [55] Grant was unusually sensitive to ridicule, and his later distaste for fancy military dress may have stemmed from these early embarrassments. It also demonstrated how little the civilian population of the time thought of the military .

At first Grant was stationed at Jefferson Barracks near St. Louis, Missouri, where he was reunited with some of his West Point friends. Ulysses had brought with him a small brown thoroughbred from home called "Fashion", with which he was able to gallop over the picturesque lands of the barracks overlooking the Mississippi - exploring the extensive areas of woodland that still teemed with deer and making sure to avoid the sink holes that dotted the estate.

Soon after his arrival he rode his horse out to visit the home of his West Point roommate, Fred Dent, some six miles away. Dent's father, the "Colonel" , had made a fortune early in life in the fur trade . He now owned land covering over eight hundred acres with many slaves to work it and had his own steamboat to bring up life's little luxuries from New Orleans.[56] Grant had the best bit of luck in his life when he met "Colonel" Dent's eldest daughter , Julia, then seventeen years old . The apple of her father's eye, Julia was a pint-sized bundle of chat and vivacity with an easy charm . A warm-hearted and emotional soul, given to vivid dreams and psychic premonitions , she was also impossibly spoilt. Servants had done everything for her from an early age. But one thing she could do for herself was ride a horse. Young miss Dent had heard a good deal about Mr. Grant before she even met him. Brother Fred was always singing his praises, saying he was "pure gold".

When the young people went out together for their walks and rides on the plantation, Julia found that she had much in common with the new officer from Ohio. They both knew about stubbornly opinionated but doting fathers. They were keen on plants, trees and flowers. They shared a deep interest in horses. Julia herself was an accomplished, if not a particularly daring, horsewoman. (Throughout her life she showed a cautious approach to riding and seemed less than enthusiastic about speed).In spite of this her mare, "Pysche" , who was part Arab, was about the only

---

[55] Ulysses S. Grant, *The Memoirs of Ulysses S. Grant,* page 20. Penguin Classics.

[56] Pamela K. Sanfilippo ,*Agriculture in Antebellum St. Louis,* page 7 . U. S. Grant National Hist. Site.

thing that could keep up with Grant's blooded little horse, "Fashion" as she rode side-saddle beside him. This enabled them to be alone together.

Grant was smitten from the start, while Julia herself would later describe these times as "winged months". In the background her perceptive little sister, Emmy, rightly observed that the visitor " did most of his courting on horseback". It is little wonder that he did, for he was at his most impressive and attractive in the saddle, losing any awkwardness. A romantic image of Ulysses and Julia was evoked by one of Colonel Dent's slaves, Mary Robinson, who had the opportunity to observe them at close hand. The scene she conjured was one of white gloves, dainty ankles, effortless vaulting into the saddle, elegant postures on horseback. Interestingly, Robinson remembered Grant's smooth way of mounting a horse which seemed to be all his own and which Horace Porter and many other war colleagues were to comment on frequently.

Sometimes Grant and Julia ran into danger. Early in their friendship an incident occurred which never failed to make Grant shudder when he thought about it. [57] The two had set out on their horses to tour the banks of the Mississippi one morning. During the journey the porous soil at the edge of the river gave way under Julia's horse. Grant managed to grab hold of his companion just as Julia's mare disappeared before their eyes. "Psyche" was quickly swept down the river . The lieutenant pursued the horse from the river bank, never letting her out of his sight. The mare was eventually retrieved by the combined efforts of Grant and a nearby boatman who guided the horse into shallower waters.

Outings like these kept Grant away from Jefferson Barracks as any excuse was found to visit the Dents at White Haven. Back and forth he went over the barely trickling Gravois Creek, sometimes returning to barracks at a furious pace to avoid being late for dinner or dress parade. Frequently he didn't make it on time, incurring the disapproval of the mess hall superintendent, Robert Buchanan, a stickler for rules. The penalty for being late was to stand the officers a bottle of wine, and Grant accumulated several penalty bottles during this period. [58]

Grant was home on leave when he got word that his regiment was leaving Missouri. The race was on now to make his true feelings known to Julia, with whom he'd

---

[57] John W. Emerson , "Grant's Life in the West and his Mississippi Valley Campaigns", *Midland Monthly*, VI, 5 . Nov. 1896, page 4. http://www.lib.siu.edu/projects/usgrant/emerson/02nov1896.html. Accessed 31/10/02.

[58] Lloyd Lewis, *Captain Sam Grant*, page 108. Little, Brown and Co.

fallen deeply in love in the few months that he'd known her. Receiving a week's extension of leave from a sympathetic southern officer, Captain Richard Ewell, he set off for White Haven, taking his usual quick route over the Gravois Creek, which usually hadn't enough water to "run a coffee mill".[59] Ewell probably did much to alter the course of Grant's life by this good turn. Ulysses had borrowed an ungainly horse at the barracks for the journey. (He'd left his own quality saddle horse at home). Under normal conditions he could have crossed the Gravois Creek with his eyes shut. But this Spring, flash floods had caused the stream to swell up over its banks. The biographer of his early years, Lloyd Lewis, described what happened next as his best ride. In a manner reminiscent of his boyhood adventures, Grant plunged straight into the creek and was quickly swept away down stream. The horse he had borrowed for the journey was a fat, sturdy specimen. As was the custom in the army, Grant would most likely have attached a rope to the horse's bit and swam behind his mount with its tail in his hands. With the aid of the rope he could then keep steering the animal in the desired direction. Eventually horse and rider made it to the western side of the creek and scrambled up the bank. Grant picked up some dry garments at a Dent villa nearby before proceeding to Julia's home. It had been an auspicious entrance, for Julia had recently had one of her dreams in which she saw Ulysses entering the house in civilian clothes.

A few days later the same floods in the neighbourhood did Grant another good turn. The young officer was driving Julia to a nearby wedding in her father's buggy, when the couple came to a narrow old bridge that they needed to cross. The river underneath had swollen to such an extent that water was running up over the planks of the bridge. Julia thought the structure itself could be swept away and wanted to turn back rather than risk the crossing. Grant, with his almost pathological aversion to retreating, assured her that it would be safe to proceed, although Julia observed that he had gone rather quiet. This was the same person who had conveyed the two elegant ladies to Georgetown through the swollen White River Ford many years ago. It was as if he had been training for this moment. Julia recalled that in her heart she relied on him and said, "Now if anything happens, remember I shall cling to you, no matter what you say to the contrary ".

When they were safely across on the other side, Grant asked Julia if she could cling to him for the rest of her life. The flooded river, a test of trust and

---

[59] Ulysses S.Grant, The *Personal Memoirs of Ulysses S Grant*, page 23. Penguin Classics.

bravery, cemented their devotion. The two agreed to be engaged, but secretly. [60] The combative Colonel Dent would have frowned on the prospect of his favourite daughter marrying a man without means, much less a soldier, although Julia's mother, Ellen Wrenshall, always liked the lieutenant and predicted a great future for him .

Ulysses took up residence at his new camp - Fort Salubrity, Louisiana. There was growing conflict between the United States and Mexico over the disputed territory of Texas . Fort Salubrity was the height of rough quarters. Built on high ground above an alligator - infested swamp, the soldiers enjoyed few creature comforts; although the high altitude did protect them from the abundant mosquitoes. Grant in a letter home even wished for the food of West Point once more! Owing to the cost of living in the camp, it was no longer practical for officers to keep their own horses. Grant had to leave his beloved saddle horse behind, a bleak state of affairs for a restless soul with a poor walk.

Twenty miles away stood Fort Jesup, where many of Grant's West Point comrades were based, among them his old roommate at the academy , Rufe Ingalls . Rufe had been a witness to many of Sam's earlier equestrian achievements. It was with much amusement then that he observed Grant riding through the dust one morning on a scrawny, flea-infested little pony that he had rented for the social visit. Was this the same cadet who had achieved unheard of heights on "York" and tamed the dangerously spirited bay horse that was slated to be shot by the riding faculty?

Grant passed the days by writing long, newsy letters to Julia, starting a habit of faithful correspondence that was to last the length of their long separation. In time the officers acquired new horses to ride. With great amusement Grant described Robert Hazlitt's new "Jim along Josy " of a pony (after the popular Harper folksong) somersaulting on the road when returning from a ball late one night. Grant obviously thought the combination hilariously comical looking, the horse being rather small and the rider rather tall. [61]

Free time brought the opportunity for horse racing , at which Grant excelled, and gambling, at which he did not. While at Fort Salubrity, Grant acquired an unprepossessing little racing pony called "Dandy" . A West Point friend, Alexander Hays, was stationed there at the same time. An early photograph exists showing the

---

[60] Lloyd Lewis, *Captain Sam Grant*, page 112. Little,Brown and Co.

[61] Prof. John Y. Simon, ed. ,*Papers of Ulysses S. Grant*, Vol 1, letter to Julia Dent Jan 12th 1844. Southern Illinois Univ. Press.

two officers posing with their mounts, Hays considerably taller and with his horse ,"Sunshine" , Grant with his arm propped affectionately over the diminutive "Dandy's" withers.

The officers widened their social net to include the wealthy planters of the nearby Red River Valley. Although the young lieutenant lacked the dash of other officers, he became something of a favourite because of his skill in the saddle and his knowledge of horse flesh.

Chapter 5

*N*elly

In March 1845, Congress voted to annex Texas , setting the United States at odds with Mexico which also laid claim to the territory. Grant and his regiment were sent to New Orleans in anticipation of a military engagement. In September of that year , the Fourth Infantry arrived in Texas, where Grant was to come under the spell of the army's rugged, unconventional commander, General Zachary Taylor, named "old rough and ready" by his men. Taylor had a complete disregard for uniform, preferring to turn himself out in an old battered hat and jeans. His battle charger, the unflappable "Old Whitey" ,was as seedy looking as his rider with a mane that scarcely ever saw a comb. For Grant this was a no fuss, no frills type of military style that he could relate to. He provided a detailed description of Zachary Taylor in his memoirs. Their resemblance to each other in style of leadership in the field is so marked that Grant could just as easily have been describing himself.

> General Taylor never wore uniform, but dressed himself for comfort. He moved about the field in which he was operating to see through his own eyes the situation. Often he would be without staff officers……….Taylor was not a conversationalist, but on paper he could put his meaning so plainly that there could be no mistaking it. He knew how to express what he wanted to say in the fewest well-chosen words……..Taylor saw for

himself, and gave orders to meet the emergency without reference to how they would be read in history. [62]

Grant must have studied Taylor closely in Mexico and decided that this was the style of command to emulate. He noticed that Taylor was " very much given to sit his horse side-ways with both legs on one side - particularly on the battlefield. "

The terrain between the camp at Corpus Christi and the army's destination at Matamores was extremely barren and so vast wagon trains of supplies had to be transported on the marches. This proved to be a logistical nightmare. Native mules and horses were needed for the job. These were supplied in abundance by American traders and Mexican smugglers for between eight to eleven dollars a head, although sometimes the quartermasters, if they were skilled at negotiating, could buy in bulk and procure $36 animals to the dozen. Grant's observations made him familiar with the quirks of the pot-bellied Texan mule, smaller than his northern counterpart at between thirteen and fourteen hands, but much sturdier and better able to live off the native scrub . His memoirs mention in amusing detail the "training" of these unwilling animals to harness : a situation aggravated by the complete ignorance of many of the soldiers on the subject of mule-handling. Five mules were allocated to each wagon. Slip nooses were lashed around their necks which tightened if the animals became boisterous. Two men stood either side of the lead mule: and when they were in position, the restraints were loosened. Grant described how all five mules would be dancing in the air as the wagon set off . After a time the lead mules would go forward but the ones at the rear would stubbornly hurl themselves on the ground. [63] In this way the supplies of the United States army were somehow conveyed around Texas.

Grant observed the mules closely, noticed their habits and ways of going, the means by which their teamsters got them across rivers and other obstacles. They seemed to be an endless source of fascination to him. It was alright if they didn't get their ears wet. This was the one thing a mule couldn't stand. The trains were not the only fascinating spectacle at Corpus Christi. The army was in the heart of Comanche land now. Grant made mention of it in his letters. Comanche society revolved around the horse. With it the braves hunted the buffalo, fought the White Man and the Apache, and enjoyed their favourite forms of recreation - a sort of mounted games

---

[62] Ulysses S. Grant, *Personal Memoirs of Ulysses S. Grant*, page 72.Penguin Classics.

[63] Ibid., page 40.

practiced since early childhood. The artist George Catlin had this to say about their beautiful maneuvers on horseback:

> Amongst their feats there is one that has astonished me more than anything........a stratagem of war, learned and practiced by every young man in the tribe; by which he is able to drop his body upon the side of his horse at the instant he is passing, effectually screened from his enemies......he lays in horizontal position behind the body of his horse, with his heel hanging over the horse's back; by which he has the power of throwing himself up again, and changing to the other side of the horse if necessary." [64]

In their free time many of the men took in some sightseeing, very much like tourists. Always restless and curious, Grant was an enthusiastic traveller , although the outings could be dangerous, owing to the aforementioned Comanche, bandits and indeed the Texan settlers themselves. Ulysses referred to the latter as people he would not care to meet on a dark night. In his memoirs he told of a interesting journey he made with a friend from West Point, Calvin Benjamin , (killed later at the battle of Mexico city). As they rode together on the lonely plain, they heard the chilling sound of wolves howling in the distance. Grant became frightened, though he kept this to himself. He was hoping his companion would suggest that they both turn back. But Benjamin was from Indiana , a state still populated with wolves , and he was familiar with the sound. He asked Grant to estimate the number of wolves howling . Not wishing to appear ignorant, Grant deliberately underestimated the pack and put the number at twenty. Benjamin smiled and rode on. When they got to where the wolves were, Grant discovered that the entire sound had come from just two. [65] It was a lesson that stayed with him, especially in war.

At that time vast herds of strong, heavy-set horses roamed the land freely between the Rio Grande and the Nuences rivers . Grant was among the officers who took the trouble to ride out for several miles to obtain a closer look .He noted that the herd extended as far as the horizon, likening it to the famous buffalo herds of the central plains in the 1820s. Many of these wild horses were captured by the Mexicans and sold on to the American settlers and the officers of the army from between eight to twelve dollars a head. Grant commented on their appearance - strong like the "Norman horse" with heavy manes and tails. And they proved very

---

[64] George Catlin, *Letters and Notes on the Manners, Customs and Conditions of the North American Indians*. Letter 42 . 1844. Dover Publications 1973.

[65] Ulysses S. Grant, *Personal Memoirs of Ulysses S. Grant*, page 38.

useful riding horses too, surefooted in the terrain and better doers outdoors than the northern breeds . He wrote enthusiastically to Julia about the terrain. "It is just the kind of country, Julia, that we have often spoken of in our most romantic conversations. It is the place where we could gallop over the prairies and start up deer and prairie birds, and occationally (sic) see droves of wild horses or an Indian wigwam." [66]

With horses going so cheaply Grant soon acquired as many as four . Three had been broken to saddle when he paid for them. But the fourth one, a very spirited yellow stallion straight out of the plains, had hardly been backed. None of the other officers would touch this one. But Grant was confident enough to take the risk. As usual, James Longstreet was there to witness what happened . Repeating his earlier boyhood technique on the road to Maysville , Ulysses had the stallion blindfolded. He tacked him up with a strong bit and a Mexican saddle. Then he calmly climbed onto the stallion's back and the blindfold was thrown off. The stallion reared, spun, threw his head between his legs, bucked and did everything to try to unseat the weight on his back. A crowd of soldiers formed around horse and rider. Would Grant break his neck now ?

But as he had done in his boyhood days at the circus, Grant stayed firmly on board. When the stallion's fury showed the first signs of abating, his rider quickly rewarded him by letting out the reins and spurred him on over the plains. He was gone for hours and many in his regiment feared the worst . Eventually he turned up. The stallion, now dripping with sweat, was as quiet and obedient as if he'd been ridden under saddle for years. [67] Unlike the cavalry, the foot regiments could boast few stories about brave rides on horseback. But Grant's ride that day became part of infantry folklore, and was told at many camp fires throughout the territory, perhaps becoming a little embellished with each telling. The stallion became Ulysses' firm favourite and never gave any trouble after that.

Soon he was to lose his entire stable. His Creole servant, Valere ,was leading the horses down to water when he was thrown from his mount, and all four escaped to the plains from where they had come. Grant was more forgiving of the noisy, hapless Valere than of Zachary Taylor's adjutant, Captain Bliss, who remarked "Grant lost six dollars worth of horses there !". This must have been a sensitive

---

[66] Simon,John Y. ed. "Papers of U. S. G" .Vol. 1.letter to Julia Oct. 10th 1845. Southern Illinois Univ. Press.

[67] Gene Smith, *Grant*, page 42. Simon and Schuster.

point. With sly humour he made sure to contradict Bliss's remark in his later memoirs, insisting that his beloved stable of horses had cost him all of twenty ! [68]

It looked now as if Ulysses would have to undertake the one hundred and ninety six mile march to the Rio Grande on foot, until a Captain McCall of the same regiment came to his aid. The captain's servant had just purchased an unbroken mustang for three dollars. McCall hastily arranged a deal whereby Ulysses could have it for five. The mustang received all the education he would need on the long march. Grant spoke about their comedic interaction in his memoirs and as always his encounter with a new horse ended sweetly.

> For the first day there were frequent disagreements between us as to which way we should go, and sometimes whether we should go at all. At no time during the day could I choose exactly the part of the column I would march with ;but after that , I had as tractable a horse as any with the army, and there was none that stood the trip better." [69]

In April 1846, the assistant quartermaster responsible for organising Taylor's wagon trains, Colonel Cross , disappeared while out on a pleasure ride. His permanent absence was to put a huge burden on regimental quartermasters, which would soon include Lieutenant Grant. A squadron of dragoons sent out to scout the region where Cross had disappeared around Matamoras was attacked by Mexican army regulars. Sixteen U. S. soldiers were killed, making war with Mexico unavoidable.

Grant's first experience of battle was as a foot soldier confronting the splendour of the Mexican cavalry with its brightly-coloured uniforms, plumed helmets, and shining lances six foot long. [70] Of his first experience of combat he said in a letter to his friend John Lowe that he " did not feel any peculiar sensation " as he marched slowly toward the Mexican guns ,now and then hidden from view by the smoking prairie grass. Grant witnessed how Taylor had won the day by going on the offensive and how artillery innovations like "flying batteries" were now the main force in modern warfare. The Mexican army, showy and outdated , had relied heavily on its cavalry, and had paid dearly for it. Any Mexican worth his salt wanted to be in the

---

[68] Ulysses S. Grant, *Memoirs*, page 41.Penguin Classics.

[69] Ibid. Page 43.

[70] Lloyd Lewis, *Captain Sam Grant,* page 144. Little ,Brown and Co.

horse regiments. Their uniforms were so magnificent that they eclipsed the plumage of the parrots that sat in large clusters in nearby trees. This lesson wasn't lost on the young Ohioan. Grant would define an entirely different role for the cavalry when it was his turn to shape the tactics of war.

It is just as well that Grant observed the mule teams at Corpus Christi as closely as he did. When he was appointed quartermaster and commissary for his regiment in August 1846, he became a mule organiser at first hand. The reasons given for the responsibility were his steady organisational abilities, his knack with horses and his talent for driving a team. All his knowledge and experience as a teamster would be tested to the full in the following months as he tried to grapple with his duties. But as Grant was soon to learn, his talents did not always translate smoothly to the recalcitrant Mexican pack mules. The new quartermaster commented that their antics often reduced him to want to swear loudly, which says a lot for someone whose saltiest oaths were " dog on it !" or " thunder and lightning!".

Ulysses was helped by local Mexican teamsters, whom he considered indispensable to the job. Several hours were spent each morning in loading his noisy charges with all camp utensils. It was essential that the loads be made into packages of equal weight and bulk so as not to chafe the animals' backs. Moveable items like sacks of grain needed to be secured further with sticks between them and the hitching ropes, so that no uneven pressure would result during the journey. Two ropes of equal length secured the load with usually a man on either side of the mule raising the pack, putting the loops of the rope over the saddle and then securing it to the cinch hook. Several systems of hitches were used, with the complicated but beautifully symmetrical diamond hitch being the most common.[71] By the time the last of Grant's mules were loaded, the first ones would usually have rid themselves of their loads. When this happened the lash strap had to be untied and the whole laborious loading process started over again.

Years later, when Grant became Lieutenant General, his time with the U. S. mules was a popular topic of camp-fire conversation. According to one story, Grant appeared to have a nearly hypnotic effect on the breed. During his time in Mexico, he came upon a comrade who was trying to get his mule to move. But none of the usual measures had worked, from cursing to whipping. "Grant dismounted, faced the

---

[71] Emmet Essin, *Shavetails and Bellsharps*, Photograph 3,4 and 6. Univ. of Nebraska Press.

mule, and quietly cast unfavourable aspersions on the mule's paternity and chances of posterity. The animal shook himself and walked off." [72]

The terrain had grown mountainous now, making the job of loading, driving and unloading the wagons and packs even harder. But to the rank and file of his regiment he was "quartermaster extraordinaire" . Everything was set up and ready before the arrival of the troops in camp each night. Making use of his youthful years as a teamster, Grant could navigate his train patiently through seemingly impassable terrain and turn up in camp before the men.

A particularly key job involved the checking of the mules for saddle sores. The smallest trace of broken skin, and the indigenous screw worm would burrow into the animal's flesh, leading to huge abscesses. If this happened the only solution was to blow calomel into the wound, but the mule was still useless for a long time - a state of affairs that the United States army could not afford. Grant had needed all his stable management skills to ensure his animals were free of sores. It was painstaking work. There was one pack mule allowed for every eight soldiers, so Grant would have had up to fifty mules to inspect in addition to three five mule wagon teams. One wagon was set aside for the transportation of water, the other two to carry articles that couldn't be packed on the mules' backs. The crupper attached to the saddle was essential in rugged terrain but had to be broad and soft. Care had to be exercised when buckling the breast strap as if it was done too closely it would chafe the skin. The girth also had to be broad and soft to protect the forelegs ,and preferably made of hair rather than leather. [73]

The correct fit of saddle and especially saddle blankets was also vital. The army was helped in this by the use of the superlative Grimsley pack saddle. Developed in St. Louis by a local saddler, Thornton Grimsley, it never seemed to wound a mule's back. But for captured native mules, all unfamiliar with this saddle, the only tack for them would have been the Spanish-style saddle - the Aparejo - a sort of stiff padded blanket that didn't slip or cause sores. The Mexican handlers employed would have understood its use. In official circles there was some resistance to adopting the Mexican style, with General Winfield Scott in particular tending to adhere to traditional practices.

---

[72] Ibid, page 70-71.

[73] Randolph B. Marcy, *The Prairie Traveller,* page 82. Perigree Books. 1994.

From Cincinnati to the Colorado Ranger

Monterey was General Taylor's next target - a heavily fortified town of fifteen thousand inhabitants with many natural defenses. And it was to prove Grant's crowning achievement in Mexico for sheer selfless bravery. At the centre of it all was a grey mare called "Nelly" . How Grant came by her isn't clear. There was no mention of her in his memoirs or correspondence prior to Monterey . Indeed she may not have belonged to him at all. So much horse swapping went on in these chaotic few days that she may well have belonged to some other officer. And as quartermaster, Grant had access to many horses. She probably belonged to the small, tough breed of horse indigenous to the area.

At first Grant had no part to play in the combat. As quartermaster his place was in the tranquil walnut grove selected as the army's camp . But the sound and sight of battle in the distant walled town proved irresistible, and he galloped off to join his regiment. Two days later he was in the thick of the fighting - at the plaza very near the centre of town, where his own regiment was running perilously short of ammunition. If the Mexicans were to discover this, they risked defeat. Someone had to return to camp to ask for reinforcements. The journey was so perilous that the commanding asked only for a volunteer. It was his quartermaster who stepped forward.

During his time in Texas, Grant had closely observed how the " Lords of the Plains " evaded enemy fire by clinging to the side of their horses at full gallop, demonstrating unbelievable balance, bravery , strength and trust in the horse. Thus in his best Comanche style - his body wrapped around the side of the horse, his foot supported by the high cantle of the dragoon saddle, and a sturdy clump of mane in his fist - Grant galloped "Nelly" through the sniper-infested streets of Monterey where flat-roofed houses provided great vantage points for Mexican sharpshooters. "Nelly" answered the challenge. Not only did she gallop with the sort of speed that made her rider a difficult target, particularly at the street intersections, but she also jumped a four foot embankment for him on the way. Dangling from "Nelly's" side, it is a miracle that Grant stayed on. But stickability had been his hallmark from an early age. Grant made it back safely to headquarters about a mile from his starting point .

"Nelly" must have stayed in Grant's possession for the rest of the Mexican campaign, and there is some evidence that she came north with him after the war. [74] Grant always gave the credit for bravery at Monterey to his mare, while playing down the risks of the ride by saying that the men of the Fourth had made it back to

---

[74] Lloyd Lewis, *Captain Sam Grant*, page 283. Little,Brown & Co.

camp on foot through the very same streets he had galloped. After the surrender of Monterey , Grant noted the pitiful sight of the bedraggled Mexican army leaving the city, with its cavalry mounted on miserable, half starved horses who could hardly carry their riders out of town. He realised how slim their chances had been all along against his own well equipped force . [75]

Although the war appeared to be over after Monterey, fresh troops continued to pour into camp, bearing welcome news of old class mates from the academy. Grant did his bit to make the new men feel at home, bringing recruits such as Dabney Maury and Cadmus Wilcox for long rides around the countryside. As quartermaster he had greater liberty than most with his time being largely his own.

At the beginning of 1847, the regiment was ordered to return to the Rio Grande for a fresh expedition under General Winfield Scott. It was a much different style of command than Zachary Taylor's and a more ambitious mission involving the largest force ever assembled by the United States. It lead the men in the footsteps of the Conquistadors . Mexico's former president, Santa Anna, had been in the country since the previous year and was now the focus of renewed resistance against the "Barbarians of the North". Scott's Mexico city campaign would bring Grant in contact with many officers who would be key during the Civil War : Captain Joe Johnston, Major Robert E. Lee and Jubal Early, Captains Meade , Beauregard and McClellen. Undoubtedly he made many mental notes on the traits of these officers.

The two-week journey by sea to Vera Cruz on the ship, "North Carolina ", must have been a particularly bitter experience for the horse-mad Ohioan. The vessel was only appropriate for carrying freight and the intense heat added considerably to the misery of the passengers. Many of his draught horses and mules, already traumatised by a difficult embarkation which involved being winched aboard by ropes and pulleys, died during the crossing. At some point in the voyage, two ships collided sending the animals into a frenzy in the hold. Thanks to the quartermaster of the Fourth there was one affliction that the men didn't need to fear. Prior to the journey he had gone out to market and bought up all the lemons he could find in an act of great foresight.[76] It was these little touches of initiative, small but profound ,that marked Grant as an officer.

---

[75] Ulysses S. Grant, *Memoirs*, page 61. Penguin Classics.

[76] Jesse R. Grant, *In the Days if My Father*, page 7. Harper & Bros. 1925.

At the harbour in Vera Cruz, the fourteen- thousand strong army disembarked safely in a mere six hours - one of the most astonishing feats of amphibious landing in the history of the U. S. Army. But perhaps the most stunning aspect of the feat was the landing of over five hundred horses and mules a day or two later. Most of these animals, particularly the mules, were on unfriendly terms with sea water, yet somehow they were coaxed ashore. For the mules, the bell mare was the key to this operation, for her long-eared herd would walk over fire to follow her. Officers' horses were the first to be disembarked. Then the draught animals were loaded onto the steamboat "Petricia" and brought as close to shore as wind and tide would allow. If the bell mare went into the water, the others would follow. The animals were then swum ashore in tow of the vessel.[77]

Grant took no part in the fighting as surrender was swift. The problem now was the scourge of yellow fever which forced the army to go on the move again to higher ground. Tensions between Scott and Washington bedeviled the transport situation, probably for political reasons. Scott had requested five hundred extra draught horses from the north to enable his ten thousand strong force to undertake the march. President Polk believed that the general should use native horses and mules. Wagons were an encumbrance : the Mexicans didn't use them so why should Scott. "Fuss and Feathers" stood staunchly by his demands. Chief quartermaster ,Thomas Jesup , sided with the president on the issue but tried his best to meet the general's requirements . Such was Scott 's desperation that he sent members of the Fifth Infantry down the coast as far as Alvarado to trawl for anything on four legs that could carry a load . It was a full eleven days from the surrender of Vera Cruz before the quartermasters received enough wagons and pack animals to proceed on the march. The train eventually consisted of five hundred wagons and two hundred and fifty pack horses and mules.

Grant and the other quartermasters faced a hard time as the one hundred and eighty mile expedition to Mexico City was begun. The need for draught animals had been so urgent that the purchasers weren't as choosy as they could have been. Many of the horses were untrained to harness - often kicking their equipment to bits. Initially there was no road and the march had to be undertaken through heavy sand in blistering heat. Rations would last only six days. After that the army would have to live off the resources of the terrain. These fertile lands formed part of the vast estates of Santa Anna, and no doubt the wily Mexican' s beef herd wound up on many a U. S. army dinner plate.

---

[77] Emmet Essin, *Shavetails and Bellsharps*, page 38. Univ. of Nebraska Press.

Frequently Grant had to call on the services of the men to pull his derailed wagons out of the bottomless sand through which he lead his team. Hard driven on the march by a restless commander, General Worth ,the men dropped like flies. Grant's job at the back of the column now included collecting the fainting soldiers and putting them in his already overburdened wagons until they were fit to resume the march. So many men fell that the best he could do was to make them comfortable beside a tree or a rock on the journey, until the doctors could attend to them. Many men died on the way.

The twelve thousand men of Santa Anna's army, some of which included Irish and German deserters from the American regiments, were waiting for Scott's men at the top of a dramatic mountain pass, "Cerro Gordo" . Here Grant was to witness the wizardry of Scott's engineering corps. Both Robert E. Lee and Gustav Beauregard, at great physical risk to themselves, managed to map out a path up the mountain that would enable Scott's force to surprise the enemy behind its own defenses. Cannons and ammunition were hauled piece by piece up and down this treacherous route by ropes, since the way was even too steep for the mules. The invaders were protected by a spur in the mountain that allowed them to approach at close range without being seen. When Scott's artillery finally opened fire on the Mexicans , the forces of the one-legged commander were so startled that they fled at once. Santa Anna himself narrowly avoided capture by sliding down the mountain on top of a hapless burro. His baggage, wooden leg and carriage (pulled by six mouse-coloured mules) were all left to the invaders.

The way was now clear for the march towards Mexico City, with its imposing natural defenses and one hundred thousand inhabitants. When the force reached the town of Jalapa , Scott had a core force of six thousand well trained regular troops. Grant was very taken with Jalapa and its environs. He thought it would be blissful to live in such a place, provided Julia was by his side of course. There was time for a little recreation in the mountains in the form of horse racing. Grant was competitive in these high speed duels. According to one colleague attached to the Sixth Infantry, (who rejoiced in the name of "Cerro Gordo Williams" after his valour in the battle of that name,) Grant inadvertently killed a Mexican who strayed onto his path during a furious race. Williams had been lagging far behind when he saw the hooves of Grant's galloping horse clip the man's head in front of him. Not wanting to upset his colleague, he kept the tragedy from him until a card game between the two men years later brought the horrifying details to the surface. [78]

On their way to the capital the men of Winfield Scott's army passed through many places - the barren Pedregal , Churubusco , Molino del Rey and Chapultepec : "the Hill of the Grasshopper", on the outskirts of Mexico City. At each point the Mexicans made a stand, joined now by what was left of the predominantly Irish deserters of the army, under the emerald San Patricio banner . It was said that these men, mostly gunners, fought with particular abandon since they were fighting in the shadow of the hangman. [79] During this time official acknowledgment for bravery came to Grant when he received a brevet captaincy for "gallant conduct". The honour arose after he saw the potential of placing a cannon in a church belfry overlooking the San Cosme gates to the city. His idea wreaked havoc on the defenders below . By the following day the city was in American hands. In all this period Grant's conduct was characterised by a marked independence and self reliance, with a tendency to use his initiative way beyond his duties as quartermaster.

The Fourth Infantry remained in Mexico on garrison duty for a further eight months. The troops were stationed at Tacubaya , four miles from Mexico City. When free from his duties, Grant usually spent his spare time galloping into town to take a look around on one of the horses he had at his disposal. He always had the knack of choosing a horse with great ability, and even after the war he was enhancing his reputation for getting his mount to do the impossible. The officer in charge of Chapultepec was the Fifteenth Infantry's Colonel Joshua Howard . Howard 's headquarters were surrounded by high breastworks, and everyone who called tended to leave their mounts outside these imposing barriers. Not so Lieutenant Grant. Riding over from regimental camp one day, he leapt over the breastworks and continued down the steep, narrow steps to the colonel's door. "How do you expect to get him out?" asked Howard. "Ride him up the steps instead of down ", came the confident reply. Grant did just that without the least effort and flew back out over the defenses, leaving the colonel open-mouthed with disbelief. [80]

---

[78] Henry Watterson, *Marse Henry an Autobiography* by Henry Watterson. Volume 1, pages 213-214. Accessed 05/01/2012 via website, *Documenting the American South*, http://docsouth.unc.edu/fpn/watterson1/watterson1.html.

[79] Lloyd Lewis, *Captain Sam Grant*, page 234. Little, Brown & Co.

[80] Lloyd Lewis, *Captain Sam Grant*, page 186.

During this time death claimed the life of a young Mexican friend in a riding accident. The young man, attached to the monastery in which the Fourth Infantry was billeted , had latched onto several members of the regiment and hero worshipped Grant in particular, owing to their shared interest in horses. Nothing would do the Mexican but to ride out with the lieutenant on a horse that he had admired from a distance. Hot and forward-going, Lieutenant Henry Prince's horse was no novice ride. Prince , a hard-bitten veteran of the Seminole wars of the 1830's, had been severely injured at Molino del Rey and could not ride. Most likely the horse was being ridden by Grant in his absence from the saddle. Grant had seen the young Mexican on horseback and had felt privately that his skill in the saddle was not equal to the task. But he also realised that the young man put a high price on his opinion. Not wanting to hurt his feelings, he arranged the excursion for him. [81]

After a boisterous lunch at the officer's mess, during which a great fuss was made of the young man, the two set out on their horses. But at some point on the journey, Henry Prince's horse took off on the Mexican . In a desperate attempt to gain control the rider pulled too hard on one rein, causing the horse to swerve off the causeway. The animal careered over a ditch, throwing the young man to his death. The tragedy weighed heavily on Grant and may have been a poignant reminder of the Bailey tragedy in Georgetown many years before.

Quickly the invaders turned to sightseers with the climbing of the seventeen and a half thousand foot volcano, Popocatepetl being a particular challenge. Grant was particularly interested in the fate of a mule that had accompanied them. Laden down with two large sacks of barley for the horses, the animal had bumped against a steep wall of rock beside the narrow path and tumbled helplessly into a ravine. The men assumed the mule had been smashed to pieces in the fall and continued on with their climb. They were surprised to find him advancing on their camp that night, having been cushioned from serious injury by the sacks of feed. [82] In speaking of the mountain adventure, Grant said more about that mule than he did about the difficult ascent .

Ulysses didn't quit Mexico without seeing the national sport for himself. For a confirmed animal lover , the bull ring was a particularly painful and baffling

---

[81] Henry Coppee , *Life and Services of Gen. U. S. Grant,* page 25. Richardson & Co. 1868.

[82] Ulysses S. Grant, *The Personal Memoirs of Ulysses S. Grant,* page 97. Penguin Classics.

experience. His sympathies were not only with the bull, but also with the scrawny, debilitated horses of the picadors that he reported were barely able to move around the arena. Unfortunately , during the fight that he witnessed one of these horses was gored by the bull and died in the ring. Grant could barely endure to stay to the end and must have vowed that he would never sit through one again. Many years later he had occasion to visit Mexico in an official capacity and a bull fight was staged in his honour. Although he wasn't able to prevent the occasion from going ahead, he firmly gave his excuses and failed to attend. [83]

When the campaign in Mexico came to an end , Grant wasted no time in returning to St. Louis, complete with Mexican horse. He was much changed from the fresh-faced, boyish soldier that the Dent family had known . In his own estimation exposure to the sun had aged his features about ten years. But his feelings towards Julia were unchanged. If anything the absence had intensified them. He had been prolific in his letters to Julia during the Mexican War. His writing reflected his preoccupation with returning to her some day although he often expressed his frustration at her infrequent replies . His experiences in Mexico had given him both dash and depth, while his kindness to Julia's injured brother, Fred, during the storming of Molino del Rey - propping him up on a wall so that he would be conspicuous to the regimental doctor - had not been overlooked either; even if his kindly act had given rise to even greater injury when Fred awoke and fell off the wall.

In his memoirs it can be seen that Grant was quietly building his own military theories in Mexico. He had learned to study and interpret maps in detail to support his ideas. His combat experience at Molino del Rey and Chapultepec taught him the importance of pursuing a retreating enemy to avoid subsequent unnecessary combat. Grant observed that the officers commanding at Molino del Rey in particular failed to pursue the fleeing Mexicans up the slopes of "Grasshopper Hill" , which resulted in further casualties .

He had experienced sieges, forced marches , marching in file in front of the enemy, and the command of two great but contrasting generals. During this time Grant learned a lot about what enabled an army to sustain itself away from the fighting. The possibilities of a force living off the land was brought home to him on the journey from Vera Cruz to the Mexican capital. At Cerro Gordo he saw how it was possible to attack an army in position - and a seemingly unassailable one at

---

[83] Ibid, page 94.

that. He had seen how Winfield Scott was always magnanimous to the opposing forces when surrender had been secured. These lessons proved invaluable in years to come.

Not least he had learned a grudging respect for the hard-bitten Mexican mule. Grant gave a personal illustration of how tough the breed could be when he recounted the story of how his quartermaster wagon had driven over one on the road to Mexico city. The exhausted animal had flopped down in the wagon's path and Grant hadn't time to take evasive action. He was certain he had crushed the little burro to death in the collision. But instead the animal got up, shook himself, and trotted away with no trace of the encounter except a look of mild disgust on his face.[84]

---

[84] Frank Burr, *The Life and Deeds of General Grant*, page 110. J. B. Furman & Co.

Chapter 6

The Cicotte Mare

Back in St. Louis, Colonel Dent's stubborn resistance to the idea of Julia's union with lieutenant Grant yielded, and the couple were free to name the day. They resumed their friendship with long horseback rides through the Missouri countryside, before Grant returned home to become the toast of Bethel, Ohio and the apple of Jesse's eye as never before. On August 22nd , 1848, the couple were married in Colonel Dent's St. Louis town house . It must have been disappointing for the groom, decked out in his best uniform, that neither of his parents could attend the ceremony. The Dent's plantation lifestyle, with slavery at its heart ,would have been completely unacceptable to Jesse Grant. And Hannah was no traveller. But many army friends from Mexico and Jefferson Barracks were there, including James Longstreet, a distant relation of the Dents.

In the autumn of 1848, Grant resumed his quartermaster duties ,this time with Julia by his side. He was stationed at Sackets Harbour on Lake Ontario - a bleak and freezing outpost at the time of the couple's arrival. Their quarters were in the barracks. Julia, who had been used to slaves all her life, plunged herself into the art of keeping house and various "culinary experiments" with characteristic joie de vivre. Her presence did much to liven the place up, and many of the unmarried officers envied Grant his domestic bliss.

In the course of his duties Grant corresponded often with the Quartermaster General of the army, Thomas Jesup, requesting money for repairs and other improvements that needed to be done about the barracks. His duties kept him busy, though in an uneventful way that he always found hard to endure. Grant asked Jesup if he could buy an extra horse and cart in addition to the existing team of two for the delivery needs of the regiment. [85] It is not clear whether he owned a horse at the garrison or hired one for his own use, as it would not have been practical to bring one of his own to Sackets. What is certain is that he involved himself with the horse racing that was popular there, striking up an acquaintance with a young lawyer, Charles W. Ford, in the process. It was to be a lifelong friendship. For a change of scene, Grant rode out to Watertown, ten miles away, to play checkers and cards. And in spite of the weather he was able to make the trip in a swift forty-five minutes. Watertown was also the destination for Julia's shopping sprees in a horse and buggy. She recalled these trips with some fondness in her memoirs.

The following Spring the Grants were transferred to Detroit - a hard-drinking, wooden-housed, adventurer's town, completely unpaved. Funds were tight and the officers shared accommodation to cut down on expenses. The Grants took a small house with Major Gore and his wife. At the back was a good carriage house and stable. Julia did her best to add colour to the garrison, organising a fancy dress ball, (at which Grant staunchly refused to costume himself), and other social dinners. Initially Ulysses had no horse of his own at his new post, but he was soon on the hunt for a good one at a reasonable price. In spite of his aversion to music, Grant numbered among his friends in the town a band musician who observed of him: "His only dissipation was in owning a fast horse. He still had a passion for horses and was willing to pay a high price to get a fine one".[86]

Julia never begrudged her husband his taste for pricey horseflesh. If anything she encouraged it. She was, by her own admission, "unpardonably extravagant" herself, and saw no harm in his only real indulgence. Buggy racing was even more popular in Detroit than in Sackets Harbour. To the citizens of the town Grant's driving ability became proverbial. As usual he coveted a particular

---

[85] John Y. Simon ed., *Papers of U. S. G.* .Vol. 1. Letter to Thomas Jesup. Jan 27th 1849. Southern Illinois Univ. Press.

[86] Hamlin Garland, *Ulysses S. Grant: His Life and Character*, page 111. Doubleday & McClure 1898.

horse from a distance at first, although she appeared to be nothing special to the casual observer. In fact the garrison surgeon, doctor Charles Tripler, called her " that little rat of a horse ". Yet people remembered her. When the opportunity arose Grant bought her for $200 from her French Canadian owner, local politician Dave Cicotte, who himself enjoyed celebrity status as a lover of fast horses. [87] Under Grant's training the "little rat's" speed under harness couldn't be matched.

Grant was always as much at ease driving a horse as riding one, and the long reins were merely the extension of his hands. According to the custom of the day, these reins passed between the little and third finger, came up over the little finger again, then under the other fingers and over the thumb. Grant would have held the slack of the reins between thumb and forefinger of the left hand . To shorten the left rein, the thumb and forefinger of the right hand grasped the rein behind the left hand and the left fingers were slid forward on the left rein. In this way the driver always had a hold of the horse's head. Grant would have derived great satisfaction from the challenge of keeping the horse within the one gait. Breaking to a run could be rectified with a timely, subtle rotation of the wrist on whichever rein his horse was caught with more readily. He would know from observation which one. But he had to avoid the temptation to snatch at the horse when he broke, as this would lose too much ground. And any jerking or pulling could cause a dangerous swerve. [88] A subtle play on the bit was all that was needed to refresh the horse's mouth, collecting him for a further spurt, and making the risk of breaking from trot less likely.

The tiny black mare , a natural pacer, was known to all as the "Cicotte Mare", but Mrs Grant liked to refer to her as "Nellie Bly" (no doubt after the Stephen Foster song that was popular at the time.) In her memoirs Julia spoke of the carriage house and stables behind the house where the " fleet little mare of which the captain was so proud" was kept. [89] There seemed to have been much folk lore in Detroit about the "Cicotte Mare". Had Stephen Foster lived in the town at the time, she might well have furnished him with a song about her fast exploits down a muddy or snowy Jefferson Avenue. Major Bob Forsythe raced his fast pony "Spider" against her , as did members of French Detroit - the Campaus ,the Beaubiens and of course the Cicottes.

---

[87] Ibid, page 113.

[88] Hiram Woodruff, *The Trotting Horse of America*, pages 394-396. J. B. Ford & Co. 1869

[89] John Y. Simon ed., *Personal Memoirs of Julia Dent Grant*, page 80. Southern Illinois Univ. Press.

According to one inhabitant, H. C. Kibbee ,Grant won a $50 bet when he wagered that his mare could carry himself and a passenger from Dequindre Street Bridge to the Michigan Exchange in record time. The normally undemonstrative Grant lit up with delight when she came in fast and won the bet for him, and he stood the locals a free round of drinks at a nearby tavern.[90]

In wintertime , the race track at Detroit repaired to the River Rouge, where horses picturesquely pulled cutters across the frozen expanse , their drivers muffled in buffalo hides. These iced over rivers and lakes provided the participants with the perfect smooth highways that they could never find on land. It was a risky but skillful pursuit in which the trot or pace was favoured because these gaits were safer than the gallop. Bystanders sipped hot toddies and warmed themselves beside open fires, whose flames also served to take the chill off the horses' bits before they were placed in the animals' mouths.

Years later Grant told his successor at the White House, Rutherford Hayes , that he had been offered an eighty acre tract of land in a valuable part of Chicago if he would part company with the "Cicotte Mare" .[91] He turned down the offer. Although naive in business ,Grant's dealings with horses seemed to be among the few areas at which he could potentially turn a profit. But as with most horse deals, potential buyers are numerous until the horse needs to be sold. Grant's return to Sackets Harbour in the summer of 1851 prompted the sale of the "Cicotte Mare", since he wouldn't have been able to take her with him. It appears that he had to settle for the less than princely sum of $110 for her.[92] Grant sent half the money to Julia who had returned to St. Louis to see her relations.

Sackets Harbour was a different world in the summertime, losing all its bleakness. But Grant seemed to miss Detroit immediately. He must have spotted the mare's name in a newspaper and wrote to his colleague , Lt .Col. Grayson back in Detroit : " I see from my Detroit paper that sporting is on the ascendent in your place and that some of the nags make good time. I should like very much to change back again to Detroit ."[93]

---

[90] Lloyd Lewis, *Captain Sam Grant*, page 290. Little ,Brown and Co.

[91] *Ulysses S. Grant Homepage*, http://www.granthomepage.com/inthayes.html. Accessed 5/01/2012.

[92] John Y. Simon ed., *Papers of U. S. G.* . Vol. 1. Letter to Julia, June 7th 1851. Southern Illinois Univ. Press

[93] Ibid, Vol. 1. Letter to lt.. Col. Grayson . Nov 12 1851.

Subsequent events would seem to confirm that the "Cicotte Mare" possessed a class way beyond her price tag. After her sale she became a popular sight on the old Abbey Trotting Racetrack in St. Louis, west of Grand Centre. [94] Later she won a race there for a thousand dollars and was then sold on for a princely fourteen hundred dollars. As usual it was left to others to turn a handsome profit on a Grant horse.

The "Cicotte Mare" wasn't the only thing that Grant missed from his life at Sackets. Julia had gone back to White Haven to give birth to their first born in May 1850 and stayed for a lengthy period. This lead to a furious bout of letter writing from her husband. In his correspondence, he appeared to be on tenterhooks, emphasising how nice everything would be for her return. Several times he mentioned that he had got himself a horse and buggy, and an elegant one at that, so that " all to-gether (sic.) you would enjoy yourself very much ". [95] He must have owed for a new saddle or harness because he enquired of Julia in St. Louis whether she had " paid Grimsley " there. It is clear that Grant couldn't wait to get his newly born son, Fred, started on the horses. He was already making plans to take him whizzing in the buggy.

This correspondence afforded a glimpse of what social life was like at the post, as Ulysses gave Julia all the news and gossip. He wrote to her many times about their friends and other characters at the barracks: the Gores, the Wallens, the Gaynors, the Triplers, and the long rides they took nearly every evening in the countryside. He referred to little incidents like how Mrs. Wallen's horse ran away with two buggies on two successive days, dashing both vehicles to pieces. Gore, Forsythe and the garrison surgeon, Dr. Tripler, were majors and so enjoyed a better salary. Although Grant was now a captain it was a brevet rank and his pay and conditions remained that of a lieutenant. There is an impression given that Grant found it difficult to keep up with the lifestyle of his new friends at the barracks. Dr. Tripler's description of Grant's " little rat of a horse " as being " the best he could afford " had a whiff of condescension about it. (According to Tripler's hard-minded but adoring wife, Eunice, the good doctor himself drove a fine span of Vermont Morgan mares).[96]

---

[94] Walter B. Stevens, *Grant in St. Louis,* page 17. The Franklin Club of St. Louis 1916. Republished by Applewood Books. Accessed via Google Books. Jan. 30, 2012.

[95] John Y. Simon, ed., *Papers of U. S. G.* Vol. 1. letter to Julia, July 27th 1851.

[96] Eunice Tripler, *Some Notes on her Personal Recollections*, page 103. Grafton Press 1910.

Then came the order to go west with the regiment in June 1852. It was a stroke of good luck that Julia was pregnant again and unable to accompany Grant on the journey that would ultimately take him to Oregon and California . Many soldiers' families did undertake the trip ,paying for it in some cases with their lives. At that time the favoured route west involved a long voyage to Aspinwall , followed by a trek across the Isthmus of Panama and then on by sea up the coast to the western territories. Commanding the expedition was the beaver hat-wearing explorer of the West, Colonel Benjamin Bonneville. Perhaps Grant had read of his commander's exploits in the library at West Point, where he was given to reading the works of Washington Irving and other romantic novels of the West. If so the romantic vision would contrast starkly with the experience about to unfold . Grant spoke more about his harrowing expedition through the Isthmus of Panama than any other part of his career. [97] It produced in him a life-long interest in the notion of a canal to join east and west, although he favoured Columbia rather than Panama as the location.

Exhausted and underweight after the Isthmus journey, ("Captain McConnell and myself when we got across were in prime order for riding a race or doing anything where a light weight was required") [98], Grant took up his post as quartermaster at the picturesque Fort Vancouver on the Oregon Washington State border. The West proved to be an eye opener. People paid premium prices for the barest essentials there. He saw how easily fortunes were made and lost. Julia's older brothers were already making out well in a small town on the Stanislaus River.

    At Fort Vancouver - founded in 1849 on the site of an old Hudson Bay company settlement - Grant at least had the company of an old friend. His roommate from West Point, Rufe Ingalls, was also stationed there. They occupied the finest house at the fort, dubbed "quartermaster's ranch", which became the social hub of the settlement. To pass the time, he and Ingalls took long rides over the Oregon countryside, sometimes crossing the broad Columbia River, which froze in winter . Grant's outlook was initially positive because he invested in livestock and bought himself a fine horse at Dalles . He had every expectation that his family would be joining him in due course also. In the Summer, Grant's quartermaster duties kept him busy organising provisions, pack mules and horses for an army expedition to the Cascade Range. Apart from that he had little to do. The four

---

[97] Lloyd Lewis, *Captain Sam Grant*, page 307. Little, Brown & Co.

[98] John Y. Simon, ed. *Papers of USG* . Vol . 1st Aug 20th, 1852. Letter to Julia. Southern Illinois Univ. Press.

cannons at Fort Vancouver stood in an orderly line facing the Columbia River. Perhaps only Ulysses Grant could have thought of turning them into a jumping lane for entertainment. Much to the amusement of the other officers, who stood outside "quartermaster's ranch" to watch, he set his horse to leaping the big guns one after the other, as if they were a row of hurdles.

In imitation of the early settlers of the region, the officers were always on the lookout for money-making schemes. But Grant's never quite came off, establishing a pattern. They cleared large tracts of land for planting potatoes and the Ohio man did most of the ploughing. Again his skill with horses came in handy. He acquired a couple of half-starved specimens from the plains. Under his care, they picked up and became efficient farm animals. But the river flooded the fields and the enterprise foundered, bringing with it the first inklings of disillusionment. Fort Vancouver was a notorious breeding ground for malaria, with vast numbers of the indigenous Indian population wiped out by it in the 1830s and 1840s. [99] In the damp and drizzle of the Oregon climate, Grant's health and morale were beginning to break down.

---

[99] Margaret Humphries, *Malaria,* page 21. Johns Hopkins University.

Chapter 7

*E*clipse

The death of Captain Bliss - the officer in the Mexican War who insulted the quality of Grant's horses - lead to the appointment of Ulysses as quartermaster to a remote fort in the extreme north of California . Sandwiched between a vast, dreary bay and a dense, impenetrable forest, Fort Humboldt was like the last outpost on earth. Before he even arrived there, Grant knew it as a "detestible" place, populated around by either miners or lumberjacks. The fort had no family quarters , so Grant had little prospect of being united with Julia and his family of two young boys. For such a family man this was a terrible blow. His children were growing up and he barely knew them. One of them he hadn't even seen. The bitter experience of crossing the Isthmus had no doubt changed Grant's view of life. He had seen families supposedly under the protection of the army perish on the journey.

Unfortunately the job at Fort Humboldt had little in the way of challenge and Grant fought a monumental battle with boredom. There was a constant drizzle that Spring , and he became susceptible to fever and chills . Letters from the east came from ships in the bay and often months elapsed between deliveries. Julia was no letter writer, but those she did write always contained old news. Grant also had no horse of his own now since he'd had to part company with his cannon-leaping mount before leaving Fort Vancouver . And those that knew him well would say that he was never entirely happy without one. [100]

Grant's short, miserable stay at Fort Humboldt was brightened by a borrowed horse called "Eclipse" . Owned by a pioneer family , the Duffs ,whom the captain had become friendly with in the nearby town of Eureka, "Eclipse" was a large roan horse of Australian origin. [101] According to Captain Grant, he was " the finest horse I ever rode west of the Rockies" . Grant rode "Eclipse" into the woods at every opportunity, jumping over logs and any other obstacle suitable for hurdling. Although there were wolves in the forest, they held no fears for him now. His travels in Mexico had taught him not to overestimate their menace. As usual, horses set off the wilder side of the captain. According to local legend he drove three of them in single file attached to as many buggies through the streets of Eureka, no doubt to the delight of the bored habitués of Ryan's store or Brett's saloon . [102]

To relieve the loneliness, and also perhaps his chills, Grant drank a little . But with his ability to metabolise alcohol compromised by chronic malaria, a small amount could produce a dramatic effect ,leading to mistaken assumptions that he was drinking heavily. There was the added complication that the symptoms of malaria -sweating, headaches, tremors, unsteady gait - bore an unfortunate resemblance to hangover. Fort Humboldt was a gold fish bowl where minor incidents could be magnified out of all proportion. No doubt this had a huge bearing on the persistent rumours concerning Grant's departure from the fort.

This came four months after his arrival when an unsympathetic commander , "Old Buck" Colonel Robert Buchanan ,Grant's old adversary from Jefferson Barracks, came down heavily on Grant when he reputedly found him under the influence at his post one day. After fifteen years of service , Grant decided he couldn't be a soldier under these circumstances and resigned. It was a brave move. The army had been his only career. Now at thirty- two years of age, he starting out all over again.

Characteristically , he had lent money to various people during his time in the West, and now he had no savings when he needed them. Procuring transport east

---

[100] John W. Emerson, "Grant's Life in the West and his Mississippi Valley Campaigns", *Midland Monthly*. Vol. VI, 5 .Nov. 1896., page 7. http://www.lib.siu.edu/projects/usgrant/emerson/02nov1896.html. Accessed 31/10/02.

[101] Charles G. Ellington, *The Trial of U. S. Grant,* page 153. Arthur H. Clark Co. 1987.

[102] Ibid, page 147.

through the army quartermaster, he arrived in New York without enough funds. His Mexican War friend, Captain Simon Boliver Buckner, had to go guarantor for an unpaid hotel bill. Years later it was a small kindness that Grant was destined to repay in unexpected circumstances.

Chapter 8

Tom and Bill

Grant's time as a Missouri farmer is especially interesting because it was what he really wanted to do in life, and was possibly his happiest period. It was a natural choice that he should gravitate to this new occupation after leaving the army. Farming was in the blood. Since the early Seventeenth Century in Ulster , and before that in the Scottish Lowlands, his maternal ancestors had grown cereal, flax and potatoes on tiny holdings of land with grim, uncomplaining tenacity. In such communities the skillful use and care of the farm horse meant the difference between survival and pinching want. (Grant may have heard of some of their old customs from his grandfather : how they ground gorse bushes on the whin stone to feed to the horses, since it made their coats glossy and toughened their mouths for the harness bit.)Besides it suited his temperament. He always favoured what his friend Ned Beale called the "quiet, contemplative life mixed with the activity of outdoor work". [103] No doubt his ambitions included some notion of owning and

---

[103] George Childs, *Recollections*, page 138 . J. B. Lippincott & Co.1898

training young horses on the farm in time. He returned to this idea frequently throughout the Civil War.

Grant believed that the West was the land of opportunity for the farmer: "I left the pacific coast very much attached to it, and with the full expectation of making it my future home." [104] It had always been his intention to return there with his family so that he could try his new occupation in more lucrative markets. But in the short term an opportunity came up to farm eighty acres of timbered land at Carondelet that had been a wedding present from Julia's father. The couple quickly set about establishing a home for themselves there.

Although Julia was no doubt delighted to be reunited with her husband on home soil once more, close to the familiar places of her childhood, the couple were largely starting from scratch. The land hadn't been cultivated before, so the measures needed to get it in a fit state were time-consuming. Initially they lived in one of the Dent's villas in the woods, "Wish-Ton-Wish". But it was a mile distant from the farm, and Grant, with his fierce independence, wanted a place of his own. The land had to be cleared and a small farm house built. Grant cut the timbers and let them mature for a year, before calling on the neighbours for the " raising". This part of Missourian rural culture served a social as well as a practical purpose, bringing neighbours together in a common project. With the help of seven or eight neighbours - people like the Sappingtons, the Longs, the Sigersons and the Wrights, together with their slaves - Grant assembled much of the cabin himself. [105] Then with his usual dry humour, he dubbed the unpretentious new place "Hardscrabble".

Setting out on his own farming expedition at Carondelet, Ulysses Grant would have had few illusions about the life ahead of him. Butchering livestock in the early months of the year, mending tools, preparing for spring planting, harrowing, grubbing, harvesting, threshing, winnowing : it was an unending cycle of labour. Characteristically Grant put his back into the project. He bore the brunt of the work himself, partly because he enjoyed it but also because he had discovered in the West that working alongside hired hands increased their productivity enormously. "I moistened the ground around those stumps with many a drop of sweat" he said many years later during a visit to the old farm. [106]

---

[104] U. S. Grant, *Memoirs*, page 111. Penguin Classics.

[105] *McClure's Magazine*. April 1897. "Grant's life in Missouri ", page 515. Accessed at http://www.unz.org/Pub/McClures-1897apr. Jan 2012.

[106] Hamlin Garland, "Grant's life in Missouri ",*McClure's Magazine*. April 1897 , page 516.

From Cincinnati to the Colorado Ranger

At first the new man in the neighbourhood had little funds to buy livestock, equipment and seeds. But he did manage to get a team of horses on "easy terms" from his old racing friend of Sackets Harbour days, Charles Ford - now manager of the Adam's Express Company in St. Louis. Ford's horses, Bill and Tom, had belonged to the company, so they were unusually swift for farm horses. The team really got him up and running on the farm, and he never forgot the favour. [107]

In time the captain became a familiar sight with his " span of black and white" on the Gravois and Reavis Jefferson Barracks road; or sitting on a log outside the blacksmith's, clay pipe in mouth, waiting for the horses to be shod . [108] Wood was a ready if time-consuming source of cash , so he hauled plenty of it into the city and the barracks. A local coal mine needed mine timbers and Grant supplied much of the props for the works at a good price. But again this labour diverted much of his energies away from the farm. A neighbour, Mrs. Blow, gave Grant an "excellent rating" for denting her favourite tree with the hub of his wagon as he delivered wood, no doubt a little too speedily, to her house one day. (On a visit to the White House some years later she was quickly reminded of that rating!. [109])

In spite of these odd mishaps , he quickly gained something of a reputation among his neighbours for doing amazing things with this little team. If local families like the Sappingtons were winning prizes for their model farm, the Longs for their potato yields, and the Sigersons for their fruit at agricultural fairs, [110] then at least Grant could take simple pride in the fact that his team could haul more bushels of wheat than anyone else, and arrive faster into St. Louis with it too. And this in spite of the fact that at certain times of the year the melting macadamised Gravois road was scarred with deep rivets. Grant's destination was usually the Lucas market at St. Charles and Fourth Street. He prized his team so highly that nobody else was allowed to sit in the driving seat, with the exception of his son, Fred. Grant was keen that his eldest should emulate his own precocity as a teamster, and he would encourage the eight year old to accompany him to St. Louis with a load. Having

---

[107] Ibid., page 516.

[108] Walter B. Stevens , *Grant in St. Louis*, page 53. The Franklin Club.1916. Republished by Applewood Books. Accessed via Google Books. Jan. 14, 2012.

[109] Hamlin Garland, "Grant's life in Missouri ", *McClure's Magazine*. April 1897 , page 517.

[110] Pamela K. Sanfilippo, *Agriculture in Antebellum St. Louis,* pages 38-9. National Historic Site.

Fred to drive would also cut down on hired help. [111] Grant's horses would do anything for him and it was noted how much pleasure he took in their handling. [112] If he was hauling something heavy, he often walked along side the loaded wagon, saying that "horses had enough to draw the load without a lazy rider". [113]

Later in the day Tom and Bill were tacked up to bring Mr. and Mrs. Grant, each with a child on their back, to quilting bees and other neighbourhood socials. And they would double up as schoolmasters for Fred when Grant began teaching his eldest son to ride in his spare time. Grant always urged Fred to be brave during these early horseback lessons, and he showed his displeasure if he wasn't. For him, courage was as essential to the business of sitting on a horse as good hands and sound balance.

Grant's farming life at White Haven coincided with many scientific developments in agriculture. New machines were coming on stream : steel-bladed ploughs , mechanical threshers, better designed reapers and harrowers. [114] No doubt Grant, with his scientific mind, read about these in the many pamphlets published at the time. But he could only dream. Without a proper financial cushion, he would be unable to avail of the latest equipment. The science of soil analysis was also in vogue. Deficiencies could be identified and remedied with selective fertilising. [115] Grant was keen to put lime into the soil when he later returned to farming after the Civil War, reflecting a knowledge of what was needed to enrich the land and increase yields. [116] Letters to his father at the time show that he was principally interested in fruit and vegetable growing. Not only were they more appropriate crops for the size of his holding, eighty acres, they were also what he liked to eat. Sweet and Irish potatoes, cucumbers, corn, beet, melons : these were the crops he wanted.

---

[111] Charles Dana, *The Life of Ulysses S. Grant*, page 37. Gurdon,Bill & Co. 1868.

[112] Hamlin Garland, *Ulysses S. Grant: his Life and Character* , page 134. Doubleday & McClure. 1898.

[113] Walter B. Stevens, *Grant in St. Louis*, page 27. The Franklin Club 1916. Republished by Applewood Books. Accessed via Google Books. Jan. 14, 2012.

[114] Pamela K. Sanfilippo, *Agriculture in Antebellum St. Louis*, pages 45-51. National Hist. Site.

[115] Ibid, page 31.

[116] John Y. Simon, ed. *Papers of U. S. G.*. Letters to farm manager Nov. 24th 1870. Southern Illinois Univ. Press.

In the Winter of 1856 and again in the early Spring of 1857 (after a bad winter in which the wheat yield was down),Grant wrote to Jesse asking for a loan of $1000. This would help him buy the necessary equipment and seeds to get him up and running with his vegetable business. But it seems that the old benefactor was reluctant to help his son now for there is no record that the loan ever materialised. The fact that Ulysses had chosen to farm on Dent land with slavery at its heart would have been repellent to Grant's father , a keen amateur abolitionist. Ultimately , though, the wily Jesse may already have had other plans for Ulysses, and the promotion of the farming business would have got in the way of these.

From early on, Grant was aware that wheat didn't pay and he really only wanted to grow it for his own use. But his lack of start up funds meant that he had to fall back on it as a cash crop more than he wanted. By 1857, the end of the Crimean War saw cheap Russian grain flooding back onto the market, and the price of cereal fell. [117] Farmers had to switch to the production of butter and potatoes after the collapse. But Grant's yield of potatoes was disappointing.

On a visit to St Louis a chance encounter on the street lead to a dinner invitation from an old acquaintance of the west coast - the versatile and volatile Ned Beale. One time naval officer, surveyor and rescuer of General Stephen Kearny 's men in California in 1846, Beale was just back from leading an expeditionary party to the West. Both men probably had a laugh over Beale's decision to use Tunisian camels along with mules and horses for the expedition. The camels turned out to be a perfect choice, except for the fact that other animals for miles around could sense their presence long before they were even seen. Any horse that encountered them on the road - from carriage horse to saddle pony to wagon mule- was almost certain to bolt in terror. Not surprisingly the bright idea was shelved for future surveys .

The French called Carondelet "Vide Poche ". And perhaps the title had resonance for Grant too. Southern soil was to yield up few riches to him . Grant's droll military secretary, Ely Parker, who was to dabble in agriculture himself before the war, thought that it cost more to run a farm than a steamboat. [118] In many ways the Grants lacked the necessary unsentimental approach to be farmers - treating all the animals as pets rather than as a means of livelihood. For instance Julia was particularly proud of her collection of brahmas, bantams and shanghais, and named them all individually.

---

[117] Pamela K. Sanfilippo, *Agriculture in Antebellum St. Louis*, page 30. Nat. Hist. Site.

[118] William H. Armstrong , *Warrior in Two Camps*, page 78. Syracuse University Press.

Of his time as a farmer, Grant said: "I worked very hard, never losing a day because of bad weather, and accomplished the object in a moderate way." [119] According to Julia he was much more successful than Colonel Dent, achieving much higher yields. By 1858 he was farming two hundred acres of ploughed land belonging to his brother-in-law. Perhaps the final verdict on Grant's abilities as a farmer should be left to his neighbours at the time, many of whom had been farming the land for decades. In the words of one, Trip Reavis, Grant was good at what he did but simply didn't know how to get the results out of farming. [120]

But ill-health was to take Grant away from the plough for good. The debilitating form of vivax malaria he'd known intermittently in his younger days came back to afflict him. The onset of symptoms was devastatingly sudden, coming at forty-eight hour intervals, in keeping with the life cycle of the parasite itself. These symptoms consisted mainly of fever, splitting headache, icy joint pains, and chills that made the teeth literally chatter. [121] The lassitude that accompanied the malaria made working the land impossible now. Reluctantly, Ulysses was forced to sell his equipment, livestock and his beloved team.

Leaving his family behind in the country, he moved to the city for the first time and tried his hand at real estate with a relation of the Colonel's. St. Louis had grown explosively in both population and trade in the preceding few years. It was now a place of muddy cinder-strewn streets, plank sidewalks, crowded omnibuses, and rows of steamboats by the Mississippi wharf. Grant took an unfurnished back room with his new partner at South Sixteenth Street. He was on shanks' mare once more, and between January and March of that year he trudged the weary twelve miles out to White Haven on Saturday evening to see the family. On Sunday evening he trudged back again.

Unfortunately, Grant had little aptitude for the real estate business and was soon looking for another job. As a West Point graduate he was qualified to apply for county engineer, and he had high hopes of securing the post. Grant pulled out all the stops to get it. One of the many referees on his letter of application was the St. Louis saddler, Thornton Grimsley. Grant failed to get the position however, possibly

---

[119] U.S. Grant, *Memoirs*, page 111. Penguin Classics.

[120] Walter B. Stevens, *Grant in St. Louis*. The Franklin Club 1916. Republished Applewood Books, 21 Feb 2008. Accessed via Google Books. Jan. 12, 2012.

[121] Margaret Humphreys, *Malaria*, page 9. Johns Hopkins Univ. Press.

because of his association with the slave-holding Dents . The city fathers sought to surround themselves with county officials of unquestioned loyalty to the Union. It was a disappointment. Even his attempts at selling his brother Simpson's horse in St. Louis were a disaster. In a letter to "Simp" at the end of 1859, Grant described how he'd given the horse out on trial to a man who promised to pay $100 if he liked him; but after two weeks there was no sign of either horse, saddle or buyer. [122]

On Julia's advice, Ulysses went to see his father. Jesse Grant, who had been nearly wiped out by malaria as a young man, found a clerking job for his eldest son at the family leather goods store in main street, Galena, Illinois , a town that had become prosperous through its lead mines and steam boat traffic. [123] There was a good reason for installing Ulysses in the shop. Grant's younger brother, Simpson, who ran the store, was dangerously ill with the family curse, tuberculosis. Perhaps Jesse envisaged that Ulysses would fill his brother's role in time.

Jesse Grant's store on main street Galena must have been an interesting shop to step into. Its stocks of saddles, bridles, harness, and French and Ohio calves would have reached right up to the high ceiling. The smell of leather would have hung strongly in the air, and in the vast storeroom and counting room at the back. The store would have been a meeting place for many diverse groups - farmers, fur traders, cobblers, livery owners, passengers off the steamboats. A relaxed and perhaps indifferent Grant would be seen reading a newspaper with his feet propped up on the counter. But he moved fast enough when a customer came into the shop, frequently retreating in haste to one of the back rooms. [124]

One thing that made him highly useful in the store was his ability to sling a hide. Many of them weighed up to two hundred and fifty pounds. Yet Ulysses made light work of them. He was also a good judge of a hide and was sent to the country to negotiate with rural sellers, particularly as Simp was increasingly unable to make the journeys. He enjoyed the travel and the open air. The men in the shop, including his brothers, respected him as a man who had seen a great deal of the world and had been through the sort of trials that they could scarcely imagine. Yet on the whole,

---

[122] John Y. Simon ed., *The Papers of U. S. G.* .Vol. 1, Oct 24th 1859. Letter to Samuel Simpson Grant. Southern Illinois Univ. Press.

[123] Kenneth N. Owens, *Galena,Grant and the Fortunes of War*, pages 2-3. Pick and Gad Publications. 1963.

[124] William H. Armstrong, *Warrior in Two Camps*, pages 73-74. Syracuse University Press.

Grant showed little aptitude for the retail trade. He was an indifferent and unpersuasive salesman who often trusted people with prices too much.

Grant's time in Galena was significant. Many of the people who made his acquaintance there became key members of his staff during the war. These included William Rowley, Ely Parker and especially a young attorney with swarthy complexion and eyes as black as the charcoal he had once burned for a living, John Aaron Rawlins. Rawlins handled any legal matters associated with the leather goods shop. Grant's involvement in the Mexican War made him interesting to many people, and Rawlins was no exception. The serious-minded young lawyer succeeded in drawing the ex-captain out when many others failed. Similarly Ely Parker, the Seneca Indian who worked as a civil engineer on the Galena customhouse, had no problem with the Grant reserve: it reminded him of many of his friends among the Iroquois .[125] According to Grant's biographer Lloyd Lewis, both men shared a passion for horses and silence. Grant always had an instinctive sympathy and fascination for the American Indian , perhaps because he himself possessed the "woodcraft" of the native American: "...... knew places, localities, the lay of the ground, what the skies had to say as to weather and other mysteries." [126]

Now there was talk of another conflict, potentially bloodier than the Mexican War. The papers wrote of little else. In the evenings after work Ulysses would read the articles aloud to Julia, whose eyesight was poor. Every speech for and against secession was carefully read out.

For the moment Grant had very different matters to deal with : customers in the shop, collecting money, filling out invoices, putting up boxes, selling goods, finding the price of things. He had no horse in Galena - he had no need of one. His house was situated on a steep bluff at 121 South High Street, and was accessed from Main Street by a vast network of wooden steps that were as tedious to negotiate as the work below.

---

[125] Ibid , page 74.

[126] John Russell Young, *Men and Memories,* page 474. F. Tennyson Neely. 1901.

Chapter 9

*R*ondy

Within three years of leaving Jesse's leather goods store in Galena, Grant was the highest ranking officer in Lincoln's vast army, with the finest selection of battle chargers at his disposal. It was some compensation for his failure to gain a cavalry appointment in his early career. Indeed Grant had more mounts at his disposal than some of his cavalry generals.

Because of the way in which Grant conducted his campaigns, he was seldom out of the saddle. As the war progressed he made sure he had several choice rides at any time, often with contrasting traits. Grant was fortunate in his medium height and weight . It gave him the flexibility to ride anything from a fourteen hand pony to a seventeen hand giant. Several criteria were at play in his choice of mount : speed, comfortable paces and endurance for the long journeys and marches, height for difficult terrain, presence and good movement for ceremony, long legs for the mud. And while their rider was usually dressed informally like his hero of old, Zachary Taylor, with a battered hat and a private's coat (although he made sure it was that of a cavalry private),the Grant horses were immaculately turned out in full caparison . He took his horses very seriously. According to an early biographer ".. friends used to say that to disparage his charger or to ride a better one, was a sure way to lose favour". [127]

This was all a far cry from the early weeks of the war when Grant purchased an unprepossessing horse from a small livery yard in Galena to serve as his first war horse. Events had moved swiftly in the Spring of 1861 to take Grant away from his monotonous clerkship in Illinois. Confederates had opened fire on a garrison at Fort Sumter on April 12th, prompting civil war. Six days later Grant attended a meeting in Galena courthouse to organise volunteers and from that day on "… never went into our leather store after that meeting, to put up a package or do other business." [128]

    The horse, "Rondy", was acquired in Galena by Grant's youngest brother, Orvil, from a local livery owner, John C. Calderwood ,who had a yard at 60 Commerce Street just north of the De Soto Hotel. "Rondy" seemed to have reflected his modest price. In a letter to Julia, it is clear that Grant was already itching for a replacement.[129] He asked her to tell Orvil to look out for another "fine horse" in Galena, saying that "Rondy" would "do him" for the march to Quincy that he was about to undertake (ninety miles). "Rondy" wasn't quite up to Grant's notion of a suitable mount for a colonel - his entry rank. The problem may have been that the horse was a little long in the tooth. Grant liked to give his horses nicknames: "Old Nuisance", "Mankiller", "Kangaroo", "Hippadrome", "Bucephelus" ,"The Waif", "Flying Cloud" to name a few. About this time Fred Grant ,then eleven years old, remembered his father riding a horse called "Methuselah" and this may have been a reference to "Rondy". Shortly afterwards Grant borrowed a horse from one of his staff. [130] "Rondy" was then donated to Fred, who, in spite of his tender years, had accompanied Grant to camp. Fred would be the recipient of his father's equestrian cast offs many times , both then and in years to come.

    As Grant's rank increased, so too did his apparent need for a more impressive horse. By August 1861, he had been appointed brigadier general of volunteers,

---

[127] Albert D. Richardson, *Personal History of U. S. Grant* , page 259. American Publishing Co.1868.

[128] U. S. Grant , *Personal Memoirs of Ulysses S. Grant,* page 122.Penguin Classics.

[129] John Y. Simon , ed. *Papers of USG.* Vol. 2. Letter to Julia June 26th 1861. Southern Illinois Univ. Press.

[130] Ibid, Letter to Julia ,July 7th 1861.

thanks in large part to the Galena congressman who saw his potential, Elihu Washburne . Although burdened with huge workloads, he found time to write to his friend in St. Louis, Charles Ford, advising him that there was a horse belonging to him at Jesse Arnot's livery stable and that one of his staff would pick it up. [131] It is not known who this horse was or whether Grant ever took possession of him . It may have been the horse shot from under Grant at Belmont later that year.

Arnot's and other similar livery establishments were busy and impressive places. The St. Louis establishment was located at Chestnut Street and was five stories high. Horses were kept in the basement level with carriages and buggies taking up the entire first floor. Arnot's took great pride in the quality of its stock, claiming in an early advertisement that many of its horses for rent were easily capable of doing a mile in two minutes forty seconds, either as a buggy or saddle horse . The stables were run by an expert trainer, accomplished in both horsemanship and veterinary skills. [132]

Many horses were being seized around Missouri at this time for use in the War . At first Grant disapproved of the practice and asked for its suppression in a letter to a colonel of Missouri volunteers. But by August of 1861 he had become more ambiguous on the subject. Perhaps this was in response to the aggression shown to his men by the inhabitants of the district . He proposed the setting up of a mounted home guard , in which members could obtain a horse from "good secessionists who have been aiding and abetting the southern cause". [133] As the War progressed Grant became an enthusiastic recipient of good Confederate horses . It was one of his favourite ways of making "war support war."

Throughout the war, Grant was to use his own Grimsley saddle instead of the standard federal issue, the McClellan. By May 1864, Horace Porter, Grant's aide de camp, described the general's Grimsley as being " somewhat the worse for wear" , as he had used it in all his campaigns from Fort Donelson to the present time . He was obviously very attached to it. During his time in St. Louis , he would have known the colourful, bellicose saddle maker who designed it , Thornton Grimsley . Orphaned early in life, Grimsley was apprenticed to a saddler in his

---

[131] Ibid, Grant to Charles Ford ,Sept 1st 1861.

[132] Taylor and Crooks, *Sketch Book of St. Louis* , pages 306-7.

[133] John Y. Simon, ed. *Papers of USG*. Vol. 2. Letter to Captain Speed Butler, Aug 22nd, 1861. Southern Illinois Univ. Press.

teens, before striking out on his own in 1830s St Louis . He traded at No. 37, North First Street, making a fortune out of supplying good, long- distance saddles to fur traders. His distinctive saddles were also used extensively by the United States army in the war with Mexico and this is most likely where Grant became familiar with the saddle that he was to favour so much. [134]By the time Grant was living near St. Louis, Grimsley had become one of the city's most prominent citizens and , like Grant's father-in-law, had the title "Colonel" to prove it. Grant even asked for his signature of recommendation when he applied unsuccessfully for the position of county engineer in 1859. In spite of his enthusiasm for war, Thornton Grimsley saw little of the conflict that was to feature his saddle so prominently. While working at his store in 1861, he took ill and died soon after.

The Grimsley saddle was light ,with a compact tree and a high pommel and cantle. Its predominant feature was its durability . This was because the tree was encased in rawhide, put on green and drawn tight by contraction in the drying process. Writing in the 1840s bible for emigrants travelling west, *The Prairie Traveller* ,Capt. Randolph Barnes Marcy considered the Grimsley the best saddle he had ever come across. Marcy had used Grimsleys on the mules when making his harrowing forced march across the Rocky Mountains in the middle of winter . He observed then that not one of the animals' backs had been injured. The Grimsley was lighter but with a more elaborate finish than the McClellan, and probably allowed for a deeper seat on the part of the rider. What 's noticeable about the Grimsley is that the stirrup bar is located much further back in the saddle, positioning the rider's leg underneath his trunk and thus creating the desired straight plumb line going from shoulder, hip to heel. But without prominent knee rolls, it would have needed skill to keep position in the saddle. In the McClellan, the stirrup bar was located much farther forward. Although this was more comfortable for the rider it would have put him automatically into the less classical chair position .

Grant's leather shop in Galena traded extensively in horse tack, and Grant must have owned and appreciated the best of horse furniture. In an army inventory of August 26th, 1861, he was listed as already having three saddles and bridles ,valued at $600 in total. [135] This was a good sum then , reflecting the quality

---

[134] Lawrence O. Christensen ed., *Dictionary of Missouri Biography* , pages 356-7.

[135] John Y. Simon, ed. *The Papers of U.S. Grant*. Vol. 2. August 26th ·1861.

of the tack . Three months later this precious equipment was lost at the battle of Belmont .

Grant was kept extremely busy between drilling his regiment and dealing with more official correspondence and letter-writing than he had ever known in his life. The workload kept him up until the small hours of the morning in spite of signs of a looming malaria attack. He still managed to write diligently to Julia, as he had done in Mexico. Julia must have been interested to hear about his horses, because he would tell her little details about them, referring to them by name and commenting on their qualities. In one letter, he complained that he had no time to ride out on his horse, which "as you know always keeps me well." [136] Five days later, however, his correspondence indicated he had rearranged his schedule to do just that every evening after four o'clock, perhaps on Julia's advice.

---

[136] Ibid, Letter to Julia ,20th Sept 1861,

Chapter 10

Jack

Everybody noticed "Jack" , from Julia Grant to the officers in the field, to the war reporters who accompanied the campaign from 1861 to the end of 1863. There are more references to Grant's "clayback" horse than almost any of his other war mounts, with the exception of "Cincinnati" . Perhaps it was his unique appearance that caught people's attention: flowing mane and tail of bright silver, black eyes and a coat variously described as cream, yellow, dun or light sorrel. His striking appearance made him ideal for ceremonial occasions. Julia recalled him vividly at a review in Cairo , 1861, where he seemed to enjoy the pomp and ceremony of reviews better than his rider !

> ……Old Jack, a beautiful light sorrel, with sweeping white mane and tail, would come dashing up to the flagstaff near which our ambulance was placed, and turning around, would proudly stand for the regiments to pass him in review". [137]

---

[137] John Y.Simon, ed. *The Personal Memoirs of Julia Dent Grant*, page 9 .

According to eleven year-old Fred, Grant first came across "Jack" when he took his regiment to Missouri in July 1861. There a local farmer brought a stallion to his father's makeshift camp on the Illinois river. The horse appealed to Grant right away. He purchased the stallion with borrowed money since he had few savings of his own. [138] Perhaps the youngster might have been mistaken in his recollection however. A letter from General John McClernand to Grant after the battle of Belmont (November 12th, 1861), contains a description of a captured stallion with white mane and tail that is too similar to "Jack" to be a coincidence. McClernand's servant had caught the horse and turned it over to the brigade quartermaster for appraisal. McClernan added that the horse was subject to "any transfer of possession" that the general might be pleased to order. [139] Many horses were captured at Belmont and the horse Grant was riding had been shot from under him. It is highly likely that he would have been happy to receive a captured horse at the time.

Unlike most of Grant's horses, "Jack" seems to have been a lazy, phlegmatic type, in spite of being a stallion. Sturdy rather than fast or blooded, he required both whip and spur under saddle, in which case he was, according to his rider, "the best saddle horse you ever rode". Maybe this is why the general took to calling him the "Old Nuisance". This laziness must have been a distinct liability on the battlefield however, where speed and maneuverability were paramount. But for endurance and toughness on long marches, "Jack" apparently had no equal. Grant evidently had the measure of him and was able to overcome his idleness with skillful riding. Besides, the general must have valued his fine appearance. There is no record of how big he was, but he was probably not a large animal. The fact that Grant always rode him in a curb bit and with spurs, as indicated in a letter to a friend in 1864, indicates that he was probably a small, compact type that needed to be held together - in marked contrast to, say, "Cincinnati".

"Jack" carried the general during all the campaigns of 1862 and 1863 and many key journeys of the war were made on his back. It was "Jack" that bore him swiftly away from Admiral Foote's ship the night before the attack on Fort Donelson. It was "Jack" that made the hard reconnoiters in the bottomless Tennessee mud before and during Shiloh. It was "Jack" who undertook the

---

[138] Cadwallader, Sylvanus, *Three Years with Grant*, page 18.

[139] John Y. Simon, ed. *Papers of Ulysses S. Grant*. Vol. 3 notes. Nov. 12 1861.

harrowing journey to Chattanooga through the Cumberland Pass in November 1863 . The latter was Grant's first real journey on horseback after a serious riding accident at New Orleans the previous September , and he suffered greatly on the way ."A description of the roads would give you no conception of them" he wrote to Julia shortly afterwards. On at least one occasion "Jack" lost his footing in the dark and fell on his rider, pinning the injured leg to the ground . "Jack" had an unfortunate habit of falling on his rider. He had almost certainly done the same in the mud of Tennessee before the battle of Shiloh in 1862.

After the Chattanooga campaign Grant decided to retire "Old Nuisance". When the general was called east in March 1864, "Jack" was sent to Grant's business advisor and U.S. marshal for Northern Illinois , J. R. Jones , for his personal use . The general wrote a letter to Jones enquiring whether "Old Jack" had arrived safely into his care in Chicago ,and even gave tips about how he should be ridden : curb bit,use of spurs etc. Grant added that "Jack" could also be driven to carriage, although not surprisingly, his speed was nothing to write home about. [140]

At the end of the war, Grant donated the "Old Nuisance" to the Chicago Fair to raise money for the Sanitary Commission, which oversaw the work of improving camp and hospital conditions for the troops. Grant wrote to one of the organisers, Ellen Sherman , with his usual recommendations: "If I was not deceived in the purchase of Jack, he is now eleven years old . He is a very fine saddle horse, very gentle in harness, but requires whip and spur." [141]

"Jack" had celebrity status now, owing to Grant's fame. His arrival in Chicago was greeted with terrific fanfare . As huge crowds thronged the entire length of the route, Grant rode his old stallion from the train station to the fair grounds. The only snag was that he now found himself without the obligatory whip and spurs, while "Jack" had grown even more deliberate in his retirement. Grant could do little to prevent his famous charger from sauntering aimlessly along on the journey. Five hundred tickets at $2 a head were sold that day, and the winner was Jirah D. Cole of Erie Street, a member of the Schubert Male Quartette . It was at Cole's peaceful stables that " Old Nuisance" saw out the rest of his eventful life, dying four years later at the age of fifteen. [142]

---

[140] John Y. Simon,ed. *Papers of Ulysses S. Grant* Vol. 12. Letter to J.R. Jones, Nov 13th 1864.

[141] *New York Times*. Letter to Ellen Sherman , June 18th,1865.

[142] Philip A. Pines, *The Complete Book of Harness Racing*, page 260. 1982.

However, Grant's correspondence to his farm manager in 1874 gives a tantalising clue that he used "Jack" as a breeding stallion on at least one occasion . In the letter he mentions the existence of a filly that was sired by a "yellow Mexican saddle horse" that he once owned - "of great beauty but not blooded of course." [143] If this was the case, "Jack" was the only war horse to produce a foal for the general.

When it came to Grant's exploits on horseback, rivers were never far away. One incident early in the war involved the biggest of them all . In November 1861 Grant, now promoted to brigadier general of the Twenty-First Illinois Volunteer Infantry, was mounting one of his first campaigns in Missouri , a state with very mixed allegiances. The operation was both a training exercise and a chance for real action for the men under his command.

Using the Mississippi River for access, Grant moved his troops on a Confederate camp at Belmont . The camp was duly routed, although during the battle the general's horse, a bay , was shot from under him. In all likelihood this is the horse that he had either brought out from Arnot's Livery Stables in St. Louis or had bought from Lt. Col. Alexander for $140. According to John Rawlins the same horse was a hopeless liability in the field, refusing to go where it was bid unless it had a lead from another horse. [144]

Grant quickly borrowed the horse of his friend from St. Louis, William Hillyer - now a member of staff with the rank of captain. Hillyer drew the short straw when he was given Fred Grant's pony as a replacement . The pony was soon killed in battle under Hillyer . In one day, Grant had lost two horses, and two pricey saddles and bridles as well. The most expensive part of his horse furniture, however, seemed to have been his saddle cloth, which he had left behind in camp.

Owing to inexperience, Grant lost control of his men who commenced looting the camp, enabling enemy troops to regroup and counterattack . The Federals were now surrounded and cut off from their boats. There followed a desperate scramble to get back to the transports before the enemy had them in their grasp. Without a staff officer accompanying him, Grant rode a borrowed horse that he was completely unfamiliar with to within a hair's breadth of the enemy. A nearby field planted with corn as tall as a house, gave him good cover from the Confederate

---

[143] John Y. Simon, ed., *Papers of U.S.G.* Vol 25. letter to Nat Carlin, April 14th 1874.

[144] James Harrison Wilson, *The Life of John A. Rawlins*, page 66. Letter of Rawlins to mother, Nov 15th 1861.

troops, a mere fifty yards away. Grant was the last Federal soldier on dry land now as his troops had already embarked and were ready to pull out. It is a credit to his iron nerve that he didn't dash for the boats. Instead he walked the horse calmly towards the river . What followed is best told in his own words - one of the few Civil War adventures with horses that he described in his memoirs:

> The captain of a boat that had just pushed out but had not started, recognised me and ordered the engineer not to start the engine . He then had a plank run out for me. . . .my horse seemed to take in the situation. There is no path down the bank and everyone acquainted with the Mississippi River knows that its banks do not vary at any great angle from the perpendicular . My horse put his fore feet over the bank without hesitation or urging ,and with his hind feet well under him, slid down the bank and trotted aboard the boat twelve or fifteen feet away over a single gang plank .I dismounted and went at once to the upper deck. [145]

It would be easy to imagine Grant - his shoulders nearly touching the tail of his horse - plunging down the massive bank . Enemy bullets posed little threat to his men on board because the river banks were higher than the heads of the men standing on the upper deck of the steamer. With the river virtually in flood and enemy fire whistling through the air, he could easily have been swept helplessly along by the current. It was a stroke of luck that he had lost his original horse earlier in the day, as this horse would almost certainly have refused to take him down the bank. Grant's Civil War career might have ended here. Characteristically he gave his horse the credit for his narrow escape.

Later on as the two sides met on a truce boat, the new commander discovered how close he had come to death. The troops he had been hiding from had, in fact, spotted him in the cornfield. Their commanding officer, General Leonidas Polk, had invited them to take a pot shot at him, but the rebels decided not to bother. Back in Galena , Julia Grant had had one of her dreams. As she dozed on her bed, she saw her husband raised up as if on horseback ,gazing at her reproachfully . When she woke up she was greatly disturbed. Julia and the children were supposed to have gone down to the camp some days before, but she had delayed the visit. Later Grant confided to her that as he made his escape, he was wondering what would become of them if he was to die that day. [146]

---

[145] U.S. Grant, *The Personal Memoirs of Ulysses S. Grant* , page 148. Penguin Classics .

[146] John Y. Simon, ed., *The Personal Memoirs of Julia Dent Grant,* page 93.

It was either on his yellow stallion, "Jack", or a horse called "Fox" that Grant made his fateful and hazardous journey to and from Admiral Foote's flag-ship before the attack on Fort Donelson. "Fox" was a spare horse that Grant used when he needed to rest "Jack" . His red coat suggested his name and he was described as fast and spirited. Roads had been cut up deeply and then had frozen hard, so that the horse had all his work cut out to convey his rider safely with reasonable speed. The general had envisaged a combined army and navy initiative to force the Confederates to surrender the fort. But the injured Admiral Foote was unable to give assistance. Grant knew as he travelled away from the ship that he must go it alone, formulating a new plan in the saddle as his horse trudged along in the wintry night.

Twenty-one thousand Confederate soldiers were well entrenched within the fortified walls of Donelson on the Cumberland River. Grant had only fifteen thousand men shivering in front of it in appalling weather . Yet he was determined to take it . Conspicuous on his clay-coloured horse, he rode tirelessly up and down the front to make sure the line was held. The cigar remained embedded in his fingers throughout . He was a welcome presence among the officers and men, many of whom were disheartened by the misery of cold and hunger. Panic broke out in the ranks when the troops realised that the Confederates were trying to force their way out. Grant insisted they must not escape, saying :"the one who attacks first will be victorious". Riding his horse, he coordinated the decisive assault that drove the enemy back into the fort.

Knowing he was trapped, the general commanding the troops inside the fort , Simon Bolivar Buckner , sent out a note requesting surrender terms. Grant famously demanded "unconditional surrender" of his old Mexican War comrade. When the two met inside the fort Grant put his private purse at the disposal of the man who had bailed him out in his time of financial distress many years before. Donelson put Grant on the map. In spite of himself, he was now a national hero. He won promotion to major general of volunteers and was now the highest ranking officer in the field of the western theatre. The papers portrayed him as the general who smoked a cigar on his yellow horse throughout the battle. And a legend came into being, with "Jack" an intrinsic part of this image. Grant never had to buy another cigar for himself for the rest of the war.

One of the distinguishing features of Grant's horsemanship during the war was that he never needed roads to get from one place to another. At the drop of a hat he would ride across fields and over hedges or swim his horse through any amount of streams if it meant getting to his destination quicker. [147] Night time wasn't a barrier to his activities either . For Grant, riding during the hours of darkness was as good a time as any, and he frequently risked falls in the process. There are many instances during the war when Grant made key journeys at night and suffered significant tumbles in the process. Running into trees was an additional hazard in the pitch dark. The endless reconnoitering in the saddle often served as an opportunity to discuss tactics with staff and finalise plans. They provided a chance to cross-question natives, fugitives and slaves for intelligence purposes and to formulate maps. Whether reconnoitering , marching , or directing a battle ,these journeys on horseback were a stiff test of riding at its boldest . As a result there were many adventures en route: some recorded by those who took part, but undoubtedly the vast majority left untold. Grant's style of command could pose a problem for staff members, particularly those who lacked endless reserves of physical stamina and coordination on a horse. Grant's officers had to become hard-riding soldiers quickly or face falling by the wayside.

The general's horse, again probably "Jack", was to fall on his rider two days before the battle of Shiloh in April 1862. It was a bad omen. The Tennessee ground was sodden, thanks to many days of torrential rain. Everyone knew that something big was going to happen in the surrounding countryside - a mixture of dense woodland and scattered farms. But exactly when was uncertain. Returning late from reconnoitering the enemy's position on the night of April the 4th , Grant and his small group of staff officers were riding in the pitch dark . Investigations of the topography would have shown that the land was bounded by three creeks, each of them in flood. All the officers could do was trust their horses to stick to the path . No doubt Grant was riding ahead at a more adventurous pace than the others when the horse lost his footing over a log and fell. His ankle was pinned under his mount, but because the ground was so yielding he escaped major injury. Although unbroken, the limb swelled so much that his riding boot had to be cut off and he was unable to walk without crutches for a week.

On Sunday morning ,the sound of enemy cannons was heard in the distance. The south's commander , Albert Sydney Johnston, had seized the initiative, attacking before the Federal troops in front of him could be reinforced. The officers in camp breakfasted early and had their battle chargers tacked in readiness. Preparing Grant's horse for the day's action was a French orderly whom everyone dubbed "Napoleon" . After "Jack" and the other horses were loaded onto a steamer,

---

[147] William H. Armstrong, *A Warrior in Two Camps - Ely Parker*, page 91.

Grant hobbled aboard with his officers. When the boat arrived at Pittsburg Landing he was helped to remount by one of his staff. But once in the saddle the leg injury was forgotten. Nearly leaving his entourage behind with his speed, he galloped "Jack" to the front.

Grant rode the lines throughout the long day : promising reinforcements, organising ammunition supplies , telling leaderless brigades where they might be most useful, offering practical advice and encouraging stragglers daunted by the intensity of fighting and their inexperience in battle. He deployed some cavalry to urge the stragglers back to their positions and to guide General Lew Wallace to the field, although the latter went astray and failed to arrive . Grant's omnipresence at Shiloh ,especially where the firing was at its fiercest, caused much anxiety to his staff officers, including the normally verbose aide de camp, Captain Hillyer, now reduced to silence by the danger. At one point Grant's scout, Carson ,had his head blown off within a few yards of the general, splattering everyone with blood. Firing became so intense around Grant's small party ,that bullets ricocheted under "Jack's" legs. His rider took shelter behind a small cabin which was soon ripped to pieces. Grant usually never rode with his sword, saying it hurt his hip. But he had reason to thank his decision to wear it that day ,as his scabbard deflected a Confederate bullet, causing the sword itself to fall to the ground.

Other officers had very close shaves that day. Major Hawkins had his hat, and General McPherson his horse, shot down . In a different part of the field General Sherman had three horses shot from under him. In his memoirs Grant wrote about McPherson's horse in surprising detail, observing that the charger kept on running until they were out of the enemy's range . It was only when the party stopped that the animal began to show signs of distress. Grant must have helped to examine the wound because he was able to say that a ball had struck the horse on his side behind the saddle and had gone straight through . The animal dropped dead some minutes later. [148] Grant had much sympathy for McPherson on the death of his horse. Perhaps this sympathetic account allowed him to vent his feelings on the loss of his own battle chargers.

By the end of the first day defeat looked inevitable. But a large line of cannons helped to block the Confederate advance to the river. The sound of this enormous battery was the loudest thing that had ever been heard in the war, causing noses and ears to trickle blood. In spite of pain and exhaustion, Grant visited every

---

[148] U.S. Grant , *The Personal Memoirs of Ulysses S. Grant* , page 190.

division commander on horseback that night, arguing in favour of an advance at dawn. Reinforcements had arrived by river and Grant was one of the few to express confidence that the situation could be turned around. Colonel Theophilus Dickey of the Fourth Illinois Cavalry was with Grant and his staff on the Sunday night. According to Dickey, Grant listened impassively to a "doleful rehearsal" of the results of the day's battle from his subordinates. Then he straightened out his good leg, turned to the cavalryman and remarked: "Dickey, do you like this kind of cavalry boot? ", bringing their despondent mutterings to an end. [149]

The following morning he was again lifted into the saddle and made his way to the front. Grant firmly believed that when two armies fought to the brink of exhaustion, whichever side was first to attack the following day was certain to win out . By Monday afternoon the tide had turned. The only sound to come from the Confederates now was intermittent musket fire. Though reputedly tone deaf, Grant often gauged a battle by ear, and the sound told him that the enemy was in retreat. Gathering up all the men at his disposal, he directed a final charge against the southerners, again sitting astride his palomino stallion.

Two of America's ablest generals had faced each other at Shiloh. But they suffered different fortunes. In spite of coordinating the final advance on Monday with an injured leg ,Grant came out of the campaign unscathed. Riding his magnificent bay thoroughbred, "Fire-eater ", into the face of the Union line the previous afternoon, Grant's southern counterpart Albert Sydney Johnston was shot in the leg and needlessly bled to death for want of a tourniquet .

But the losses on both sides had been difficult to justify. After Shiloh General Halleck, never over fond of Grant, [150] had his officer removed from field duty and reassigned to a reserve force . Halleck himself would take command in the field. The national army now turned its attention to occupying Corinth ,Mississippi , under the field leadership of a man who "couldn't ride his horse faster than a walk". [151] Grant must have felt the injustice keenly. Many years later in an informal conversation with an aide , he mentioned Shiloh as the place where his tenacious

---

[149] Colonel Nicholas Smith, *Grant, the Man of Mystery*, page 117.

[150] John Y. Simon, *Grant and Halleck : Contrasts in Command*, page 19. Marquette University Press. 1996.

[151] Colonel Nicholas Smith, *Grant the Man of Mystery* , page 126.

presence had been most influential in turning the battle. Grant considered resigning but his persuasive comrade, William Tecumseh Sherman ,who had given him such unflinching support during the battle ,was able to talk him out of the idea, arguing that his fortunes would be sure to rise if he stayed. Grant was allowed to move his headquarters to Memphis . He had only a few staff members and a small convoy of Illinois Cavalry to accompany him as he set out on the journey. Shortly after he came within a whisker of being captured by Confederates when he stopped to have dinner in a planter's house on the road. Only the exhaustion of the southerners' horses was to deny them.[152]

Grant's friend from his days in Galena, John Aaron Rawlins, had accompanied the general from the outset of the war and was the only staff officer to stick it out for the duration, progressing from adjutant to chief of staff. He was devoid of military training and was very different in personality to Grant, but the two men worked well together. Much is made of how indispensable Rawlins was to Grant's success. But if "Black John" had been a poor rider - unable to jump countless hedges or swim his horse across streams - this indispensable quality would have been to no avail. As a young man Rawlins had abandoned the family farm to pursue a career as a lawyer, but his early life as a farmer's son might have served as a better preparation for life in Grant's camp than his legal studies. Other members of staff thought Rawlins inexcusably rude to Grant - calling him "old skeeziks" within earshot. [153] Rawlins was rigid and uncompromising - as adept at saying "no" as Grant wasn't. His talents were to spare his chief a great deal of grief from petitioners and from the machinations of military rivals.

    The chief of staff was very proud of his war mount : a long-legged, high-withered horse with a beautiful tail called "General Blair". But one morning he awoke to find his horse's tail had been reduced to the appearance of a shoe brush. Turning white with anger , Rawlins vowed to shoot the perpetrator, whom he assumed to be a mischievous comrade within his own ranks. Grant roared with laughter at the outburst, knowing well who the culprit was. He finally explained to a disbelieving Rawlins that the beautiful tail had almost certainly been eaten by a mule that had got loose in the night. Rawlins and his horse's tail remained the butt of Grant's jokes for many weeks after. Finally, the chief of staff could take no more and

---

[152] U.S. Grant, *The Personal Memoirs of Ulysses S Grant* , page 210.

[153] William H. Armstrong, *Ely Parker : Warrior in Two Camps,* page 94.

retaliated by asking Grant how he would like it if some old mule came and attacked the tail of his precious yellow stallion . [154](The demands of the front ,with constant wettings on the tough journeys in all weathers, robbed Rawlins of his health. After the grueling journey to Chattanooga over the Cumberland Mountains in the winter of 1863, he was more or less unwell. He died early of tuberculosis in September 1869.)

By all accounts Grant's other staff members were a motley crew, particularly in the first years of conflict. Many had been friends and acquaintances in Galena and St. Louis and were more familiar with a desk, pen and bar stool than a sword and uniform. Charles Dana of the War Office painted a grim picture of these individuals, noting that they compared badly with the staff of even minor generals . Dana questioned whether they had any worthwhile contribution to make at all , since their general seemed self-sufficient in the field and in writing his own dispatches .

It seems that Clark Lagow had been appointed a staff officer by Grant for no other reason than that he came out of his original Illinois regiment. Lagow was renowned for few things, except perhaps his penchant for fine liquor and horses. Like Grant, Lagow was a daring horseman, risking all manner of stunts on horseback, although frequently they didn't come off. The cavalry officer, Col. Dickey, got lost in thick woods with Lagow as they were making their way back to camp from Iuka . When Dickey's horse refused to go any further, Lagow spurred his mount down a ravine in front of them, but landed in a heap in the stream below.

The rock-like Ely Parker was assistant adjutant general on Grant's staff, eventually becoming military secretary - writing some of the general's orders in his distinctive and beautiful hand. Parker, like Grant's other military secretary Adam Badeau, was not a man for the outdoors. But he had a good mastery of a horse and proved fearless and impassive on the battle field. Adam Badeau cut a ridiculous figure on a horse at the best of times. Completely unfamiliar with the art of riding before the war, his entry into the field marked a true baptism of fire in the saddle with many dangerous and exhausting rides.

Captain Audenried of the Fifth Regular Cavalry had the job of riding out after Grant, sometimes carrying his overcoat strapped to the back of his saddle. [155]

---

[154] Albert D. Richardson, *Personal History of Ulysses S. Grant,* page 259. American Publishing Co. 1868.

[155] Horace Porter, *Campaigning with Grant*, pages 41-42.

Grant also used a small contingent of that regiment for escorts. William R. Rowley, the county clerk whose desk in Galena Grant had once measured and then covered with new leather, served on the staff from February 1862 until October 1864, when ill-health forced his resignation. The intensely loyal Theodore Bowers had served with Grant since Donelson and was a great favourite. His abiding post-war ambition was not unlike Grant's - to retire to a quiet farm in Indiana - a dream cut short by his untimely death under the wheels of a train in New York shortly after the war.

It was known that Grant frequently and deliberately rode out without an escort, and this, together with the fact that there was nothing on his plain blouse to indicate rank, is why he was seldom recognised by the enemy. But perhaps his style of riding made it difficult for his staff members to keep up anyway. They would undoubtedly have had to be well mounted to do so.

In July of 1862, Henry Halleck was recalled to Washington to coordinate operations from where he felt most at ease: behind a desk. This allowed Grant to enter active service once more. By October, he was back in charge of the Army of the Tennessee with headquarters at Jackson. Since there was a relative lull in activities at this time he returned his horse ,"Jack" ,to Illinois for a month's rest . *The Northwestern Gazette* proudly announced the arrival of "General Grant's noble war horse" by the cars in Galena, Illinois . The horse was stabled at Calderwood's livery yard where Grant had purchased his first and most unglamorous war mount, "Rondy" . [156]

The following month "Jack" was back with Grant at headquarters. Member of the press , Sylvanus Cadwallader, remembered accompanying the general to camp. During the journey, a despatch rider rode up to the general and managed to tread on "Jack's" heels. Grant rebuked the soldier sharply, saying there were few things he disliked more than having his horse's heels trod upon. The depth of Grant's irritation took the newspaperman by surprise and he had to wait several years before he saw Grant this nettled again. [157] Grant rarely lost his temper but the sight of anyone mistreating a horse would be sure to evoke a strong reaction. An orderly who had been a great favourite fell out of favour forever when he was seen striking "Jack". [158]

---

[156] *Northwestern Gazette,* Oct 21st 1862.

[157] Sylvanus Cadwallader, *Three Years with Grant* , pages 18-19.

[158] Albert D. Richardson, *Personal History of Ulysses S. Grant* , page 259. American Publishing Co. 1868.

Newspaper accounts of the general's style of riding during this period were numerous. Again Cadwallader described his way of going when mounted. Grant seemed to be an early practitioner of the forward seat. If he wanted to travel any faster than a walk he would incline his body forward from the hip as if he was anxious to get to his destination quicker than the horse could carry him. [159] Many bystanders who had only seen the general mounted in the field thought him tall, and were surprised at his average height when they saw him standing. [160] Frank Wilkie of the *New York Times* gave a more flattering account of Grant's bearing in the field, contrasting his pitching, stooped way of walking with his proud posture on horseback. He also pinpointed the likely secret of Grant's success in the saddle - his ability not only to sit on the horse's back but to make himself part of the horse through his seat and posture.

> On horseback he loses all the awkwardness which distinguishes him as he moves about on foot. ... he seems a portion of his steed, without which the full effect would be incomplete………..[161]

Perhaps "Jack" summed up the quality of Grant's early campaigns in the West. Not the fastest or the best bred horse, not without his faults, he none the less built up a reputation as a solid and dependable stayer.

---

[159] Sylvanus Cadwallader, *Three Years with Grant*, page 351.

[160] S.H. Byers, *With Fire and Sword,* page 195.

[161] Francis Bangs Wilkie, *New York Times,* June 12, 1863.

Chapter 11

Kangaroo

With his new authority, Grant felt confident to suggest an assault on Vicksburg. Perhaps his amazing qualities were never so well demonstrated as during the campaign to take the town that proved the key to the Mississippi River. For Grant it had been like a second chance after his removal in the wake of Shiloh. Now he acted like a man possessed, showing a quick-thinking inventiveness and an urgency not seen before. Never was he so heedless of his own physical safety or comfort and never was his stamina in the saddle so tested.

Geography afforded Vicksburg unparalleled defense against attack. Jefferson Davis dubbed it the "Gibraltar" of the Confederacy. In the early spring of 1863, Grant hatched a plan that would rewrite the military textbooks. His intention was to march his army south through difficult terrain. Then with the help of the navy, they would cross the mile-wide Mississippi and come out underneath Vicksburg, some sixty miles from the town. They would break free from their supply base and March through hazardous territory, laying siege to Vicksburg from the rear. The town would then have its back to the river and would lose its impregnability.[162] The plan

---

[162] U.S. Grant, *Memoirs*. page 228 ,249.

called on his army to virtually live off the land as they went. Grant had seen how this could be done when Nathan Bedford Forrest's cavalry had destroyed his supplies a few months earlier, forcing his retreat.

In order to get below the town, Admiral Porter's navy first had to run the gauntlet of Confederate batteries situated on the Vicksburg bluffs. From a nearby boat Grant, together with his family and officers, watched as Federal boats, protected by bales of cotton, were pounded by the most formidable cannon power that the rebels could muster. The outcome for the flotilla was inconclusive in the darkness. And the minute the guns fell silent, Grant dashed ashore and mounted his horse. He spent the whole of the following day galloping across the bends to New Carthage, over treacherous, rickety corduroy roads.

With him on the journey was Illinoian staff officer James Harrison Wilson. A wizard in the saddle like Grant, Wilson had also been given the job of training intractable mounts as a West Point cadet (1856-1860) and had many close shaves in the process. Always well mounted, he was able to keep up with Grant's lightning pace while serving on his staff at the front. The round trip of seventy-five miles took two days. Grant travelled at top speed, perhaps using the blood horse, "Kangaroo". The swift ride had a happy outcome and Grant's plans could go ahead. The Mississippi was in flood that early Summer. Ginhouse and plantation timbers were needed to provide bridges and pathways for the determined soldiers who made slow but steady progress to the point of embarkation. [163]

Using Colonel Benjamin Grierson's cavalry raid to divert attention away from his own activities, Grant sent twenty-three thousand men across the Mississippi. Shortly before the embarkation, he had a miss-hap with his own horse when the animal tripped and fell badly in the darkness. Grant's companion on the journey, government official Charles Dana, expected to see the general being pitched out of the saddle. Instead he kept his seat, rebalanced the floundering horse and rode on without so much as a curse. To Dana it was a signal of the unusual calmness of the man he'd come to spy on. [164]

When Grant made the Mississippi crossing, he himself had nothing except the clothes he stood up in and a toothbrush. The following few weeks were a test of sheer physical endurance for everyone. Grant allowed a small contingent of cavalry to cross over to act as couriers and scouts. He borrowed their horses from now on,

---

[163] James Harrison Wilson, *Under the Old Flag*. page 169.

[164] Charles A. Dana, *Recollections of the Civil War*, page 59.

along with a saddle that consisted of nothing but a naked tree and some rudimentary stirrups. [165]This same saddle doubled up as a pillow, accompanied by a saddle cloth for a blanket, on the few occasions when sleep could be snatched in a nearby farmhouse or church bench. Initially Grant was mounted on a good horse from Colonel Mudd's Illinois Cavalry, obtained for him by Colonel James Harrison Wilson . There are many accounts of Grant on his borrowed horses during this period . It is here that the legend of the "dust covered man on a dust covered horse" takes root . He was a highly influential presence on the rapid march as his men filed by, urging them on in person with his customary quiet, confident air . "Men, push right along; close up fast, and hurry over.." [166]

The speed with which the Federals moved was the key to the success of their plans . Grant's style on horseback reflected this urgency . He rode incessantly for the first three days and most of the nights. [167] Food was scanty and irregular . The weather provided many discomforts - torrential rain , a mixture of cold nights and stifling heat, and dust up to the ankles. Grant was constantly in the saddle, pressing the men to move on swiftly, then galloping ahead of the infantry to the next flash point . It was common to set off at midnight on a journey to confer with one of his generals and return to headquarters through woods in the small hours of the morning.

In spite of the seriousness of the mission, Grant made a point of making the march as pleasant as possible for everyone, with a geniality and cheerfulness that was infectious . He would say to James H. Wilson who often rode up beside him because he was well mounted: "Wilson , there's a fallen tree you haven't jumped yet . Put your horse at it and let us see how he takes it." [168] The spectacle of the horse leaping was light relief to Grant and helped to ease the tension of these times. Wilson would have had no problem with these leaping challenges . According to himself, nobody in the army could out-jump him . (Later when he assumed his

---

[165] U.S. Grant, *Memoirs*, page 266.

[166] Major S. H. M. Byers, *With Fire and Sword*, page 65.

[167] James Harrison Wilson, *Under the Old Flag*, page 174.

[168] Ibid, page 194.

cavalry command, he favoured the jumping of ditches and other cross-country obstacles as a form of drill for his men). [169]

The army wasn't long in demonstrating that it meant to live off the land in earnest. Horses and mules were gathered up furiously from farms and plantations everywhere . Joe Davis's plantation near Bruinsburg was raided early by Sherman's men and, among other things ,a fine petite black horse of imported blood was seized.

During the journey Grant was surprised to come across his twelve year-old son, Fred, who had stolen across the Mississippi against his father's wishes . Fred was perched like a pea on the back of an enormous old grey draught horse that he had seized along the way . Fred was without stirrups and using a bridle made out of an old clothes line . He had fallen off many times already . The first thing that Grant did was to lend him his own borrowed horse, the general himself taking a spare horse, a spirited bay, from cavalry commander, General A. J. Smith.

The army engaged the rebels and fought battles at several points - Port Gibson , Raymond and the capital, Jackson. Any onlooker on the road to Jackson would have caught sight of Grant with his officers in the woods parallel to the road - jumping anything in their path, from logs to brush, as they galloped along at speed. [170] Grant's life was endangered many times. En route to Jackson, his party was ambushed by Confederate sharpshooters and the general had to risk racing his unfamiliar horse into the woods from where the firing was coming to find cover. Actively present during the fighting at Champion's Hill. S.H. Byers, (a soldier with the Fifth Iowa) observed Grant joining the men at the front when they were coming under fire from Confederates in the woods.

> He was mounted on a beautiful bay mare, and followed by several of his staff. For some reason he dismounted. . . . . here was Grant under fire. He stood leaning against his horse, smoking the stump of a cigar. His was the only horse near the line, and must naturally have attracted the enemy fire.........what if Grant should be killed? I am sure everyone who saw him wished him away; but there he was and there he remained, clear, calm and immovable ,with no sign of inward movement upon his features". [171]

Grant and his army reached the outskirts of Vicksburg on May 18th. Initial assaults were disappointing and the troops faced a lengthy siege. Fred was by his

---

[169] James Pickett Jones, *Yankee Blitzkrieg*, page 17.

[170] Major S.H.M. Byers , *With Fire and Sword* , page 72.

[171] Hamlin Garland, *Ulysses S. Grant -His Life and Character.* , page 230. Doubleday & Mcclure Co. 1898. (Quoting Maj. S.H.M Byers.)

father's side throughout the siege until illness caused his removal from camp. There were visits from other members of the family too , including Julia. Their presence did much to ease the strain. Julia's calm and level-headed nature made her a great favourite with the staff officers who saw her as a way of getting their petitions or grievances seen to. On her arrival at the front, Grant would sometimes ride out to meet her ambulance. Drawing his horse up beside the vehicle ,the couple would proceed to headquarters holding hands. [172] Their romantic devotion was looked on with a mingling of admiration and amusement by the young staff officers.

When the western troops were established around Vicksburg , it became the general's habit to ride over his army's lines each day, a distance of twelve to fifteen miles through difficult terrain studded with ravines, cane-brake and forest . To add to the danger, Federal lines came uncomfortably close at times to the enemy .Grant kept himself active in this way during the six-week siege , hoping always to increase the stranglehold on the town, or identify a weakness in its defense . He reconnoitered, toured the lines and visited field hospitals or occasionally a nearby plantation. Sometimes the routes chosen for his inspections were so swampy that impromptu corduroy roads had to be hastily constructed so that the little party on horseback could proceed. [173]

One of Grant's favourite ,if quirky, mounts during the Vicksburg campaign was "Kangaroo". He had had an unpromising introduction to the Federal leader the previous year as a scrawny, poorly- conditioned Confederate horse found wandering on the field at Shiloh . The Federal troops who found him sent him as a joke to Grant's wayward staff officer, Colonel Clark Lagow, who always liked to think that he kept a fine horse. Lagow of course saw no reason to keep the "gift" . Always partial to thoroughbreds, Grant recognised his potential immediately . He would have the horse for himself if the colonel did not want him, he said. History doesn't record the colour or shape of "Kangaroo" - only the peculiar habit that gave him his name, because he would always spring up in the air when first mounted (perhaps indicating he was cold backed.) In time, he became a horse of unrivaled magnificence , and Grant used him extensively.

---

[172] John Y. Simon,ed. *Memoirs of Julia Dent Grant* , page 102.

[173] James Harrison Wilson, *Under the Old Flag*, page 214.

Later "Kangaroo" played a part in one of the most notorious stories that circulated about Grant during the lengthy siege. [174] In a way the horse serves as a silent witness to the inconsistencies of the tale . In early June 1863, the general set out by steamboat on the Yazoo River to make a fact-finding mission to Sartartia ,with a view to ascertaining enemy movements there. Grant had already experienced some of the worst pressures and physical privations of his career the previous month, and was very likely in poor health by now, perhaps even fighting off the onset of another malaria attack.

Unluckily for Grant ,"Chicago Times" reporter, Sylvanus Cadwallader, was also on a steamboat on the Yazoo River at the same time, heading back from Satartia. According to Cadwallader, when the boats met on the river, Grant decided to transfer to the newspaperman's vessel. This would have meant the movement of Grant's horse, "Kangaroo", and those of the cavalry detail accompanying him . The Yazoo River has a restless current . The transfer of horses from one steamboat to another in the middle of its waters would seem a risky and unlikely maneuver to attempt. But according to Cadwallader, this was done.

The journalist went on to paint an unflattering picture of the commander on the steamboat, describing how he saw him downing whiskey by the bottleful, even though anyone that knew Grant would testify that he only needed a few glasses to become very drunk. Cadwallader maintained that the general was in no fit state to do anything when he got to his destination. But according to the newspaperman, he stubbornly insisted on going ashore, despite reports that the town was crawling with rebels. Always the hero of the hour, Cadwallader made himself ready to shoot or hamstring every horse on board, including "Kangaroo" , to prevent the party from riding away from the boat. One can only guess how angry Grant would have been had the horses been deliberately harmed in this way . The pressman would doubtless have been banished from camp for such an action, which would have been the kiss of death to a war reporter. Perhaps Cadwallader felt safe in making this threat because there was never any danger of Grant or the horses disembarking.

When the vessel returned to Vicksburg , Cadwallader left the boat with the general. Grant, reputedly still tipsy, mounted "Kangaroo" to return to headquarters . But the horse reared up dramatically and Grant only just about stayed on. He galloped on ahead of the newspaperman , whose own horse was no match for the general's fireball . Grant's subsequent journey on "Kangaroo" in the failing light, conducted at a flat out gallop, would have witnesses open-mouthed. Shelby Foote

---

[174] Sylvanus Cadwallader, *Three Years with Grant* , page 103.

humorously described the scene as follows: "The road was crooked, winding among the many slews and bayous, but the general more or less straightened it out".[175] According to Cadwallader, Grant mowed down virtually anything in his path, clouds of dust and angry shouts rising high in his wake. Of particular concern were the bridges that had to be crossed. Sentries were posted there to prevent anyone from going too fast, and in theory they could have fired at the galloping rider.

After many miles "Kangaroo" finally slowed down to a walk and the newspaperman was able to catch up with him. Even though Grant was now riding at a walk, Cadwallader saw fit to grab the reins from him. According to the reporter, there followed an unseemly tussle between the two men with Grant trying to grab back his reins. Convinced of the commander's drunken state, Cadwallader insisted that Grant get down off his horse, and even went so far as to call for an ambulance. The story goes that Grant then fell asleep on the road, his head propped on his beloved Grimsley saddle. When they eventually made it to headquarters in the ambulance, a concerned John Rawlins, a fanatic teetotaller, was waiting for his chief outside his tent like a mother hen. Grant simply got out of the ambulance, said nothing, and went straight to bed. [176]

This baffling episode was of course attributed by Cadwallader to Grant's abuse of liquor. But the reality may have been more mundane : less to do with the state of the rider and more to do with the state of his horse. "Kangaroo" had been on a boat much longer than scheduled. The planned cavalry reconnaissance at Satartia had not taken place. "Kangaroo" was a blooded horse and now was full of pent-up energy that needed to be released. Grant had no option but to let him off. The newspaperman would have known nothing about Grant's sprees on horseback throughout his life - how he thought nothing of galloping at breakneck speed since boyhood. Alcohol had no part to play in this behaviour. Often during the campaigns, it was Grant's chief way of banishing the splitting headaches that plagued him. And Charles Dana had stated that Grant was ill during the steamboat journey. [177] Sylvanus Cadwallader described himself as the best friend Grant could have had in the Army of the Tennessee but in his own way "Kangaroo" told a different version of events.

---

[175] Shelby Foote, *The Civil War: a Narrative.* Part 2, page 419.

[176] Sylvanus Cadwallader, *Three Years with Grant*, pages 107,109.

[177] Charles A. Dana, *Recollections of the Civil War*, page 90.

Grant's skittish mount seemed to fade from the scene after Vicksburg. He was rarely mentioned after the siege ended. Possibly he was sent away from the front and back to Galena. But a small incident at Natchez in August of 1863 indicates that "Kangaroo" was still in circulation and may have been up to his old tricks. Grant, who was being feted in the town at the time, lent one of his horses to the mayor to ride. It appears that the mayor was leading this horse over some bad ground, when the animal reared up suddenly and struck General Kirby Smith's horse in the foot. The mayor went flying and so did Kirby Smith, who was thrown to the ground in the melee. [178] Was this "Kangaroo"? It seems to fit in with his previous form. Perhaps the arrival of "Cincinnati" and "Jeff Davis" in Grant's camp eclipsed "Kangaroo's" popularity with the general. There is some evidence that the horse made his way back to his original "owner", the indifferent Colonel Lagow, when the latter resigned from Grant's staff towards the end of 1863. Lagow would have been in need of a horse then to take back home. In a letter to Julia, Grant mentioned that he wanted his brother Orvil to send back the horse he had in Galena to Lagow, adding that he would tell his old staff officer that he "had no means to keep it". [179] Like "Kangaroo", Lagow had been found increasingly unsuited to the demands of the campaign, sometimes getting lost with important dispatches in his possession. [180] But Grant seemed to have had a nostalgic attachment to him, and the offer of the horse was a reflection of this.

    The citizens of Vicksburg endured forty-six days of shelling and starvation before General Pemberton offered a surly surrender to Grant on the third of July 1863. Grant's terms to his Mexican War comrade were generous. When the Confederate troops marched out of the town, most of them walked straight back into the ranks. After Vicksburg Grant's army was dispersed, but the campaign had made him everlastingly famous with the northern public. His quick-thinking flexibility during the campaign seemed to take many commentators, both then and now, by surprise. But in fact he had been refining this skill on the back of a horse from an early age.

---

[178] William Mcfeely, *Grant*, page 140.

[179] John Y. Simon, ed. *Papers of USG*. Vol 10. Letter to Julia, Feb 17th 1864.

[180] Ibid, Vol. 9. Notes on letter to Julia, Oct 24th 1863.

Chapter 12

Charlie

Grant was always lucky around horses, avoiding serious injury in spite of the many hours he spent in the saddle. But his luck finally ran out a few months after his Vicksburg triumph . The events surrounding his accident at a review at New Orleans in late August, 1863, demonstrated how he could be a victim of his irresistible attraction to difficult, challenging horses.

His host at New Orleans , General Nathaniel P. Banks, knew how to put on a good review. An ambitious , well connected man, Banks had been one-time governor of Massachusetts and speaker of the House of Representatives . As a politically appointed soldier, he belonged to a breed that never found favour with Grant. Banks was also extremely proud of his own horses whom he considered the fastest in the army. The day before the review, he brought Grant for a carriage ride and his visitor asked if he could take the reins . True to form, the general rode the team hard and achieved an amazing speed . When they got back to the stables, the groom was alarmed to see the horses steaming like locomotives. [181]

Banks seemed to have been a daring and accomplished rider, fond of riding his rangy, coal black stallion called "Shenandoah " in reviews. But he also had a track record of testing the mettle of other horsemen . At a review on the plains of Baton Rouge earlier in the year, he subjected Admiral Farragut and his saddle-rusty

---

[181] Bruce Catton, *Grant Takes Command*, page 23. Castle Books. 2000.

naval officers to a bizarre trial by ditch on horseback, which only ended when a member of Bank's own staff disappeared down an enormous drain that he had urged his guests to jump on the way home. [182] In a later interview Banks is reported to have rather condescendingly referred to Grant's seat in the saddle as "secure. . . . . but not at all elegant". [183]

    The day after Grant's interesting carriage ride ,there was to be a grand review of troops to celebrate victory at Vicksburg . After a long lunch, the guest of honour was given one of Bank's horses, "Charlie ", to ride . To many onlookers in the town, the sight of a band of officers on horseback in full uniform riding off to a review was a sight to behold . But there was more to the splendour than met the eye. Grant later described his horse for the day as "vicious and but little used" - strong language by his standards. [184] According to one eye witness two men were needed just to hold "Charlie " - an enormous Virginia-bred bay thoroughbred. General Lorenzo Thomas who was present at the review, summed up the horse as a hard-mouthed brute. It is baffling, then, that Banks chose this horse for his guest of honour. Was Grant , like Admiral Farragut, being tested by having to ride this "vicious and but little used" horse ? Or perhaps Grant himself asked Banks if he could ride the most powerful and spirited horse in his stables . Throughout his life he was never able to resist a challenge on horseback . The fact that his horse was green or partially broken would , if anything , have added to the attraction.

    All appeared to go well at the actual review . The Thirteenth Corps that had shared so many of Grant's battles, was stretched out across the field at Carrolton. Grant, now dubbed the "Seahorse of the Mississippi", galloped passed the line at top speed, leaving his entourage scrambling to keep up . He stopped below a huge spreading oak and doffed his hat as the national colours filed past . It was a moving experience for both guest of honour and troops. [185]

    But on the return journey to the hotel, Grant received the worst injury of his career. The horse appeared to spin out of control on the road and nearly crossed

---

[182] James G. Hollandsworth, *Pretense of Glory. The Life of Gen. Nathaniel P. Banks*, pages 102-03. Louisiana State Univ. 1998.

[183] Bruce Catton, *Grant Takes Command*, page 24. Castle Books. 2000.

[184] Ulysses S. Grant, *Memoirs*, page 320.

[185] Kenneth Williams, *Lincoln finds a General*. Vol. 5, X11, Publisher's preface.

paths with a hissing locomotive on the New Orleans to Carrolton line. The charger shied at the noise, lost its footing on the slippery surface, and fell on his rider. Mrs Grant maintained that the horse reared and fell back on her husband, which would account perfectly for the nature of his subsequent injuries. In a way Grant was a victim of his secure seat. Because he stayed on instead of being thrown clear, his entire left side was pinned underneath the horse. When "Charlie" scrambled to his feet Grant lay motionless on the ground underneath him and had to be stretchered to a nearby hotel. He had apparently suffered a dislocated hip and possibly a fractured skull as well. [186] A vivid account of his agonies was given in his memoirs.

> When I regained consciousness, I found myself in a hotel near by with several doctors attending me. My leg was swollen from the knee to the thigh, and the swelling, almost to the point of bursting, extended along the body up to the armpit. The pain was almost beyond endurance. I lay in the hotel something over a week without being able to turn myself in bed............ I was then taken to Vicksburg, where I remained unable to move for some time afterwards. [187]

Luckily there was a lull in western military operations at the time and Grant missed less of the war than he might have done. The length of the confinement did much to weaken his strength however. He was confined to bed on his back for twenty days and, for once in his life, was forced to dictate his letters. When he returned to Vicksburg to recuperate, Julia joined him. Grant remained on crutches for months afterwards and it is arguable that he never really fully recovered from his New Orleans accident. (When he slipped on the sidewalk in New York twenty years later, he aggravated the injury to his left side and remained lame until his death.)

It seems that the general was still suffering from this injury when he was given command of the military division of the Mississippi with orders to proceed to the strategically important Chattanooga in October of 1863. Although the population living in the rugged hills around this part of Tennessee was staunchly unionist, the area remained under rebel control. Rail lines there connected the east of the Confederacy to the west and allowed free movement of troops and supplies. In view of the previous month's accident, the forty mile trip in the saddle from the railway

---

[186] Shelby Foote, *The Civil War. A Narrative*. Part 2, page 774.

[187] Ulysses S. Grant, *Memoirs*, page 321.

depot at Bridgeport to the front was a severe test. Grant endured a two-day long ride over the notorious "steep as a horse's face" Walden Ridge, during a bad storm and over what he himself described as "some of the worst roads it is possible to imagine". [188] It was Grant's first real outing on a horse since his injury.

On the way there was ample evidence of the carnage and confusion that had taken place there earlier in the month, when vast teams of army mules and horses, abandoned by their terrified teamsters, had run wild in the wake of a Confederate cavalry attack. [189] The bones of the perished animals made an eerie sight over the roads and bridle paths for eight miles. [190]

Grant and his staff cut loose from their wagons and baggage so that they could travel faster. Because of the mud, knee deep in places, the injured general might have needed a relatively long-legged mount for the journey. This would have ruled out "Jeff Davis", who was an obvious choice because of the comfort of his paces, particularly in view of Grant's delicate physical state. Instead Grant's steady old servant, "Jack" ,was drafted in for the trip. At one stage the "Old Nuisance" slipped and fell in the dark, giving his rider another bad bruising. Grant was still severely lame from the accident and couldn't walk unassisted. Often he had to be lifted and carried by his men when it wasn't practical to proceed on horseback.

When he arrived at his new headquarters, he had to be lifted again out of the saddle. His new hosts in the Army of the Cumberland were fascinated by the pools of water that accumulated on the floor underneath him as he held a quick council at their headquarters, choosing to remain in his wet clothes. [191] Incredibly Grant was back in the saddle early next morning for a day-long reconnoitre, having been lifted like a baby onto his horse by John Rawlins. At least later on in the journey he was able to dismount on his own, stopping at Brown's Ferry within full view of the enemy pickets at the other side of the river. Far from setting his recovery back, the hard ride over the mountains rapidly freed up his leg , so much so that he was soon able to mount his horse again without too much difficulty, and could even throw away the crutches. [192]

---

[188] John Y. Simon, ed. *Papers of USG*. Vol. 9, Letter to Julia Grant , Nov. 1863.

[189] Theo Rodenbough, *Photographic History of the Civil War. The Cavalry*, page 162.

[190] Ulysses S. Grant, *Personal Memoirs*, pages 329-30.

[191] Horace Porter, *Campaigning with Grant*, page 2.

[192] John Y. Simon, *Papers of USG*. Vol. 9. Letter to Julia Grant, Oct. 27th 1863.

The situation of the Cumberland Army was dire. After its rout at Chickamauga ,it had retreated to the south side of the Tennessee river, and had become boxed in at Chattanooga by the Confederates. The southerners occupied virtually every bit of high ground. Union supply lines had been cut off, leaving the men dangerously short of rations. Although no soldier had died of starvation yet, ten thousand animals had. Accounts at the time tell of mules gnawing through pine trees and harness traces to alleviate starvation. On his arrival, one of the first things Grant did was to order all animals that could be spared to be driven back to forage at Stevenson. [193] Then a route was found to the base of supplies at Bridgeport, some forty miles away. Grant and his men dined on hardtack, dried vegetables and canned meat, until the "cracker line" was opened up. The general's stallion "Jack" would have fared equally badly after his journey over the mountain. There was no fodder available and a couple of ears of corn would have been his only fare.

Grant's presence in camp gave renewed impetus for the opening up of the supply line. Just ten days after his arrival , a way was found through a planned river assault at Brown's Ferry with a contingent of a few thousand men. Grant's second favourite animal, the mule ,was to play a significant part in sabotaging the Confederates. Teams of famished mules from Geary's division had got loose from their supply wagons and "with heads down and tails up", had proceeded to run amok in blind panic towards the rebel line. The southerners mistakenly believed they were the subject of a cavalry charge and deserted the line. With a gesture that Grant would have appreciated from his Mexican days , the quartermaster in charge of the mules sent the following communication to headquarters: "I respectfully request that the mules, for their gallantry in this action, may have conferred on them the brevet rank of horses". [194] In a campaign short on amusing incidents, the ex-mule handler of the Fourth Infantry appreciated the joke very much. The "cracker line" was now open.

With Sherman's division added to the Cumberland Army, Grant now had sixty thousand men at his disposal, some twenty thousand more than the Confederates who occupied a front six miles long. He set about inspecting these six miles immediately. The rebel lines went from Lookout Mountain to Chickamauga and these he reconnoitered closely to check for weakness in fortifications. Close

---

[193] Horace Porter, *Campaigning with Grant*, page 7.

[194] Horace Porter, *Campaigning with Grant,* page 10.

examination of the rugged hillsides yielded rich results. He found a weakness at the right flank. Only a small rebel cavalry detail guarded certain points of the Tennessee River , and some good roads were out of view of rebel positions. In a giant leap of faith, Grant decided he could attack the enemy from its existing positions.

Early on he had a risky encounter with some of General Longstreet's blue-clad veterans who had come down to draw water from Chattanooga Creek. During a reconnoitre on his own, (he wouldn't subject his staff to the risk) he sat on his horse by the creek and, assuming the men were under his own command, engaged them in conversation . He was only spared by the fact that they did not recognise his rank because of the unassuming plainness of his uniform. [195]

The first day of battle started with a reconnoitre on horseback, accompanied by General George Thomas ,whose stately physique necessitated the use of a heavy weight bay horse called "Billy", named after Sherman . Early in the fighting a vantage point called Orchard Knoll was taken . From here the the progress of the entire field could be observed : first at Lookout Mountain, then at Missionary Ridge two miles distant . Grant had rightly judged that a weak force had been left to defend these vantage points.

When it looked as if Confederate forces were crumbling, Grant asked for his horse so he could go down and see for himself. Quick as lighting he was off down the plain to ride along the lines. It was a miracle that the bullets never reached him. By this stage "Jack" was enjoying a well- earned rest . So the general's mount for the day was a little, cat-like horse that he had borrowed from James Harrison Wilson . The horse was ideal for the rugged, hilly terrain . Since he had been found wandering near Vicksburg , the general dubbed him "The Waif", and he always showed a keen interest in him. Wilson thought him the most capable and best broken horse he had ever encountered during the war. [196]

The men cheered wildly when they saw their commander among them, some clinging to his stirrups and hugging "The Waif" in uninhibited joy. The Confederates abandoned their positions and retreated behind the ridge. From his good vantage point ,Grant was able to observe a young division commander called Philip Sheridan pursue fleeing rebels to the crest of Missionary Ridge and down the other side,

---

[195] Ulysses S. Grant, *Personal Memoirs*, pages 337-8.

[196] James Harrison Wilson, *Under the Old Flag* , page 318. D. Appleton & Co. 1912.

capturing an abundance of artillery and prisoners.[197] It was just the sort of tenacity that appealed to Grant. Grant rode in the direction of the pursuit as far as Ringgold, some twenty miles south east of Chattanooga, in order to satisfy himself that the retreat was wholehearted and final. In spite of recent catastrophic injury, Grant's time at Chattanooga was characterised by his usual tireless reconnoitering, coupled with alacrity and omnipresence in the field. All achieved on the back of a horse.

---

[197] Roy Morris Jnr, *Sheridan*, page 147.

Chapter 13

Egypt

Grant lived a Spartan existence during the war, often going without food and sleep for two days, and allowing himself few living comforts in the field. But one indulgence he allowed himself was a fine selection of large, powerful battle chargers. And his rank provided him with a marvelous choice. Although unassuming himself, Grant seemed fully aware of the horse as an emblem of power . Nothing gave him more delight than to know that his battle charger had been purchased for a good sum of money and was admired around camp. Many times in his life Grant was unable to afford the horses he wanted. But during and after the war he received many gifts of valuable thoroughbreds from well-wishers he hardly knew.

In the last month of 1863, a special gift arrived at Chattanooga in the shape of a fine thoroughbred . The gift had been the idea of a group of prominent citizens from the region of Egypt in Southern Illinois , spearheaded by prosperous merchant and one time saddle maker, Orval Pool of Shawneetown , an uncle of James Harrison Wilson . The gift horse could not have come at a better time. Wilson would have known that Grant was in need of a new horse as he had obviously decided to retire "Jack" after two long weary years of campaigning . And the "Waif" had only been on loan. (Wilson used him on his subsequent cavalry campaigns in Virginia ,Alabama and Georgia). The general wrote a letter of thanks to Pool, saying what a great personal compliment the gift was. Grant dubbed the horse "Egypt" in honour of the citizens who had donated him . In his letters home he spoke with obvious pride of his new mount, saying that not less than a thousand dollars would have purchased him. [198]

"Egypt" must have earned every dollar spent on him during the subsequent journeys to and from Chattanooga to Nashville and Lexington that Grant undertook in the following weeks. They were the first stiff test for the new horse . The general had made his new headquarters at Nashville . And again he faced a harrowing journey of three days to get there, this time over the Cumberland and Wild Cat Mountains in January - a hazardous route even to this day. Grant and his staff endured temperatures of -10c over ice-covered slopes with little food and shelter. They had to walk and lead their mounts over many miles and fell frequently in the process . The sparse extracts from staff officer Cyrus Comstock's diary convey something of the hardships of the journey.

> **Jan.7**. From Cumberland Gap to Barboursville Ky to London ....roads very icy and ride through only 24 miles, very tiresome. Stayed last night at Mrs. Eve's hotel.
> **Jan 9.** London to north side by hill 35 miles. Still sick but bear it well..........
> **Jan 10**. Lexington Ky. Today on to Lexington ...43 miles. Still sick not having eaten anything for three days, but bear the ride well and told the gen. I could stand three days more. His $1000 horse and himself were nearly used up today......[199]

Grant had obviously made Comstock and presumably everybody else aware of "Egypt's" handsome price tag ! The journey may also have demonstrated to the general that "Egypt" was too fine to risk in the field. His subsequent letters indicated a desire to send him away from the front, perhaps to serve as a carriage horse for Julia.

Standing sixteen hands high," Egypt" was an exceptionally beautiful dark bay who , like "Cincinnati" ,was of Kentucky thoroughbred stock. He was seven years old when he came to camp . He was distinguished by two white hind fetlocks , which were often hidden by muddy going. In spite of his reservations, Grant used "Egypt" extensively in the field during the Virginia campaign, although

---

[198] John Y. Simon, ed. *Papers of USG*. Vol. 9. Letter to Orval Pool. Dec 11th.1863.

[199] Merlin Sumner, *The Diary of Cyrus B. Comstock*, pages 251-52.

"Cincinnati" seemed to have been preferred for key occasions . There is some evidence that "Egypt" may have been unsuitable for the big event , and like his rider he wasn't particularly keen on music. Young Jesse Grant mentioned that he tended to become restless and dance around at City Point when the band struck up, in contrast to the placid "Cincinnati" who seldom bat an eyelid at anything. [200]

Though slightly smaller and more compact than "Cincinnati" ,"Egypt" had his own presence and was a better model of a horse than his stable mate . His appearance without his tack in the 1864 photograph taken by Mathew Brady at Cold Harbour exudes quality . In spite of the age and lack of clarity of the photograph ,it is still possible to observe much of how the three principle horses of Grant's Virginia campaign were put together. "Egypt" was built uphill and would have found it easy to carry himself in good form. But there is some visual evidence that he may not have been all that comfortable to ride . He had upright pasterns and a rather straight shoulder, so he would have had a bouncy, jarring stride . It is no wonder that Grant's other ride," Jeff Davis" was so much sought after for his smooth action, particularly following the New Orleans injury. To compensate, "Egypt" was powerful behind the saddle with a thick, strong neck well set on his body. His legs seemed sturdier and shorter than those of "Cincinnati".

Grant had a special way of mounting a horse, peculiar to himself . It was of sufficient interest to staff officer Horace Porter for him to make note of it at Spotsylvania. Keeping his body straight, he would grab the mane of the horse above the withers, put his left leg in the stirrup, and in a smooth easy motion reminiscent of mounting a step, he would rise up by simply straightening this leg so that he could place the right leg over the horse. [201]

Grant was to use "Egypt" extensively at both Spotsylvania and Cold Harbour. He also served as a spare horse for visitors to headquarters, if they were competent riders. Grant would also use him when President Lincoln visited the front and "Jeff Davis" was unavailable.

In the meantime, life in the winter camp at Nashville in the early months of 1864 was a relatively restful time for the general and his men. Most of the time was taken up with planning military operations before the opening of the next campaign in the Spring. The general could now do a little riding out for pleasure- "for an hour in the

---

[200] Jesse R. Grant, *In the Days of my Father,* page 23.

[201] Horace Porter, *Campaigning with Grant*, page 164.

evening on horseback or in the buggy. This you know always keeps me feeling well". [202]

Around this time a large spotted horse dubbed "Hipa-drome" came to Grant. He was excited about the prospect of sending him to Julia because he drove beautifully, was big enough for two horses and then she could get a decent carriage for four persons. Grant now had the opportunity to try "Egypt" in the buggy for the first time and he was delighted with the results. He found him the best horse he had ever driven and was so gentle that he thought even six year old Jesse could manage him. Again he considered sending him away from the front. "I must find some person to send him to keep during the next campaign. He is too fine to risk loosing. (sic.) I presume not less than one thousand dollars was paid for him.". [203]

Meanwhile, the public appetite for donating horses to the general continued. This time a four-legged gift came from a New Jersey well-wisher, H. Williams. But it was too late for Grant to collect the horse or use him in the coming campaign. Although he thanked the donor profusely, he instructed one of his aides in Washington, George K. Leet, to use him as his own. [204] Grant took a short visit to St. Louis and received the gift of another horse there: one that would soon be well known about camp.

---

[202] John Y. Simon, ed. *Papers of USG*. Vol. 10, letter to Julia Grant, Feb. 14th 1864.

[203] Ibid, Letter to Julia, Feb 17th 1864.

[204] Ibid, Telegraph to Capt. George K. Leet, May 3rd 1864.

Chapter 14

Son of Lexington

By the time Ulysses S. Grant met Robert E. Lee on the Virginia battlefields, he had cut his teeth on some of the most testing campaigns of the war. And he had already out-generaled many of the south's ablest commanders : Joseph Johnston, Albert Sydney Johnston, and Braxton Bragg. Unlike many of his officers the prospect of meeting Lee and his seemingly invincible army didn't faze him in the least. "I …. knew that he was mortal ; and it was just as well that I felt this." [205] As the campaign against Lee's army resumed in earnest in the Spring of 1864, Grant chose to position himself alongside the Army of the Potomac. Commanding this distinguished force was Mexican War veteran George Meade, whose irritable ways earned him the nickname, "damned old goggle-eyed snapping turtle ". A peculiar source of annoyance to the general, a careful unadventurous rider with poor eyesight, was the habit that some of his cavalrymen had of jumping ditches and fences as they escorted him. [206] Meade's presence in the field had been associated

---

[205] Ulysses S. Grant, *The Personal Memoirs of Ulysses S. Grant*, page 101.

[206] *New York Times*, Aug 17th 1880. (Interview with Gen. Alfred Pleasonton .)

for many years with the famed and indestructible battle horse, "Baldy", wounded four times at Gettysburg, and in many previous campaigns. "Baldy", with a mane as sparse as his rider's, was now enjoying a well earned furlough and the commander of the Potomac was mounted on a steady substitute horse for the upcoming campaign.

By moving below the Army of Northern Virginia, across the Rapidan River, Grant would have access to the river ways for movement of both injured troops and supplies. Although he had the considerable advantage of fighting in his own territory, the Confederate commander would have to be on the defensive now. And Lee hated waging a defensive war nearly as much as Grant.

In the days before the crossing of the Rapidan River, Grant had the chance to get to know another fine new blood horse, possibly the best bred in the Federal army. He made excursions to General Meade's headquarters and further afield to Cedar Run Mountain some twelve miles from camp at Culpepper Courthouse. An old boyhood friend, Daniel Ammen, paid a visit to headquarters in early May, 1864. The two friends rode out in the afternoon as they had done in childhood and spent hours on horseback touring the Federal camp - stretched out across the plain as far as the eye could see. Grant was mounted on "Cincinnati", and Ammen on "Egypt". Ammen gave a very vivid description of Grant's mount: " A large powerful bay with a free easy stride of great scope", and the "finest horse that he, Grant, had ever mounted".[207]

These outings on horseback were an opportunity for the staff officers - those new to camp mingling with the veterans - to become acquainted in a pleasant, informal setting as they travelled side by side. One aide recalled riding with his new chief to Meade's headquarters. It was only two months since Grant had gone to Washington to receive the rank of Lieutenant General from the president. Now he occupied the highest position in the army - commanding well over five hundred thousand men - an unprecedented figure in American military history. The young staff officer was surprised at the commander's ability as a conversationalist, given his sphinx-like reputation. Amazingly, Grant's old West Point dream of being a cavalry commander had never dimmed. He revealed that the height of his ambition back in 1861 had been to command a cavalry brigade in the army of the Potomac, because his fondness for horses would make him feel most at home in command of cavalry. Only a long-held superstition about not lobbying for a post prevented him

---

[207] Adm. Daniel Ammen, "Recollections and Letters of Grant". *North American Review.* Oct. 1885. Vol. CXLI, No. 347, page 364.

from applying. Now his command was far in excess of anything he had expected, due perhaps to the fact that he had not been commissioned into the cavalry. The aide, Horace Porter, noted the sprightly fashion in which the general mounted "Cincinnati". Grant insisted that he had fully recovered from his recent riding accident, although he admitted that his leg sometimes went numb. [208]

Grant needed a collection of fast, sound, and sure-footed horses for the job ahead of him. It would be nothing to travel fifty miles a day, in all weathers and jumping all manner of hedge, brush, fence, or stream. Riding at night was a common occurrence. With these demands on his horses, it was essential that they could be rotated and rested at will so that they would always be fresh. By the start of the Virginia campaign ,Grant was also surrounded by a small group of fourteen officers - tough, young, hard-riding staff members who were able to transmit the general's orders to various parts of the field and report back on troop organisation with maximum speed.

Horace Porter, Orville Babcock and Cyrus Comstock were West Pointers and so had had formal training in the saddle. Colonel Comstock might even have been glad of his "tearing rides" as a cadet, for they were some kind of preparation for the job of accompanying Grant in the field. Colonel Babcock was particularly fearless at the front. Grant would often select him for dangerous, unpopular missions. His bravery in the war earned him Grant's undying loyalty after it.

On the morning of May 4th, the vast army of the Potomac crossed the Rapidan River. In honour of the occasion Grant was kitted out in his sword, sash and spurs - a rare sight - and was mounted on "Cincinnati". "Cincinnati" was similarly dressed in full caparison : a double bridle, Grimsley saddle, (Grant's own), with breast strap and crupper attached to prevent movement, a boot on the right front for Grant's carbine, a smart blanket over the saddle trimmed with gold and embroidered with the figure of an eagle; and over the eagle's head the three stars denoting the general's rank. The heat and dust of the day wouldn't have diminished "Cincinnati's" presence and quality in the field.

Of all the horses associated with Ulysses Grant," Cincinnati" was the most celebrated. His arrival in camp somehow embodied the growing breadth and depth of his rider's leadership. Standing nearly seventeen hands high, this imposing horse would convey him swiftly on the field until the end of the war.

---

[208] Horace Porter, *Campaigning with Grant*. Page 25.

He was reputedly sired by the famous thoroughbred, "Lexington ", out of a Kentucky thoroughbred mare. Lexington won six out of his seven races before becoming partially blind. He was then bought for $15,000 in 1856 and retired to stud at R. A. Alexander 's Woodburn farm in the Blue Grass region : the foremost thoroughbred nursery in the country spanning over three thousand acres. If the patrician Alexander thought that his British citizenship or "Lexington's" blindness left him immune from raiding parties, he was mistaken. Such was the demand for mounts during these years that Woodburn Farm became a happy hunting ground for southern cavalry, who plundered it in October 1864 and again in February 1865. Among others, the renowned "Asteroid" and the trotting sire "Abdallah 15" were taken. "Asteroid" , "Cincinnati's" half brother and one of the fastest four milers in the United States, was returned to Woodburn after a ransom was paid. But "Abdallah 15" died of exhaustion in the hands of Confederate raiders. Alarmed by these events, Alexander moved a grumpy and uncooperative "Lexington " at night to the safety of Illinois for the remainder of the war . He remained the leading stallion in America until 1877, and by 1865 could command a stud fee of $500, the highest in the country.[209]

Yet Grant's introduction to "Cincinnati", while on a rare leave of absence in St Louis, was eerie and inauspicious. The purpose of the visit was to check on the health of young Fred ,who had caught camp dysentery and had been sent to Julia's cousin to recuperate. Naturally Grant's trip to the city created a stir . He received a letter from a man begging him to call at the Lindell Hotel, then the largest hotel in America. The writer signed his name S. S. Grant - the initials of Grant's beloved brother, Simp, who had died of tuberculosis two years before . The uncanny coincidence aroused his curiosity and he went to the man's apartments. The bedridden stranger, a Cincinnati man, said he wasn't long for this world . He confided in Grant that he owned a special horse that he considered to be the finest animal in America . He knew he could never ride again, so the best home he could think of for such a magnificent animal was the general 's. But the conditions of the gift were strict. The horse must never be ill-treated or be allowed to fall into the hands of anyone who would do so. [210]

---

[209] Robert and Frazer Hunt , *Horses and Heroes*, page 120.

[210] Ibid, page 120.

It is not recorded whether Grant cast an eye over the horse before accepting the gift, but he was evidently unable to resist the deal. He called the horse "Cincinnati" in honour of the donor. Later he was given to calling the horse by the Latin version of his name, "Cincinnatus" [211], perhaps after the Roman general - a simple farmer called from his plough in a time of turmoil, who then returned quietly to it after the crisis had passed.

A strong and powerful ride, and an extravagant mover, "Cincinnati" quickly became the apple of Grant's eye, just as he had been of his previous owner's. He had many valuable qualities for a war horse. He was exceptionally even-tempered and rarely over-reacted to noise or mayhem. If the general ever needed to dismount to take a closer look at things, he would stand and wait, scarcely moving from the spot. [212] There is a wonderful photograph by Mathew Brady of Grant standing beside his horse after the Cold Harbour campaign. He isn't holding the horse in any way - he is just standing beside him - yet "Cincinnati" remains still enough to have been clearly developed in Brady's negative. Although he is gazing at the camera, cigar in left hand, Grant's body is turned in towards "Cincinnati" with his right hand lying on the animal's shoulder. The sheer size of the charger is immediately evident, as he stands in profile. But Grant's posture is also interesting. He seems to be drawing the viewer's attention to the horse, as if showing him off. It is a revealing gesture of personal pride in a man who usually gave nothing away in front of the camera.

Although undoubtedly a magnificent presence, photographs show that "Cincinnati" was far from ideal in his conformation. His hindquarters were evidently powerful but he shows a rather straight hock and he was "camped out" behind. Had he gone to the race track like his famous father it is doubtful whether he would have shone. "Cincinnati" had a pronounced ewe neck, giving him a high head carriage. He would have had long, rangy paces that might have been tiring to sit to. If the rider was not relaxed in his seat, it would have been difficult to go with the movement of this horse. It is no wonder that Grant allowed few to ride him. Given his pedigree he could have been very explosive under the saddle if the rider couldn't sit still.

In another photograph, the horse's face is more visible. He shows a large, intelligent head, generous ears, and a slightly Roman profile. What stands out are his

---

[211] Sylvanus Cadwallader, *Three Years with Grant*, page 232.

[212] *Chicago Tribune*, Aug 9, 1885, page 20.

big bulging shoulders, which are accentuated if anything by thin, gangling legs that seem to have less bone below the knee than the ideal. Also noticeable is the enormous depth of his chest, which would have given him great stamina.

Only two other people, both natural horsemen from the rural west, were allowed to sit on "Cincinnati's" back. One was Daniel Ammen, who had saved Grant from drowning in their local river at the age of eight. The other was the only man that outranked the general, Abraham Lincoln . None of Grant's subordinates were ever invited to ride him, no matter how well they rode . Lincoln took quite a shine to "Cincinnati" at their first meeting. In fact the horse's enormous size would have suited the president, who was often the subject of unkind remarks from bystanders when mounted. Horace Porter gives an account of Lincoln's visit to the front in June of 1864. Mounted on "Cincinnati" , he rode out to see the men of Meade's and Butler's commands, accompanied by Grant riding "Jeff Davis" . The two men would have made a strange picture indeed : the lanky Lincoln straddling the gargantuan "Cincinnati" , beside the slightly bent figure of the commander on his dainty, pet-like pony.

> Mr Lincoln wore a very high black silk hat and black trousers and frock-coat. Like most men who had been brought up in the west, he had good command of a horse, but it must be acknowledged that in appearance he was not a very dashing rider. By the time he had reached the troops, he was completely covered in dust and the black color of his clothes had changed to Confederate gray. As he had no straps, his trousers gradually worked up above his ankles, and gave him the appearance of a country farmer riding into town wearing his Sunday clothes . A citizen on horseback is always an odd sight in the midst of a uniformed army , and the picture presented by the president bordered on the grotesque. [213]

Grant's movement over the Rapidan culminated in the rendezvous of the two sides at the infamous "Wilderness" - seventy square miles of second growth thickets and scrub, interspersed with swamp: a natural abatis . Both sides were revisiting an old theatre of war. But this would be a battle of a very different complexion . Nature, not generals, shaped its course . Lee wished to give battle in such a place, realising it was the best way of capitalising on his army's dwindling resources. His officers knew the area better than the other side,and they had the advantage of interior lines. Significantly his veterans were expert trench diggers. Grant's superior artillery would count for nothing in such terrain.

---

[213] Horace Porter , *Campaigning with Grant,* page 218.

Riding "Cincinnati", Grant tirelessly inspected the local terrain in the few days preceding the battle, returning to camp with a uniform that was unrecognisable from the mud . The enormous son of "Lexington" would have seemed an unlikely choice of mount for the Wilderness. Certainly his presence would give an added visual power to the campaign, and would also guarantee the general speed of movement on the roads. In a campaign where minutes counted, "Cincinnati's" unrivaled pace would have been invaluable. But the landscape of thick forest and tangled undergrowth would hardly have suited a horse of such size . No doubt the occasion was the biggest factor in the selection of horse . The battle of the Wilderness opened Grant's campaign against Lee . It was an historic battle whose outcome would determine the fate of the Union. And Grant always seemed to want "Cincinnati" for the big occasion.

Figure 1. Riding at West Point Military Academy.

Figure 2. Egypt, Cincinnati and Jeff Davis at Cold Harbour, 1864. Cincinnati had the added distinction of carrying President Lincoln whenever he visited the field. (Courtesy of the Library of Congress.)

Figure 3.
Jeff Davis became a favourite mount for long reconnoiters in the field. His small, angelic appearance belied a tricky temperament. (Courtesy of the Library of Congress.)

Figure 4.
John Aaron Rawlin's horse, General Blair, circa 1864. Grant was highly amused when a hungry mule chewed off the horse's tail. The photographer obviously improvised by etching in a false one. (Courtesy of the Library of Congress.)

Figure 5.
Grant chose not to be mounted for this portrait of Cincinnati at Cold Harbour, 1864. Perhaps he wanted the viewer's attention to be concentrated on the horse. (Courtesy of the Library of Congress.)

Figure 6.
 Trotting men of the city just called it "the road". Harlem Lane, New York in the 1860s. (Library of Congress.)

Figure 7. "Four white legs-feed him to the c r o w s ". Grant drives Dexter with the horse's owner, R o b e r t Bonner, c i r c a 1 8 6 8 . (Library of Congress.)

Figure 8. Maude S. harnessed to high wheeled racing sulky. Record 2.08 and 3/4 .

Figure 9.
   Grant's four in hand at his holiday cottage, Long Branch. Albert Hawkins at the reins. (Harper's New Monthly Magazine. Vol. 53. Issue 316. September 1876.)

Figure 10.
Leopard caught Grant's eye at Sultan Hamid's stables in Constantinople in 1878. He would sweep the boards at any show in which he appeared. (Drawn by equestrian artist, Herbert Kittredge in 1880.)

Figure 11.
Linden Tree was chosen by Grant out of the seventy stallions on view at Sultan Hamid's stables in 1878. (Drawn by Herbert Kittredge in 1880.)

Chapter 15

𝒯raveller and Cincinnati

Facing Grant on a grey horse at the Wilderness was a man who strove for excellence in everything he did in life . And horsemanship was no exception. Robert E. Lee had a life-long fondness for animals , reserving the fiercest flashes of his considerable temper for any artilleryman caught abusing his horse. [214] Unlike Grant, Lee had the distinction of serving as a cavalry officer in the decade before the war. During this time he rode many of the valuable blood horses that proved so tragically unsuited to the barren terrain in which they were deployed. [215]

By the time Lee encountered Grant in the Wilderness in the early summer of 1864, Lee and "Traveller" were an established partnership, having seen the Antietam, Fredericksburg , Manassas , Chancellorsville ,and Gettysburg campaigns together over a two year period . In a letter to his wife's cousin, who wanted to paint a portrait of "Traveller" , Lee paid this detailed tribute to his horse:

---

[214] Gamaliel Bradford, *Lee the American*, page 156.

[215] James R. Arnold, *Jeff Davis's Own*, page 36.

Such a picture could inspire a poet, whose genius could then depict his worth and describe his endurance of toil, hunger, thirst, heat and cold, and the dangers and sufferings through which he has passed . He could dilate upon his sagacity and affection and his invariable response to every wish of his rider. He might even imagine his thoughts through the long night marches and days of battle through which he passed. [216]

"Traveller" was described as a sharp, nervous, spirited, grey saddlebred gelding, sixteen hands high, with "bred" blood on his sire's side through the "Sir Archy" line. Lee bought him in 1862 for $200 when he was a four year old. Consequently he was much younger than most of Grant's war mounts. Foaled at Blue Sulphur Springs, he was obviously very forward going as Lee didn't need either whip or spur when riding him. Ironically, the horse's original name was "Jeff Davis" and it was under this title that he won first premium in the showing classes at the Lewisburg Fair.

When war broke out, "Jeff" was purchased by Captain Joseph M. Broun, quartermaster of the Third Virginia Infantry, and was renamed "Greenbriar". Based at Sewell Mountain, the horse was much admired in camp for his high springy walk and equally high spirits. "Traveller" was a five gaited saddlebred. The "high springy walk" referred to by bystanders during the war was most likely the highly collected slow gait characteristic of the breed. "Traveller" also possessed "the rack" : smoother and faster than the conventional trot . It is apparent from photographs that Lee rode very long, with his feet nearly fishing for his stirrups. And it would have been "Traveller's" smooth rack that enabled him to do this.

When Lee took command of Captain Broun's brigade, he noticed the horse and immediately took a fancy to him, calling him "my colt" whenever he spoke to the captain. Subsequently Lee was stationed in South Carolina, and by coincidence Captain Broun followed him to the same camp in the spring of 1862. When he met up with Lee there, the general once again enquired about "my colt". At this point , Broun asked Lee if he would accept the horse as a gift. Lee said he could not do such a thing, but would buy the horse if the captain was willing to sell it. With characteristic correctness ,Lee asked if he could have the horse on a week's trial to learn about his qualities. "Traveller" passed the test and a week later Lee completed the sale. [217] The first thing the new owner did was to put his own stamp on the horse,

---

[216] *Stratford Hall*. http://www.stratfordhall.org/learn/lees/leehorses.php . Accessed 22/06/2002.

[217] Major Thomas L. Broun, "General R.E. Lee's War-Horses, Traveller and Lucy Long". *Southern Historical Papers*. VOL. XVIII. Jan-Dec., 1890, page 1. Richmond, Va. Via http://www.civilwarhome.com/leehorses.htm. Accessed June 2002.

and he renamed him "Traveller" . Lee and "Traveller" quickly formed an enduring and warm partnership, becoming virtually synonymous with each other in the field.

The Confederate commander, a dignified and stately presence on horseback, had the use of other horses . One such was "Ajax ", a chestnut thoroughbred that Grant would probably have liked very much . Although Lee kept him with him for the rest of his life, "Ajax" proved to be too large for the general to ride comfortably. So from the time of the battle of Malvern Hill, "Traveller" was his principle horse. Saddlebreds had been bred mainly in the southern states for wealthy plantation owners to tour their enormous estates in comfort. And the use of the breed in the war was a natural extension of that use.

Yet not everyone was enchanted with "Traveller" and he was every inch a horseman's horse . Lee's son, also Robert, described borrowing the grey gelding for a thirty mile ride to Fredericksburg that became memorable for all the wrong reasons. "Traveller" refused to walk for the duration , and his high stepping walk, alternating with his elevated trot, tired his rider out so much that he swore it would have been easier to have done the thirty miles on foot.[218]

Lee and his horse did have their occasional disagreements as well. Out on a rainy field during the Second Manassas campaign in 1862, the general was standing nearby when "Traveller" was startled by a sudden noise. Lee grabbed the bridle as the horse darted away, and he slipped and fell down a steep bank, breaking both hands . Lee was unable to ride "Traveller" for quite some time, prompting Jeb Stuart to offer the general the use of a small quiet mare with easy paces, "Lucy Long". Lee used her continuously during his disablement . But during the siege of Petersburg she was found to be in foal and was sent to the rear, where Lee lost track of her. [219]

In terms of horse tack, Lee used a Grimsley saddle instead of the ill-fated regulation Confederate model, the Jenifer (after its designer, Walter Jenifer). A rare photograph of Lee mounted in the field shows the distinctive Grimsley pommel . He also received a gift of two McClellans from the Clarksville Arsenal at the end of 1864, although there is no evidence that he used them.

---

[218] Robert and Frazer Hunt, *Horses and Heroes,* page *138.*

[219] Major Thomas L. Broun, "General R.E. Lee's War-Horses, Traveller and Lucy Long". *Southern Historical Papers.* VOL. XVIII. Jan-Dec., 1890, page 2. Richmond, Va. Via http://www.civilwarhome.com/leehorses.htm. Accessed June 2002.

After crossing the Rapidan, Grant was anxious to engage the enemy as quickly as possible. From his headquarters on a small hill at an intersection of the Germanna and Orange Turnpike roads, he rode out frequently to the front, to learn about the exact character of the location through personal inspection. He travelled many miles on his mission along these roads, characteristically leaving his entourage behind with the speed of "Cincinnati" . It was at the intersection of the two aforementioned roads, near the derelict Wilderness Tavern, that Grant directed Meade's army to attack, on May 5th. Quickly the life of one of his dearest friends was taken. Alexander Hays, then with Hancock's Brigade , had shared many of Ulysses' adventures since West Point. They had raced their ponies together as young officers Fort Salubrity and had both come through the Mexican War with distinction. Hays was killed instantly while trying to plug a hole in the union line. The news left the undemonstrative Grant visibly upset .[220]

   Lee attempted to strike at the vast Federal army in flank, before it had time to get into position across the river. Grant correctly read his adversary and thwarted the plan by swift action. According to Horace Porter, Grant's aide de camp, there was a "spur in the heel of every order he sent ". The following day, the general breakfasted early in the mess. His meal would have done a flat jockey proud: a cucumber sliced in two and doused in vinegar, accompanied by a strong cup of coffee. It was no easy matter to cater for the tastes of the General in Chief in the field. Red meat had to be cooked black before he would eat it. And he never ate any animal that "went on two legs". Cucumbers were a favourite delicacy, as were fruit and oysters. But these couldn't be all that readily obtained at the front. During this time some of Grant's staff officers fretted about how little the "old man" ate. [221]

   The battle recommenced with a dawn assault on rebel positions between the Orange Plank and Orange Turnpike Roads, driving the enemy back a mile behind their line. By mid morning, Confederates had counterattacked fiercely, with Lee giving further weight to the mission by directing the attack on horseback in person. Members of the Texas brigade reputedly grabbed "Traveller's" bridle and with cries of "Lee to the rear! Lee to the rear !", bade the general retreat because of the danger he was in. Reluctantly, he heeded their advice, visibly moved . [222] Grant, only three

---

[220] Horace Porter, *Campaigning with Grant*, page 52.

[221] Horace Porter, *Campaigning with Grant*, page 215.

[222] Robert K. Krick, *The War in the East*, page 41.

miles away as the crow flies, had his own troubles. Union forces were driven back so close to his headquarters that enemy shells began to rain down near the stump of a felled tree where he sat. "Cincinnati" was kept saddled behind the hill in case of a quick retreat. Staff officers implored him to move back , much as the Texans had insisted of Lee. The only movement to come from Grant, however, was the constant puffing on his cigar, as he turned the rapidly changing situation over in his head. The cigar smoke that enveloped him seemed to be indispensable to the clarity of his thought and he smoked a record number that day - twenty in all. [223]

The following day Grant twice rode out to various points of the line, together with Meade and two staff officers. In spite of the seriousness of their mission, the officers were briefly engaged by a cattle driver to help get a steer out of the river - Grant taking a hand in the task in person by roaring at the animal with his arms raised. [224] These reconnoiters afforded the conclusion that nothing could be gained by engaging Lee in this place . He must be forced out into the open, where numerical advantage would count against him.

For most of the rest of the day Grant chose to stay in camp ,where he could be easily located in the confusion, issuing orders calmly as fortunes changed by the minute. Little could be achieved by riding out now, such was the chaos and lack of any real vantage points. But a stiff test of coolness was to come. Lee again tried to alarm his adversary by launching an evening assault on Grant's right flank. Officers in camp, especially those from the east who had come up against Lee in the past, feared that the rebel commander was trying to cut off the Federals from their supply lines. An attack so late in the evening, well after six o'clock, and after two days of grinding battle, might have disabled another commander . But Grant, although shaken, failed to overreact . If nothing else, his long work with horses had taught him the importance of never panicking. In spite of grave warnings of impending doom from his officers, he simply gave directions for reinforcing the besieged corps and went to bed. [225]

On May the 7th ,Grant gave orders that the entire army was to pull out of the Wilderness and move towards the village of Spotsylvania Court House twelve miles away. Soon after nightfall, the enormous army started out. Despite their desperate

---

[223] O. O. Howard and Ely S. Parker, "Some Reminiscences of Grant", *McClure's Magazine* , II, 6 , May 1894, page 533.

[224] Horace Porter, *Campaigning with Grant*, page 67.

[225] Ibid, page 71.

fatigue, the troops were buoyed up by the knowledge that they were heading south instead of retreating, as they had always done under past commanders. In fact, Grant never had any intention of going back, having already ordered the pontoons to be taken up from the Rapidan River. The night-time scene on the road was unforgettable. Whenever Grant was recognised on the distinctive "Cincinnati", he was greeted by wild cheers from the men who used dry leaves to light flares in his path. In the darkness the cavalcade had to ride carefully to avoid trampling the men who lay resting or sleeping on the road. Porter observed that the excitement was infectious ; and even "Cincinnati" "over which General Grant possessed such perfect control, became difficult to manage". [226] But Grant could take no pleasure in this moving tribute, fearing that the noise would give their position away to the enemy.

This nearly proved to be the case soon afterwards. The general's camp was advancing to Todd's Tavern when word came of enemy troop movements nearby. For safety reasons, the guide (Colonel Comstock) decided to return to the Brock Road. But this meant backtracking on the route - a maneuver that Grant always opposed. Members of his staff could testify to how entrenched this superstition was. "When he found he was not traveling in the direction he intended to take, he would try all sorts of cross-cuts, ford streams and jump any number of fences to reach another road rather than go back........" [227] . The general strongly objected to the plan and advised the guide to come up with another solution. If Grant had had his way, he would probably have walked himself into the hands of Longstreet's brigade. But for once in his life he accepted the wisdom of retracing his steps and the officers arrived at their destination safely.

When Lee observed that the vast army was moving in an easterly direction, he misread the signs and assumed that Grant was retreating to Fredericksburg. But by a stroke of luck he had sent some troops through interior lines to Spotsylvania. Lee got there before his opponents, setting the scene for another lethal showdown.

---

[226] Ibid, pages 79,81.

[227] William H. Armstrong,*Warrior in Two Camps. Ely S. Parker* , page 91.

Chapter 16

Jeff Davis

Grant switched horses at Spotsylvania. On the morning of May 9th he mounted little "Jeff Davis" for the campaign ahead. No doubt he was giving "Cincinnati" a rest. But the change of terrain was also a likely reason for the switch. The countryside was now more varied, and there was much distance to be covered in the hot sun : examining the topography, the strength of enemy entrenchments, or any weaknesses in the Confederate lines.

None of Grant's horses could have differed more from "Cincinnati" than "Jeff Davis". Little more than a pony at fourteen hands, he first came to Grant's notice during the siege of Vicksburg, in the Summer of 1863. General Sherman's men came upon a secluded plantation, and in their need to "make war support war", they made off with the carriage horses that they found. The elderly man who owned both house and horses turned out to be Jefferson Davis's older brother, Joe.

Originally "Jeff" was presented to Fred Grant since the horse was an ideal size for the youngster. Fred reported that the pony was in poor condition when it first came to headquarters after a long arduous march. But with some care it soon picked up and became a pleasant horse to ride, even carrying himself in a good shape. [228] By this time Grant was suffering greatly from boils, possibly as a result of riding

---

[228] Theo Rodenbough, *Pictorial History of the Civil War. The Cavalry*, page 296.

continuously on a naked saddle tree on the march to Vicksburg . One day he left his usual restless mount behind, most likely "Kangaroo" , and rode "Jeff Davis" out to the lines instead . He found his paces so smooth that Fred lost his pony there and then. Grant sent his new find to be appraised as a Federal war horse by the board of officers appointed for this job. No doubt eyebrows were raised among the board members at the size of the animal. But "Jeff" passed the assessors in spite of it. Grant then purchased the pony for himself and named him "Jeff Davis" in honour of his origins.

The image of Grant in the field will always be associated with "Cincinnati" . But that honour could just as easily have gone to the diminutive "Jeff Davis" instead. He was the one that Grant favoured for the long journeys and reconnoiters . "Little Jeff" was a conspicuous figure on many key journeys in the Virginia campaign, and Grant was to make the historic crossing of the James River on him. After the Wilderness campaign the general needed to make long daily rides, reconnoitering enemy positions and examining the topography. The undulating landscape around Spotsylvania was challenging - streams with steep wooded banks, marshland, dense scrubby forests, and the occasional patch of cleared land . The small, agile, gliding, sure- footed "Jeff Davis" proved invaluable in this terrain. Grant soon discovered that "Jeff" could go all day and come in fresh as a daisy at the end of it. [229]

But "Jeff's" pre-eminent quality was comfort . And we can see how he provided this from the photograph taken of him by Mathew Brady in the field a Cold Harbour. The fact that he appears untacked affords the viewer an even closer look at his conformation.   The key to his comfortable paces is evident in his sloping pasterns and equally sloping shoulders, with a wither set well back from his chest. However his withers are also very flat, indicating that correct fit of saddle would have been a problem for "Jeff", with the saddle tending to slip back readily. It may be significant that in another photograph of "Jeff" in a tacked up state, he is carrying an unusual saddle. The cantle is Grimsley model but the pommel is different and is set very high off his withers. Perhaps "Jeff" had to have his own specially made saddle. In addition the woolen saddle pad is folded over several times underneath to give extra padding. "Jeff" was also very low in his croup but had good hip to hock angle indicating power in his hind quarters. The same good hip to hock angle would have indicated that he was a scopey jumper. He had a short back so his stride was

---

[229] *New York Times*: Oct 3 1886, page 3.

likewise short. Not surprisingly he was a natural pacer. "Little Jeff" appears to have been a sharp horse, and in spite of his comfortable way of going, he may not have been that easy to ride.

Spotsylvania's brand of prolonged , positional warfare made reconnoitering the key to Grant's operations there. His time as a young teamster in the formidable woods of southern Ohio had been a perfect preparation for this phase of the war, where a feel for geography and ground was all important. During these days Horace Porter noted that : "he possessed an almost intuitive knowledge of topography.........he was a natural "bushwhacker", and was never so much at home as when finding his way by the course of streams, the contour of hills, and the general features of the country." [230] It was an invaluable trait in a commander who was fighting an adversary in his own back yard, and who had to rely on maps that were inaccurate or even fictional.

Grant was in constant danger in the course of his travels . During the morning of May 9th, he rode out on the little horse to Major General John Sedgwick's line. The two officers spoke about the battle plan for a while and when Grant went on his way, he asked a member of staff to return to the general to emphasise a point. As the aide arrived back to Sedgwick ,the general's body was already being laid out on the ground where he and Grant had met just minutes before. Shortly before his fatal wounding he had famously insisted that the Confederates couldn't shoot an elephant from that distance (650 yards). The highest ranking Union general to fall in the field, Sedgwick had fought gallantly at the Wilderness.

The Confederates were massed in a formidable, well defended, hoof-shaped line about a mile deep. This "mule shoe" of trenches and abatis was a flawed tactic, since any breakthrough left the back of the defenders vulnerable. The fulcrum of the fighting was at a place known as the "Bloody Angle" or "Hell's Half -Acre" . Grant chose to mount his fiercest assault at the front of the "mule shoe". By a concerted effort, his troops managed to take the Confederates main line of earthworks. They pushed the rebels back half a mile to a second set of entrenchments. Lee, mounted on the other "Jeff Davis", made many desperate attempts to regain this principal line, again taking a personal hand in directing the repulse. The column he was riding in attracted unwelcome attention from union gunners. "Traveller" started to rear as shells exploded around him, and Lee had his work cut out to stay in the saddle. A

---

[230] Horace Porter, *Campaigning with Grant*, page 66.

cannon ball whistled under the horse's legs and more "Lee to the rear !" cries were heard from the men. Lee followed the advice, probably more out of consideration for "Traveller's" safety than his own. The position was defended with ease and Grant had to disengage his troops. [231]

A week of heavy rain suspended serious fighting and turned the roads around Spotsylvania to bottomless mud. But by May the 19th, Grant was on the move again, inching ever closer to Richmond by a crab like, left flanking movement. On the morning of May the 20th, Grant who was usually up before the rest of his aides, had slept it out in camp. When called, he was able to dress with a speed that couldn't be matched by any other staff member. Given the simplicity of his dress, it wasn't that surprising. His lifelong dislike of decorative dress had stayed intact in spite of rank. His costume invariably consisted of yellow buckskin gauntlets while on horseback at the front. His trousers were made especially wide so that he could wear them either outside his cavalry boots in camp, or tucked in if the going was muddy. (Although Grant was considered stubby, a letter to his tailors, Richardson ,Spence & Thompson in 1861, revealed that he had a long leg for his height: 49 inches from waist band to bottom outside. This would have been an advantage to him as an equestrian) [232] It was rare for him to wear his sword - it hurt his hip when he rode.

With camp set up close to farms and homesteads, Grant came in regular contact with the women of the state as they were often the only ones left in the countryside. Frequently they gave him a piece of their mind, which he took with amused tolerance. Their sense of fear often prompted them to seek the protection of a high ranking officer if the opportunity arose, even as they hated the ground he walked on. Once at Quarles's Mills near the North Anna River, a strange local woman strayed unannounced into headquarters from a nearby farm. She pulled up a camp chair and sat down beside the general. The woman spoke in a squeaky drawl of the wonderful "Conestoga hosses" that the local boys had managed to round up while they had that spot of business in Pennsylvania last year. She said that they were all around the Virginia countryside now and were the best draught animal anyone could find. Perhaps because of the equestrian tone of the conversation, Grant let the woman talk on. She proved to be uninhibited in her opinions, saying how certain she was that General Lee was going to lick him with ease. Then in the next breath, she admitted that she was scared in the house on her own. Grant agreed to

---

[231] Robert K.Krick, *The War in the East*, page 49.

[232] John Y. Simon, ed. *Papers of Ulysses S. Grant* . Vol. 2. Sept 11th, 1861. To Richardsen, Spence & Thompson.

post an officer to stay at the house , and the young man reluctantly escorted her home. [233]

Early next morning the same woman came running into Grant's camp in a state of terrific agitation. Her only horse had been stolen from the barn that night . She wanted the general to get it back. Grant replied:
"perhaps it is one of those Conestoga horses you spoke of that belong up in Pennsylvania ,and some of our men have made up their minds to take him back home".
"You've got me on that one. But you've got no business being down here anyway ", she retaliated .[234]

Indeed thefts such as these were so commonplace that many farmers were reported to have kept their horses in their houses and even their attics . Plunder of simple household goods from farmsteads along the way provided many a mounted union man with rowels for his spurs as the wheels from the inside of stolen clocks were put to imaginative good use, starting a sort of fashion within the modish cavalry.[235]

Towards the end of May 1864, Grant devised an effective diversionary ploy using the cavalry, this time involving Colonel James Harrison Wilson's Third Cavalry division. While the ailing and exhausted Lee was in his sick bed, Wilson was directed to mass around Lee's left flank to give the impression that some significant movement was about to take place in that direction. Grant's real intention was to withdraw his army to the north side of the North Anna river without Lee knowing. [236]

Wilson was the undisputed expert on horses within Grant's camp . If anything his vision of the cavalry outstripped his commander's . Grant still thought of the cavalry in terms of relatively small units making incursions as "blinds" to deceive the enemy . But Wilson firmly believed that cavalry should be organised into a huge , striking force - armed like the infantry but with the advantage of mobility and speed . With repeating carbines for weapons ,the men could dismount

---

[233] Horace Porter, *Campaigning with Grant*, page 148.

[234] Ibid, pages 150-1.

[235] James Harrison Wilson , *Under the Old Flag.* Part One, page 141.

[236] Ulysses S. Grant, *The Personal Memoirs of Ulysses S. Grant*, page 464.

and fight as needed, much as Nathan Bedford Forrest favoured doing on the opposing side.

At the beginning of June , Grant moved his headquarters to a plantation house near Totopotomoy Creek. The change of location required a change of mount. He had been using "Jeff Davis" for much of the previous week. Before Grant set out on a day's reconnoitre his attendant, Bill Barnes, enquired if he would saddle up "Jeff" as usual. But Grant said he would take "Egypt" instead, citing the increasingly swampy terrain near Totopotomy Creek as his reason for the switch. He was afraid that "Little Jeff's" legs were simply not long enough to cope with the mud. [237]

As one-time quartermaster and wagon supervisor, Grant always took an interest in the vast train of supply wagons, four thousand in all, that accompanied the Army of the Potomac. He was more aware than most of the difficulties of the teamster's job, but was intolerant of any brutality at the same time. Shortly after the move to Totopotomoy, he came upon a scene involving a supply wagon that produced a rare outburst of rage. Riding out with John Rawlins around the area of the creek, Grant spotted a horse-drawn wagon that had got bogged down in the swampy going. The teamster was going at the horses, beating them repeatedly on the face with his stick and swearing loudly as he did so. Riding "Egypt" up to the wagon, Grant began to argue angrily with the teamster, who seemed oblivious to the general's rank, and told him to mind his own business in so many words. Grant ordered him to be tied to a tree for six hours as punishment for his cruelty and insolence.

Although this was one of the busiest periods for the general and his staff, with his army maneuvering relentlessly toward Cold Harbour for another rendezvous with the enemy, Grant just couldn't quite get the affair out of his mind. Twice he referred to it during the day as he reconnoitered tirelessly with General Meade by his side. He even returned to the subject at the dinner table that night, remarking :
"If people knew how much more they could get out of a horse by gentleness than by harshness, they would save a great deal of trouble both to the horse and the man. A horse is a particularly intelligent animal; he can be made to do almost anything if his master has intelligence enough to let him know what is required." [238] The general,

---

[237] Horace Porter, *Campaigning with Grant,* page 163.

[238] Ibid, page 166.

with over half a million troops under his command, confessed to one of his staff officers that he was "looking forward longingly to the time when we can end this war, and I can settle down to my St. Louis farm and raise horses".[239] This was Grant's simple vision of his future after the war, a revealing glimpse of where he escaped to in his mind when the campaign was at its toughest.

Such incidents with draught horses were all too common at the front. On June 22nd 1864, a letter from Lt. Col. Cyrus B. Comstock of Grant's staff to quartermaster general, Rufus Ingalls, recalls: "Yesterday by Gen. Grant's direction I ordered a man who was running a horse into gateposts tress &c and who had already knocked one of the horses eyes out, into confinement. This morning I learn that he is one of your men, and wish to turn the case over to you for such action as you deem proper ".[240]

"Egypt" continued to be the general's battle horse throughout the Cold Harbour campaign. Grant had put his sights on this strategically important location because it held the short route to the James River which he was determined to cross. But Lee had drawn a six mile long curtain of troops between the Army of the Potomac and Richmond, with Cold Harbour, (shelter without heat), at the extreme right end of it. Confederate trenches were now at their best, even better than those at Spotsylvania, as Lee lived up to his long-held title, the "King of Spades". Grant's ill-fated decision to attack was based on his belief that it would shorten the conflict, now costing four million dollars a day. The sick season was nearly upon his men when heat and flies would kill more troops than any assault. There was also no way of testing any weakness in Lee's lines without taking the fight to him.

On June 3rd the battle of Cold Harbour commenced. Lee's superior knowledge of the terrain told early. By mid morning it became clear that the rebel defensive position was too strong and no advantage could be gained from an attack here. But it was too late to roll back the vast tide of casualties - some seven thousand. With the works of both armies situated so close together, recovering the dead and wounded was virtually impossible. In no man's land, a carpet of human decay formed, spanning some forty yards, the stench becoming unbearable in the hot

---

[239] Ibid, page 167.

[240] John Y. Simon, ed., *Papers of Ulysses S. Grant.* Vol. 11. Calendar, June 22nd. Col Comstock to Gen. Rufus Ingalls.

Virginia sun. This was the unique horror of Cold Harbour: one of the few assaults that Grant deeply regretted.

As the trench warfare around Cold Harbour dragged on, Grant had a visit from a political friend from the west. Against the general's advice, the visitor was anxious to experience the dubious delights of the front for himself. Wearing his silk top hat, he boldly rode out with his host. There was a particularly treacherous stretch of road that the other officers had trained themselves to ride past at top speed so they might avoid being struck. However Grant defiantly rode this stretch of road on "Egypt" at a walk, and even stopped to examine the ground in more detail. Meanwhile shot and shell were exploding all around the party, landing uncomfortably close to the visitor. Colonel Porter described the politician's grotesque rolling in the saddle as being like a "signal flag waving a message". Grant told him he was wasting valuable energy: by the time he heard the shot, it had already passed him. Realising that his life was hanging by a thread, the visitor turned his horse around and fled back to camp without Grant. He didn't even bother to retrieve his expensive silk top hat which flew off his head as he galloped away. Back in camp that night, the officers enjoyed a few jokes at the visitor's expense in a rare moment of light relief. [241]

Shortly after the battle of Cold Harbour, the darkest hour of the campaign, Grant had his three campaign horses photographed by Mathew Brady. Perhaps the exercise was to satisfy press and public interest, but it probably had a more personal significance for Grant. These horses had carried him through a month of relentless campaigning and were due some acknowledgement for their unique part in the effort. Their glossy coats and good condition spoke of the good care they had received, in spite of the rigours of the campaign. In fact their appearance strongly contrasts with the gaunt spectacle of their rider in photographs of the time. To add to his magnificence, "Cincinnati" was tacked up in full military dress. It isn't hard to imagine how impressive he must have looked when in motion. The other two horses, "Egypt" and "Jeff Davis", were presented untacked, allowing the viewer to see their conformations more fully. "Jeff" is dwarfed beside "Cincinnati" and it is amazing to think that both horses carried the same rider. We can observe how proud and beautiful the thoroughbred "Egypt" was and what extravagant paces he must have possessed. Given his thick neck and alert look, "Egypt" might have been a strong

---

[241] Horace Porter, *Campaigning with Grant*, pages 185-6.

ride: tenser than "Cincinnati" . "Cincinnati" looks the most relaxed of the three, perhaps a gentle giant. But his potential power would have been formidable. It is no wonder Grant allowed few people to sit on his back.

The grooming, care and tacking up of the Grant horses probably fell to the general's personal attendant, Bill Barnes - a runaway slave from Missouri who had attached himself to the western army since 1861. At first Bill offered his services to the promising young Colonel George Boomer of the Twenty- Sixth Missouri Volunteers . Boomer was well known for his fine horse. Perhaps too well known, for a local confederate officer put his eye on the animal early in the war and stole him at the first opportunity. When Boomer was killed during a charge at Vicksburg , Bill was out of a job. At that point it appears that he decided to divert all his considerable energies to the task of looking after General Grant. He then came east with his new employer in 1864. Grant had other servants: James Guard, a tall powerfully- built man photographed holding Grant's three horses at Cold Harbour, and a black man and woman called Douglass and Georgianna respectively. The pay of these people was negligible. Grant was able to assert in a letter to Julia that his expenditure on servants and horses did not exceed $40 a month. [242] This made little impact on his Lieutenant General's salary, now $1000 a month. Interestingly he was not entitled to the $50 monthly U. S. army allowance for horse fodder since he drew fodder in kind, or lived off the land.

As the general had very few needs, Bill's most onerous responsibility must have been looking after his horses, since Grant would have expected a high standard of stable management. Care of the hooves and legs would have been of particular importance in the perpetually muddy going in Virginia . Indeed at certain times of the year the mud would be to the belly . Bill had his work cut out for him to prevent the disabling effects of mud rash from afflicting the three war horses, particularly "Egypt" with his two white socks. Bill wasn't always around to see to the horses. Grant frequently cut away from camp and lived without any attendant. In these situations, it is assumed that a cavalry orderly belonging to his escort or attached to the camp being visited would act as groom.

By the middle of June, Grant stole away from Lee and moved his vast army across the enormous James River, using the longest pontoon bridge that had ever been built in the Civil War, two thousand one hundred feet. Dispensing with his cigar for once, he watched the crossing from a nearby bluff, no doubt paying closer attention than

---

[242] John Y. Simon, ed. *Papers of Ulysses S. Grant*. Vol. 13. Letter to Julia. Nov 1864 .

usual to the vast four thousand strong convoy of supply wagons that snaked across the river below him. Had the driver a good communication with his team , were the horses a good match, did they balk. It was his finest hour in Virginia . Lee never guessed his intentions. The maneuver left the town of Petersburg completely vulnerable to Federal onslaught. Lee quickly threw his whole force to the rescue of the town , arriving himself on "Traveller" on the 18th of June. He set about locating his trench works in such a masterly way as to make the place impregnable. Grant thought the city could be rapidly captured, but the fight seemed to have gone out of his army at this stage. Staff members spoke about the fatigue of the men at the time, of how sleeping on horseback had become an art form among the officers, and a surprisingly refreshing one. [243] A prolonged siege was in store.

Card playing, particularly whist or cribbage, was the favourite diversion among the officers during what free time they had. The men found humour where they could. Grant very seldom laughed out loud. But one subject that never failed to amuse him was foolishness on horseback on the part of his officers. One day he and his staff were riding to General Butler's lines near a loop of the James called Bermuda Hundred. They travelled in single file, Grant at the head of the cavalcade. He led the group up a steep hill, through a very narrow bridle path skirted by thick trees. Eventually the path became too narrow for even a horse to fit through, so Grant steered a path toward more open ground. Adam Badeau, his bookish, short-sighted private secretary - a "bent fo'-pence" in Grant's words - was at the rear of the column, and failed to spot the maneuver. As he continued on straight, his horse got stuck fast between two trees, leaving the rider with no room for his knees. Badeau cried out to the others for help. But it was too late. The animal finally wriggled through leaving Badeau to fall out the back door, past the horse's tail, still sitting on his saddle. The mishap kept Grant amused for the rest of the journey and for several days afterwards, when he would tease Badeau about his misfortune. [244] To Grant, clumsiness on horseback was a completely baffling and hilarious phenomenon.

Another episode that he enjoyed and loved to hear retold was admiral Daniel Ammen's near death experience on the horse of Grant's staff engineer, Cyrus Comstock. Being a navy man and therefore without a permanent horse, Ammen had borrowed Comstock's powerful grey to visit a friend in Silver Springs. The reins

---

[243] Horace Porter, *Campaigning with Grant*, page 211.

[244] Ibid , page 229.

became slippy with the animal's sweat, preventing the rider from keeping a good hold of the horse's head. When they reached the town the horse ran away with Ammen several times and nearly killed him. "The story of this ride, as told by me to Mr. Blair and General Grant, afforded them great amusement; indeed I have no recollection of seeing General Grant laugh so heartily as when the story of the ride was recounted, which he called for from time to time." [245]

Grant's pony, "Jeff Davis", was to provide many amusing incidents. At the end of June 1864, the general and some of his staff were riding out in the blistering heat to the headquarters of the Army of the Potomac, a journey of many hours. Because his regular horse was injured, staff officer Col. Horace Porter was saddled on a bay cob with a jarring, choppy stride. Grant was riding along side on "Jeff Davis", pacing along at a speed that "was too fast for a walk and not fast enough for a gallop", so that all the others had to adopt a very brisk trot in order to keep up. [246] Five miles into the journey, Grant turned to Porter and remarked that he didn't think his staff officer looked all that well. Porter described the agony that his horse was putting him through. But Grant would not believe him, insisting that all horses were more or less comfortable if the rider sat in a relaxed way on their backs. Porter asked him if he would care to swap. Keen to prove his point, Grant agreed. The young staff officer now felt he was on an armchair as he continued the journey in comfort on "Little Jeff". All eyes now turned to Grant. And it caused no end of amusement among his officers to see the jogging and saddle-pounding that the cob was subjecting their chief to. When they reached their destination, Porter noted that the general dismounted in a decidedly stiff way, and he turned to him and said "well I must acknowledge that animal is rather rough".[247]

Porter had the utmost admiration for Grant as a horseman, saying that he had never seen a better rider, or one with a steadier seat. "When he rode or drove a strange horse, not many minutes elapsed before he and the animal seemed to understand each other perfectly". [248] Porter's cob appeared to be the exception however. By this time in the war Grant valued comfort on horseback increasingly

---

[245] Adm. Daniel Ammen, *North American Review.* Vol. XLI. No. 348, Nov. 1885. "Recollections and Letters of Grant", page 421. University of Northern Iowa. *http://www.jstor.org.* Accessed Jan 20 2012.

[246] Horace Porter, *Campaigning with Grant,* page 226.

[247] Ibid, page 227.

[248] Ibid, page 226.

highly, probably due to his injury in New Orleans. War artists sometimes caught him sitting side-saddle on his horse when stationary, like Zachary Taylor. It was a good way to relieve weary hip muscles after hours in the saddle.

Grant set up his base of supplies for the Petersburg campaign at City Point, where the James and Appomattox rivers meet. It became the nerve centre of a slick, efficient military machine, lacking nothing in facilities and relative comfort for the major participants of the war. There were facilities for direct communication with all the armies of the union and with the administration in Washington , and a vast, modern hospital for six thousand casualties. The depot was served by both boats and trains. Blacksmith facilities were superb: a horse could be shod or a sabre sharpened at any time of the day or night . The City Point complex was presided over by Grant's long-time friend Rufus Ingalls as quartermaster for the Army of the Potomac . Given his own background, Grant tended to have close and cordial relations with his quartermasters and commissaries and gave them free rein in their operations.

As the autumn of 1864 set in, a line of simple huts was built to accommodate Grant and his staff on the grounds of Eppes Mansion. A short distance behind this line was the officer's mess and shelter for the horses. Nothing was wasted for the campaign. If a journalist or visitor left his horse unattended for any length of time at City Point it was likely to be snapped up by the cavalry . Some newspapermen deliberately took to keeping their horses within Grant's compound ,if they had the influence to do so, because a guard was kept over his stables at all times. [249]For the officers, camp life revolved around the fire in front of Grant's cabin, particularly in the winter months. There up to thirty officers would discuss the campaigns, chat and reminisce into the small hours of the morning, the Lieutenant General always being one of the last to leave the fireside.

In September of 1864, Grant wrote a letter from City Point to his two sons, Fred and Buck. He urged them to ask their younger brother , Jesse , if he would not like to be a brave boy and stay with his father at the front, and ride "Jeff Davis" . He signed off the letter with the words: "ask Jess if Jeff aint a bully horse!". [250] Grant was challenging his youngest and most boisterous son to graduate to the big league

---

[249] Sylvanus Cadwallader, *Three Years with Grant,* page 180.

[250] John Y. Simon ,ed. *Papers of Ulysses S Grant.* Vol. 13, Letter to Fred Grant and Ulysses Grant Jnr. ,Sept .13th, 1864.

by riding one of his father's war horses, perhaps making a visit to camp even more thrilling for the child.

But Jeff seemed to have been bully in more ways than one. This fact was illustrated the following Spring when President Lincoln paid a visit to City Point for the last time, accompanied by his son, Tad. As Jesse was also staying in camp, Grant arranged that the four of them would ride out together on a tour of the camps. As usual Lincoln was given his favourite horse, "Cincinnati", to ride. It was thought that Tad would ride "Jeff Davis" and Jesse his little Shetland ," Rebbie". Although nine years of age, Tad was not a confident horseman. The death of his brother Willie, his saddle companion, had turned him off riding. Besides he had had an earlier encounter with the little horse in June 1864 and had not liked him. He refused the ride. Jesse's seven year old heart swelled with pride when his father announced : "Jess will ride Jeff !". It would be his first opportunity to ride the battle horse, and in front of the president too! The two boys set off in front of the adults, Jesse on "Jeff" and Tad on the Grant Shetland ,"Rebbie" . A band was playing and the horses were restless. Jesse noted that his father's horse, probably "Egypt", became increasingly restless , arching its neck and dancing on the spot. All the while Lincoln's mount, "Cincinnati", remained impassive, his reins loose and floppy as a clothes line, as Lincoln liked to ride him.

The sharp, active "Jeff Davis" , carrier of the general in many of his long journeys and swift reconnoiters ,was particularly keen to get moving. Taking advantage of his young rider, he lunged forward without warning and bolted down the field. Tad Lincoln, a mere passenger on "Little Rebel" , sped off after him. Within seconds the children had left their alarmed parents far behind. Grant and Lincoln rode off in hot pursuit, but the harder they rode the faster "Jeff" galloped ahead of them. Realising this, Grant pulled up his horse and bade the others to do likewise. The terrified Jesse remarked that he was helpless to influence the pace of "Jeff" beneath him as the pony bolted away uncontrollably . Eventually an orderly's horse came upsides the bewildered child, and with the help of soldiers up ahead, who formed a human chain on the road, the unruly little pony was channelled into a mule corral where the race came to an end. Jesse's disgrace was complete when he spent the rest of the journey at the back of the cavalcade, with a lead rope around "Jeff's" neck , held firmly by an orderly. [251]Perhaps "Jeff Davis" wasn't such an easy ride after all.

---

[251] Jesse Root Grant, *In the Days of My Father*, page 25.

Chapter 17

*L*ittle Rebel

"Jeff Davis" may have been a challenge for the Grant boys, but their favourite would have been an even smaller battle charger. In spite of his tender years, six year old Jesse Grant was to get a taste of the Vicksburg campaign in the summer of 1863. As the carriage bringing him to his father's camp drew up outside headquarters, Jesse could see a little Shetland pony waiting for him, bearing a tiny saddle made by one of the army staff. Before the vehicle had even come to a standstill, the delighted child jumped out of the carriage and leapt straight onto the tiny animal's back. Many adventures awaited Jesse on "Little Rebel". Over the next few weeks he accompanied Grant on many inspections: either on the little shetland or as a pillion passenger on the general's horses, one of whom he distinctly remembered his father calling "Mankiller" because of his fierceness! During these inspections Grant would thunder along at great speed, with the six year old seated behind, clasping his father's belt. [252]

---

[252] Jesse Root Grant, *In the Days of My Father*. Page 16.

Throughout the war "Little Rebel" led an interesting double life - accompanying the children to the front when they visited camp, and then keeping them entertained back in the relative tranquillity of St. Louis or Covington . Grant wrote frequent letters to Julia about "Rebel". When the children were not with him at camp, the shetland pony represented a strong bond and point of common interest between them . Grant spoke of the comfort he thought "Rebbie's" presence at home would afford them. There is often a note of anxiety in his enquiries about the shetland. It preyed on his mind that the pony might be stolen, given his size and popularity with the children. Grant suggested that Julia keep "Rebbie" with Charles Ford at St. Louis . If the pony had to travel anywhere, the general frequently asked her if he had made the journey safely. "I would not have him lost for a great deel (sic.)". [253] The following month Grant wrote again to Julia on the same subject. He wanted to send the pony home to her so that she could harness him to a buggy and sleigh and the children could then drive as much as they pleased. He ended the letter by referring to his old dream: "I expect when this campaign ends to send all my horses home and stay there most of the time myself when I am not visiting different armies . I do wish I could tell when that would be". [254]

The children were well aware of their father's horse riding prowess. According to Fred, pa was the best horseman in the army, preferring fiery, powerful horses even if they were virtually unmanageable. But he was intolerant of any timidity in his sons, especially on horseback. Fred described how his father taught him to ride on one of the farm horses at White Haven at an early age. He would show his disapproval if the boy wasn't brave. Being the eldest son, Fred was treated virtually like a man from a young age, much as Ulysses had been in his day. At the age of twelve, he accompanied his father on much of the Vicksburg campaign in 1863, during which he witnessed all the horrors of war and was injured slightly in the leg. Surprisingly, it was Julia who was most enthusiastic about her eldest son being at the front. Grant had had his reservations, but Julia was quick to point out that Alexander had been of a similar age when he stood beside Philip on the field, famously stealing a march on his father by taming the ungovernable "Bucephalus" . Fred's adventures at Vicksburg came to an abrupt end when he contracted camp

---

[253] John Y. Simon, ed. *Papers of Ulysses S. Grant*. Vol 12. Grant to Julia, Sept. 11th, 1864.

[254] Ibid. .Grant to Julia, Oct 26th 1864.

dysentery and typhoid. In a sense, Fred's illness did Grant a good turn. While visiting his son's sick bed in St Louis, he came by the horse that would be most associated with his name, "Cincinnati". Unlike General Sherman's young son, Fred recovered and was able to rejoin his father at a later stage as an unpaid aide de camp. Eventually John Rawlins took to calling Fred "the veteran".

In camp the children could often be found wrestling their father to the ground in his tent. Grant would excuse the horseplay to his staff officers by saying: "you know my two weaknesses - my children and my horses". [255]At other times the Grant children came a little too close to the firing line. The youngest, Jesse, had accompanied his father by boat one afternoon and had been given permission to take "Little Rebel" along. After the group disembarked, they mounted and rode off to the front. In the confusion, Jesse managed to ride off with them. It was only when they came under enemy fire that Grant turned around and saw the kilted six year old in the midst of the shooting. "What's that youngster doing there!", he said. Jesse was quickly dispatched to the rear, but not without a fight. In the end an aide of the general's had to catch hold of "Little Reb's" bridle and with a sharp smack to the pony's tail end, he sent him galloping off to the rear. It was too late when the horrified aide realised that the sudden movement had made the boy a perfect target. Luckily no harm came to "Little Reb" or Jesse, who seemed to share his father's luck on the battlefield. ("Rebbie" lived to enjoy higher office at the White House stables and died at a ripe old age in 1883.)

Grant did everything to nurture his sons' equestrian skills from an early age. But according to his middle son, Buck, he was somewhat disappointed that none of them grew up to have much horse savvy. Although Fred achieved the cavalry appointment that his father always coveted and was considered one of the best horsemen at West Point, Grant didn't rate him too highly, it seems. He used to say that Fred knew a bit about horses, Ulysses nothing at all, and Jesse less than that. [256]From the time she was old enough, Grant's daughter Nellie had a string of horses at her disposal, suggesting that she shared her father's interest in the subject. "Jennie" was her saddle horse when she lived at the White House and she had several fast teams to drive, most notably "Lady Morgan" and "Queane", who were discarded just as fast after her marriage to an Englishman in 1873. From an early age Nellie was a keen socialite and a devotee of the lighter things in life. While still

---

[255] Horace Porter, *Campaigning with Grant*. Page 283.

[256] C.B. Galbreath, *Ohio Archaeological and Historical*. Vol. 31. "Centennial Anniversary of the Birth of Ulysses S. Grant", Page 286. Accessed via *openlibrary.org*, http://www.archive.org/.

in her teens, she was best known for just two accomplishments : her phaeton driving and her ability to dance all night. [257]

General Ambrose Burnside's plan of breeching the Confederate defences at Petersburg with a powerful mine seemed like a good idea at the time . The siege outside the town had been dragging on through July of 1864 and many in the whiskered general's corps were Pennsylvanian miners, experienced in tunneling . On July the 30th 1864, the plan was put into action, closely observed by Grant and a few staff officers who had bivouacked with Burnside's men. When the mine eventually exploded at dawn, much later than planned, a giant plume of earth was thrown up towards the sky, leaving a massive crater. This breached the Confederate defenses well enough, but the troops were slow in pouring into the hollow, due to poor leadership and the failure to remove the abatis that blocked the way . Once inside the crater the men had, in Grant's words, "the wolf by the ears" . T h e southerners regrouped over the vast hollow, pummeling the Federal soldiers who had no means of clambering out since nobody had thought to bring ladders.

 Sensing the confusion, Grant mounted his horse and rode as near as he dared to the scene. His mounted inspection revealed columns of men lying on their arms waiting for those up ahead to advance. Soon he was so close to the crater site that a staff officer pleaded with him to dismount for his own safety. Without further prompting, Grant jumped off his horse, handed the reins to an orderly and trudged on foot to the front in the sultry, midsummer air. Without the protection afforded by his horse, he was jostled by his own men as he made his way to Burnside's earthworks. His order was to recall any further assault. Grant made his way back to where the horses were and rode back somberly to camp. He was silent on the journey except for a few sparse observations about the plan having been mishandled and the troops insufficiently lead. [258]

Throughout the Autumn of 1864, Grant attempted to destroy the railroads that served Petersburg , hoping to starve Lee of his supplies. Again much reconnoitering was done to the west and south of the town in this objective. The terrain was a daunting combination of "natural and artificial obstacles" : slashed trees, dense wood and brush, muddy streams and even quicksand. One particularly hazardous day-long

---

[257] Ishbel Ross, *The General's Wife*. Page 218.

[258] Horace Porter, *Campaigning with Grant*. Page 269.

reconnoitre took place near Hatcher's Run, October 27th, 1864 , where enemy batteries were located. Grant on "Jeff Davis" and General George Meade ,together with some of their staff, rode in full view of enemy cannons. Quickly they were surrounded by exploding shells. As was his habit, Grant called on just one of his staff, in this case Orville Babcock, to accompany him closer to the enemy batteries. In a situation reminiscent of Lee and "Traveller" at Spotsylvania, a shell exploded in front of "Jeff Davis" , sending the animal's front hooves skyward. As he reared and plunged, his legs became entangled in telegraph wires that littered the ground nearby. Members of staff looked on anxiously from a distance. The more the horse tried to break free , the worse his entanglement became. With little thought for his own safety, Babcock dismounted to see if he could cut the wires. Grant sat perfectly still in the saddle ,warning Babcock to protect the horse's legs at any cost. Eventually the animal was cut free, suffering only superficial injuries. Grant's dangerous examinations on horseback around Hatcher's Run convinced him that he would have to detach a sizable portion of his army from City Point to break through Lee's line.

The culmination of this risky survey occurred between the 5th and the 7th of February the following year ,when Federal troops attempted to break through enemy entrenchments after the long winter . Expecting to have to surrender, Lee donned his sash and sword and galloped "Traveller" out to get a closer look. Sixty thousand troops were involved in the assault, making it an impossible situation for the Virginian . He gave the Federals the ground and retrenched.

The fate of Petersburg was sealed on 31st of March with a major union cavalry victory at the battle of Five Forks. This valuable intersection that gave the battle its name, signaled the loss of Confederate control of the south side railroad , Lee's only means of supply. Sometime after the death in the field of one of the south's key generals , A. P. Hill, Lee decided to withdraw across the swollen Appomattox before Federal assaults cut off retreat . His headquarters at Turnbull House were being subjected to much shelling now , so he rode "Traveller" to the inner fortifications of the town. He made this journey at a dignified walk, shells exploding all around him, disemboweling a horse close behind . [259]

When the end finally came at Petersburg on April 2nd, Grant himself provided a powerful image of the transfer of occupation at the outer defenses of the town. He described in his memoirs how he put his horse, "Jeff Davis", over the barricades just at the moment that thousands of Confederate prisoners were being

---

[259] Shelby Foote, *The Civil War- a Narrative.* Vol. 3, page 881.

marched out. The defeated troops showed a great deal of curiosity in the figure on the little pony who had just jumped over their works - even more so when they discovered his identity. [260] By contrast at dusk the same day, as the Army of Northern Virginia evacuated Petersburg , General Lee dismounted at a road junction and stood with "Traveller's" reins in his hands, supervising the exodus.

    Grant pursued Lee without pause, marching west with General Ord's column. He was still riding "Jeff" when a despatch came in on the road from one of General Sheridan's scouts that said, "I wish you were here yourself". On hearing this he called for "Cincinnati", whom Lincoln had ridden into Petersburg the day before. Grant had no baggage, camp equipment, sword or spur with him at this stage. But he had at least his fastest horse underneath him as he set off on a hazardous journey of sixteen miles through mainly woodland . It was to be the son of Lexington 's most grueling time. To add to the peril, most of the journey was undertaken in the dark. Grant and his little party of fourteen staff members were perilously close to enemy lines . It was well after ten o'clock at night when they were met by the disbelieving looks of Sheridan's pickets who found it difficult to take in that the highest ranking general of the Federal army had been wandering about the Virginia countryside virtually unescorted. [261]

After spending the night at Sheridan's camp, Grant took "Cincinnati" west on a day long journey to Burkeville , beside the Danville railroad, which was now in Federal hands. The journey in the rain the next day brought them ten miles further west to Farmville . Lee had achieved much needed rations at this place the day before, but he hadn't the luxury of enjoying them, such was the swiftness of the Federal pursuit. Victory seemed sure now and the soldiers felt at liberty to cheer the officers on the road and light bonfires and flares at night near camp. Grant rode swiftly to the north of the Appomattox river and joined General Meade's column where he reasoned the Confederate commander might try to find him. He had already sent out a letter to Lee requesting surrender. He had also been struck down with one of his crippling malarious headaches that night and couldn't sleep. At midnight Lee's reply was delivered into camp, but the note failed to talk of surrender. Grant, still with a throbbing head, dictated another letter urging the Army of Northern Virginia to lay down its arms.

---

[260] Ulysses S. Grant, *Personal Memoirs of Ulysses S. Grant.* page 577.

[261] Horace Porter, *Campaigning with Grant.* Page 456.

He was no better the following day, and his staff officers pleaded with him to travel by ambulance. Grant wouldn't hear of it. Instead he mounted "Cincinnati" as usual and rode to General Sheridan's front . It was difficult terrain - a mixture of hilly farmland, boggy fields and endless streams. On the way he received the despatch from Lee that he had been waiting for, the content of which had a better effect on the headache than any treatment. Grant dismounted at once and wrote a note of reply against a tree stump, selecting Orville Babcock to take it by the fastest route to the Confederate leader just five miles away. The Army of Northern Virginia ,consisting of two corps, had fought hunger and exhaustion the previous few days. Lee had shared the privations, snatching a few hours sleep in a forest on top of a wood pile with a blanket thrown over him, just as Grant had done during the Vicksburg campaign. The hardships were also making an impact on "Traveller" by now. There was no fodder and he and the other officer's mounts were reduced to feeding off tree bark in the woods.

Grant pressed on - approaching the small village of Appomattox Court House at a trot. As the road was congested with men and wagons , he characteristically put his horse across country on this his last real ride of the war. Again the party strayed perilously close to enemy lines and the union commander risked becoming a prisoner of Lee just as his army was about to surrender. [262] A decision was made to turn back; and for once the general had little objection to the retreat. The pace of the last few days didn't just show on Grant and his staff. "Cincinnati" was also falling prey to fatigue and was lame by now with a sprained foot. This meant that the meeting place with Lee had to be approached at an unusually sedate trot. When Grant reached Appomattox Court House at about one o'clock in the day, the stately southerner was already waiting for him in the red-brick house chosen by Colonel Babcock for the rendezvous. Whether by accident or design, the horse that Grant had been riding in the final days was his most impressive battle charger and the horse that he had ridden when he first engaged Lee in battle nearly a year before. Perhaps no other horse would have done justice to the occasion.

Fully expecting to be made Grant's prisoner, Lee had dressed himself in his finest uniform, complete with sash and ceremonial sword. He may even have been expecting to surrender "Traveller" to his opponent. The magnificence of his costume embarrassed Grant, who was shabby in appearance since the swiftness of the end

---

[262] Horace Porter, *Campaigning with Grant* . Page 468.

had genuinely taken him by surprise. ²⁶³ In spite of the hardships that Lee's aide de camp, Charles Marshall, had undergone, the southerner observed that it was Grant who looked like he had had a "pretty hard time." ²⁶⁴ Marshall could not have known just how close his pursuer or indeed his horse had come to breaking point. Had the rebels held out for one more day, Grant, who was depending on the land for forage, admitted later that he would have been compelled to call off his chase. ²⁶⁵

In return for laying down their arms, Lee's men were guaranteed generous surrender terms, including the right of officers to retain their side arms and horses. Lee's austere expression was reported to have softened for the first time when he read these guarantees. He pressed the issue further, however, requesting that all his men be allowed to keep their horses. Unlike the Federal army, his cavalry had not been issued with government mounts, but had ridden their own horses into battle. Now that peace was at hand, these same horses would be needed to turn the land. Perhaps recalling his early struggles at Hardscrabble ,Grant couldn't refuse this concession. Parole officers were instructed to allow Lee's men to return to their farms and homesteads with their horses or mules. Both commanders understood the immense economic and social importance of allowing the men of the confederacy to keep their mounts. It played an invaluable part in reconciling the two sides. Lee had negotiated the best possible terms for his men and looked greatly relieved at the end of the meeting. He had expected more sternness.

Outside on the front garden of Wilmer McClean's house ,"Traveller" had been untacked to graze the grass freely. When the meeting between the two commanders was over and the horse was being tacked up again, Lee, in a world of his own, was seen to take "Traveller's" forelock absentmindedly in his hand, trail it under the brow band, then smooth it down and pat his forehead gently ,as one "who loves horses, but whose thoughts are far away, might all do unwittingly". ²⁶⁶ When he rode off the same witness commented that there could scarcely have been a more elegant horseman on either side of the conflict.

---

²⁶³ Ulysses S. Grant, *Personal Memoirs of Ulysses S. Grant.* Page 601.

²⁶⁴ Charles Marshall, *Lee's Aide de Camp.* Page 269.

²⁶⁵ Ulysses S. Grant, *Personal Memoirs of Ulysses S. Grant.* Page 608.

²⁶⁶ *Harper's New Monthly.* April 1898. Article by General George A. Forsyth

Grant's delicacy prevented him from sharing in the jubilation of some of his officers or of even dwelling on the events of the day. Instead he chose to reminisce with some of the senior staff about the antics of one of the Mexican mules at Popocatapetyl twenty years before. [267] The following day he met Lee in a field convenient to both camps and the two generals talked on horseback. In spite of the constant rain it was a picturesque scene. Up to fifty officers, also mounted, were arranged in horseshoe fashion around the two figures but were out of earshot. Grant would undoubtedly have cast an eye over "Traveller", noting his movement with interest. At noon he rode to Burkeville from where he boarded a train to City Point. Shortly afterwards he was gone to Washington and away from the field for good.

Over the following days Lee dealt with the devastation of his army's defeat by maintaining an inaccessible and dignified manner in camp. But "Traveller" always did much to humanise the "marble man". In the end, Lee's men could at least bypass the icy aloofness of their commander by a quick, passing caress of his horse as he rode by them for the last time.

Like Grant, Lee showed great loyalty to his war horses, in spite of being nearly forced to sell them for want of money and forage on his return to Richmond. [268] After the conflict, he and his arthritic wife, Mary Custis, found some peace in the countryside at Derwent. But nothing gave the jaded general more solace than to ride his grey horse out each afternoon on the picturesque lands that surrounded their retreat. Lee turned his back on all things military after the war, with the exception of his battle chargers. He went to great lengths to reclaim his mare, "Lucy Long", who had been sold on to a public livery yard. When the couple moved to Lexington and Lee took up an appointment as provost of Washington College, three of his war horses - "Traveller", "Lucy" and "Ajax" - were installed in a beautiful, roomy stable behind the house. A friendly and biddable character in peacetime ,"Traveller" had free rein over the grounds, where he grazed and occasionally approached the front porch for tid bits. In time he became something of a tourist attraction, with his tail growing increasingly threadbare from the work of souvenir hunters. "Traveller" outlived his master by just one year. Having come through all the hazardous war campaigns completely unscathed, he succumbed to tetanus brought on by standing on a rusty nail in the peaceful college grounds in June 1871. He was only fourteen years old.

---

[267] Horace Porter, *Campaigning with Grant*.. Page 489.

[268] Adam Badeau, *Grant in Peace*. Page 22.

Chapter 18

*B*utcher Boy

The end of the war brought a dramatic change of lifestyle for Grant. Gone were the grueling days spent at the front with headquarters in the saddle. Gone were the detailed reconnoiters, the swift pursuits, the long marches over mountain, forest or bayou . The most demanding thing that the general and "Cincinnati" could do now was to ride in a review or pose for an equestrian statue.

In May 1865, Grant's well-worn Grimsley war saddle - the one that had carried him from Fort Donelson to Appomattox - was given as a gift to Absalom H. Markland, who had known the general briefly from his time at school in Maysville . [269]Markland had been in charge of the innovative army mail service in which letters were sent to the front by rail. Grant appreciated only too well the positive effect on troop morale of this prompt, reliable service, and the gift of his Grimsley was a token of his esteem. Strangely, in a letter marking the transfer of ownership, Grant misspelled the name of the saddle, referring to it as his "Grimsby" . (A running joke, perhaps.) The "Grimsby" resides today in the Chicago Historical Society museum.

---

[269] John Y. Simon, ed*., Papers of U. S. Grant,* Vol. 15. Letter to Absalom Markland. May 19th , 1865. Southern Illinois University Press.

Grant's new place of work in the capital was a spacious building on 17th Street opposite the White House. In the months after the war he was kept busy there with the re-organisation and disbandment of the army, with policing the surrender of the rebels, and law and order issues concerning the south . But as the horrors of the war and the chaos in the wake of President Lincoln's assassination abated, Grant returned to the notion of realising his dream of a peaceful rural life. Mrs. Grant took a more jaundiced view of her husband's preoccupation with a place in the country "where he could pasture his horses and ride out to see the meadows grow green and the fruit ripen....".[270] An old childhood friend from Georgetown, Commodore Daniel Ammen, was enrolled to help Grant find his dream farm. Julia remarked : "I listened to all their plans until the little pasturage had grown into a huge plantation of several thousand acres." At this she challenged Ammen about his knowledge of farming, and bluntly suggested that he might stick to ships instead. The Grants ended up with a practical house in Washington , No. 205 I street, near military headquarters. It was a large four-storey dwelling with ample grounds and stables. (In spite of Julia's warnings, Commodore Ammen pursued his love of the country life and ended up with a substantial tract of land in Maryland.)

In fact, Grant did have a farm to go to. Over the war years he had slowly acquired his father-in-law's lands in St. Louis by paying off his debts. With the farm now at his disposal, he could set about realising the dream that had sustained him through the difficult military campaigns. With his relative prosperity, Grant was at liberty to do what he wanted in farming for the first time. Not surprisingly he chose to concentrate on livestock, particularly the breeding and raising of fine blooded horses. In the following years he set about transforming White Haven from an old-style southern plantation into a modern stud farm.

The only ingredient missing was time. With no easing of his responsibilities in Washington, Grant had to appoint William Elrod, husband of his cousin Sarah Simpson, as caretaker. His letters to Elrod reveal his enthusiastic interest in the farm, but it is clear that he was frustrated by his lack of freedom to see anything of it. In fact the number of times that Grant managed to visit the farm between 1867 and 1875 could have been counted on one hand. Instead he wrote numerous written instructions to Elrod, accompanied by the odd agricultural pamphlet. Fortunately these letters to the farm provide a unique glimpse of Grant's theories on agriculture and his preoccupation with farming. From army headquarters and later from the

---

[270] John Y. Simon, ed., *The Personal Memoirs of Julia Dent Grant*. Page 159 . Southern Illinois University Press.

executive mansion, Grant would discuss the relative merits of manure versus lime as a fertiliser. (He preferred the latter.) He cautioned Elrod against mixing manure and lime at the same time to fertilize the grass as the lime would leech the precious ammonia from the manure, making it useless. [271] On the subject of manure, Grant favoured the use of top dressing rather than ploughing in. [272] He also advised against the use of lush clover hay in feeding his horses, believing that it damaged the wind, and could even cause founder (laminitis). He preferred timothy as a source of hay instead.

In 1867 Grant wrote to Elrod expressing his desire to have a good barn built for his livestock. Because of its importance he decided to visit St. Louis and supervise the site and design in person. [273] The structure, which was to become the centre of activity at the farm, was eventually built on sloping ground for good drainage, with an east to west orientation to minimise the animal's exposure to direct sunlight. It was constructed of sawn pine and topped off by a cupola for ventilation. With his many years spent in the army, Grant had extensive experience of military barns and he would have had ready access to their plans. The Grant barn resembled many army barns of the period and was completed around 1869. This barn still stands today and reveals some distinctive features. The horse stalls, which were made of vertical wooden boards, measured 10 feet by 13 feet, which was large for the time, allowing the occupant a good loose, airy box. As expected, each stall was backed by an exterior window allowing air circulation and light. An enormous loft space above stored the hay and this was fed into the stalls below by a chute mechanism. [274] Over time wings were added to the core structure to provide more space for Grant's growing collection of horses. [275]

---

[271] John Y. Simon, ed. *Papers of Ulysses S. Grant*, Vol. 22. Letter to Elrod, June 23rd 1871. Southern Illinois University Press.

[272] Ibid, Vol. 24. Letter to Nat Carlin Nov. 28th 1873.

[273] Ibid. Vol. 18. Nov 14th 1867.

[274] Alan W. O'Bright, and Kirsten R. Marolf, *The Farm on the Gravois*. Page 417. Ulysses S. Grant National Hist. Site. 1999.

[275] John Y. Simon, ed. *Papers of Ulysses S. Grant*. Vol. 21. Letter to Elrod, Nov 24th, 1870. Southern Illinois Univ. Press.

Now the most feted couple in the United States, Ulysses and Julia moved in a very different world : one of splendid carriages, sumptuous hotels and wealthy company. They took to it with some relish, as might be expected of people who had had to practice the art of economy for much of their married lives. The general was still getting presents of fine horses, but now fine houses were added to the list. In what little spare time he had , Grant found freedom in driving a fast horse through the streets of Washington . The exhilaration and relaxation it provided was a real antidote to the difficulties of the job, now not just military. Most of the time he drove a pair of spirited horses, though if he had a special favourite, usually a very fast horse, he would drive one in hand. [276]

The blossoming of the trotting scene, especially in New York, coincided with the end of the war, as people turned their attention to lighter matters . In the autumn of 1865, the hero of Appomattox was able to unwind as the guest of honour among New York's horsemen. Located on Manhattan 's east side was a half mile track with the Dubois mansion overlooking the home stretch. There on a bright, crisp day , November the 15th, the trotting fraternity showcased their best horses in a spectacular race meeting.

To start off the proceedings New York publisher, Robert Bonner, invited Grant to drive his fast team, "Lantern" and "Peerless", from the splendid Metropolitan Hotel to the race track. This was indeed an rare honour because Bonner never allowed anybody to drive his priceless horses. On his arrival, Grant did a few swift laps around the track before taking his seat on the Dubois balcony. That afternoon he witnessed the veteran mare "Flora Temple", the "Bob-Tailed Nag" immortalised by the Stephen Foster ditty, race for the last time in public. The young pretender who ousted her was Commodore Vanderbilt's "Dan Mace", a colt that hadn't been foaled when "Flora" was a household name. After that "George Wilkes" and the notorious "General Butler" [277] raced, followed by the highlight of the day - and exhibition of speed by the King of Trotters, "Dexter". All of the last three were sons of "Rysdyk's Hambletonian" . [278]

"Dexter's" popularity with the public was a mirror of Grant's, as his sinewy form won battle after battle on the racetracks of the north east. Though overlooked

---

[276] George Childs, *Recollections* . Page 94. J. B. Lippincott Co. 1890.

[277] ("General Butler's" driver and owner ,William McKeaver, was murdered on the track at Chicago in Sept 1866.) *Chicago Tribune* ,Sept 24th , 1866, page 4.

[278] Philip A. Pines, *The Complete Book of Harness Racing.* Page 260-1. Arco Publishing Inc. 1982

in his early career because of the "four white legs - feed him to the crows" prejudice that prevailed at the time, his victories made him the people's hero. Dexter was the greatest of campaigners - good in all ground and at all distances, good in harness, saddle or wagon . It was a memorable afternoon that whetted Grant's appetite for breeding his own stock. With numerous colts and fillies of "Hambletonian" readily available for breeding, the opportunity would have been irresistible to someone with the means and the interest.

In the summer of 1866, Lincoln's divisive successor, President Andrew Johnson, conducted the infamous "swing around the circle" tour. The proposed Fourteenth Amendment would give citizenship to everyone born in the United States. Johnson planned to speak against it to the nation, feeling it would alienate many southerners. As General in Chief of the army, directly answerable to the president, Grant was obliged to attend the tour. But he didn't wish to be present, having little taste for Johnson's style or policies, so different from those of Abraham Lincoln : "the greatest man he had ever known" . At times like these he was apt to create other forms of diversion.

On the New York leg of the journey with the presidential party, Grant produced his own version of "swing around the circle" in the pastoral setting of Central Park . Two coaches were conveying the group through the park on their way to catch the boat for West Point. They had at their disposal the best set of horses that the city could supply courtesy of quintessential New Yorker, Leonard Jerome, whose Madison Square home boasted a three -storey stable paneled in black walnut. [279]Six magnificent horses were harnessed to the president's carriage, which was driven by industrialist, Abram Hewitt . The second coach of four equally fine and highly strung horses carried a distinguished group of war veterans - Generals Meade and Custer, Admiral Farragut, and Grant himself. The four in hand was driven by the walrus-whiskered Jerome, an enthusiastic supporter of the union during the war, who had almost single-handedly made the four in hand fashionable .

In spite of his long years of experience as a teamster, Grant insisted he had never driven a four in hand before and he was keen to try it out. He asked Jerome if he could take the reins. Jerome agreed to the switch. The general immediately pulled up beside the president's carriage and challenged Abram Hewitt to a race through the park. When President Johnson unsuspectingly gave the nod, Grant set off at a terrific speed, causing his elite passengers to wonder if they'd survived the war only to perish in a park ride. They raced for about a mile, with Grant the clear winner at the

---

[279] Elizabeth Kehoe, *Fortune's Daughters* . Page 12. Atlantic Books. 2004.

end, though the odds were stacked in his favour : it would have been unlikely for a six in hand to outpace Grant's four . [280] It was the highlight of the tour for him, and the first of many subsequent fast rides through Central Park. Even President Johnson was exhilarated by the experience. But perhaps for Grant the thrilling and dangerous carriage ride represented a necessary break from the distasteful duties that now engulfed him. Soon after he left Johnson's tour, feigning illness, and returned home on his own to Julia.

By 1867 Grant had acquired several good fast mares to breed from. One who was to feature in many of his letters was "Addie" who, like General Sheridan's "Rienzi", was a foal of "Vermont Blackhawk". Grant sent her to Charles Backman's stud farm near Goshen to be covered by the stallion "Iron Duke", son of "Rysdyk's Hambletonian". ("Iron Duke's" dam was out of a son of "American Star".) The result was the first stallion colt of his own breeding, "Young Hambletonian" . The same year Grant received the gift of a brood mare from an old family friend from Ohio days, congressman Isaac N. Morris . Again in 1867 he was given an enormous brown mare from the Russian ambassador to Washington , Baron Eduard Stoeckl. This mare he dubbed " Topsey " and she became a prominent part of the breeding programme at Grant's farm. " Topsey " didn't resemble Grant's other carriage horses, being nearly two hands higher than the rest .

By 1868, Grant's status as a horse breeder was well established. He had acquired the brown thoroughbred stallion, "Legal Tender", and was starting to breed him to most of his mares on the farm. Grant used the blood horse as a stallion until the spring of 1871,and one of his last foals was the bay mare, "Flora", out of "Topsey". "Legal Tender" then came east to Washington for Grant's use as a saddle horse. [281]

Again the main ingredient missing was time. There was no let up for Grant in the years after the war with his duties as General in Chief and then Secretary of War , the attempted impeachment of Andrew Johnson followed by his own reluctant involvement in politics. Once again dreams of travel or indeed of a peaceful rural life were put on the long finger , just as they had been during the four years of the Civil War.

Grant's youngest son , Jesse , related how his father came to acquire a particular favourite in his Washington stable : the grey horse known as "Butcher

---

[280] Jean Edward Smith, *Grant* . Page 426. Simon and Schuster.

[281] John Y. Simon, ed., *Papers of Ulysses S. Grant* . Vol. 22. Letter to Elrod, Oct. 2nd 1871.

Boy". The story does much to illustrate both Grant's impulsiveness and intense loyalty regarding his horses. The general was out driving on the streets of the capital with one of his teams of fast mares with young Jesse by his side. They were traveling at the usual "fair clip" when a butcher's delivery wagon, driven by a shirt-sleeved boy, came into view. Surprisingly, butchers' wagons were pulled by many quality trotters at this time and the boy's wagon managed to outpace Grant with little difficulty. Further along the road, the vehicle stopped to make a delivery and Grant passed it by. Again, within a short time the same wagon had caught up with his own and passed it out, in spite of Grant's best efforts. The general was fascinated. He noted the name on the wagon and the next day he bought the butcher's horse for $280. Grant called his discovery "Butcher Boy". [282]

A few days later he was proudly showing off his new purchase to republican politician, Roscoe Conkling . The congressman was unimpressed and said that he'd have preferred the two hundred and eighty dollars. "That's what the butcher thought ",Grant replied. The senator turned and winked at young Jesse. [283] Not surprisingly "Butcher Boy", or "B.B. " as Grant liked to call him in letters, turned out to be one of the general's pluckiest trotters, capable of doing a mile in under three minutes with ease.

It was in January of 1868, a difficult month for Grant in Washington as his relationship with the president deteriorated, that "Butcher Boy's" career as a carriage horse was cut short at the early age of ten. Apparently the horse strained his hind leg severely when Grant's carriage encountered a dangerously uneven patch of road that typified the state of highways in Washington at the time. Indeed, the roads of the capital were still in a sorry state three years after the war, churned up by unceasing cavalry and artillery movements. Later Grant would take a special interest in their improvement, perhaps spurred on by his own experience of driving on them. [284] During his presidency, ninety-three miles of sidewalk and one hundred and fifteen miles of street were paved with Macadam, cobblestone , concrete and Belgium block . The Board of Public Works was unified for the first time. Through the efforts of committed officials like Alexander "Boss" Shepherd, the old

---

[282] Jesse Root Grant, *In the Days of My Father* . Page 113. Harper and Brothers. 1925.

[283] Ibid. Page 113.

[284] John Y. Simon, ed. *Papers of Ulysses S. Grant.* Vol. 22. Nov 1871. Southern Illinois Univ. Press. Letter of Orville Babcock to D.C. of Board of Public Works concerning the paving of Seventeenth Street.

Washington of festering pools, swirls of white sand and dust , and muddy undrained roads rapidly disappeared. By the end of Grant's first term the city had become a very pleasant metropolis with broad carriage drives, innumerable fountains and tree-lined green belts, though many old dwellings had to be pulled down in the process.

Two months after the driving mishap, Grant sent "Butcher Boy" out to the St. Louis farm to recover, writing to his friend Charles Ford to look after him until his farm manager arrived to pick him up. He also gave strict instructions to William Elrod that the horse wasn't to do any farm work.[285] Grant always seemed to harbour a soft spot for the grey horse, never losing his desire to be reunited with him. In 1869 Charles Ford wrote his friend a letter reassuring him that "Butcher Boy" was now "in fine trim" and "better than ever ".

In the mid 1870s the president was running out of horses in Washington to drive, and was anxious to be reunited with his old buggy horse. After Ford's death, Grant wrote a curiously worded letter to the man who handled his business affairs in the west, Judge Long, asking him to send "Butcher Boy" east : " If he is not too decrepit from old age . If I get him here I will keep him as long as he and I both shall live".[286] "Butcher Boy" must have given Grant a great feel under harness. They seemed to have enjoyed a special bond. Perhaps the horse's spirit or movement was what attracted, or the fact that its promise had been cut short by injury. Maybe this had been due to a careless bit of driving for which Grant blamed himself.

"Butcher Boy" was destined to end up in the Chicago home of a close associate, the self-made businessman with the midas touch, J. Russell Jones, who had once ridden into Galena a solitary and hatless teenager and left the town its wealthiest citizen. Jones had received a horse from the president on several occasions. It seemed to have been Grant's favourite way of rewarding him, or maintaining a bond . The general had discussed the possibility of sending him the grey horse as early as 1866. Jones owned a horse railway in Chicago and he had several thousand horses under his wing to power the enterprise. In their correspondence, the subject was a running joke between the two men . Would "Butcher Boy" have to earn his keep on the horse cars if Jones's fortunes failed ? Grant's very last letter to his farm superintendent in 1875 was taken up with the travel arrangements of his precious grey gelding to Jones's home.

---

[285] Ibid. Vol. 24. Mar 17th, 1873. Letter to Elrod.

[286] Ibid, Vol. 25. July 20th , 1874.

Grant's overwhelming post-war popularity made it inevitable that he would be nominated for president. With no political instinct or background, he accepted the office as a duty. He was inaugurated president in March 1869, the youngest holder of the office at forty-six. Julia's father , an unrepentant democrat, came to live in the White House and railed against his son-in-law's politics from his own fireside. Sparks would fly when Jesse Root Grant came to visit . Also taking up residence, but with greater harmony, were Grant's last three battle chargers :"Cincinnatus", "Egypt" and "Jeff Davis", together with the less impressive Shetland, "Little Rebel".

In the Summer , Grant would give instructions to have "Rebbie" shipped out with his single harness to his holiday residence at Long Branch so that young Jesse could drive him. The Grants had first come to "the Branch" in the Summer of 1867, renting an ornate cottage near the ocean with a veranda that ran the length of the house . Their presence quickly turned the quiet seaside haven into a fashionable resort, popular for its beach and also its racetrack, Monmouth Park. The track had been the brainchild of two of Grant's friends who also had summer residences nearby, John Hoey and George Childs. As Charles Ford looked after the transport of the general's horses to St. Louis, it was John Hoey, the founder of Adam's Express, who managed their safe arrival in Long Branch. Sometimes the horses were kept in the nearby stables of a Mr. Lewis B. Brown until Grant's coachman came to take them to the cottage. Like many of the general's wealthy friends, Hoey shared an interest in pedigree livestock farming. He introduced Grant to the raising of Alderney cattle by donating a small herd to the St. Louis farm. Grant tried out the experiment for a while before tiring of the project. (He had exhibited one of the bulls, a 2,000 pound specimen, at the St. Louis fair in 1873. But on the long journey home the animal dropped dead on the Gravois road.) Although Grant scaled down his riding after the war he didn't completely abandon the saddle. A neighbour at Long Branch remembered him riding out in the early morning on a frisky grey colt that had come from the St. Louis farm, teaching him the showy saddlebred gaits. [287]

In spite of work commitments, Grant continued to indulge his love of driving both at the White House and at Long Branch. Washington horsemen congregated at a speedway near the present day 22nd and H. Street, and sometimes Grant was to be seen among them. During the holiday periods, he made a ritual of driving out twice a day from the cottage on the good carriage roads that surrounded the area. He knew

---

[287] *New York Times*. Page 1. July 26th, 1885.

every by-way within a twenty mile radius of the house.[288] Although he nearly always drove with what neighbours called a look of determination on his face, sometimes he was casual - holding the reins loosely in one hand.

Usually fellow buggy drivers gave the president the road out of courtesy . But occasionally someone would have the nerve to take him on, and an unscheduled speed dual would result. Grant once told his doctor in later life about a farmer in a rough, agricultural wagon at Long Branch who threw down the gauntlet to him for over a mile. Every time he drew near enough to overtake the wagon, the farmer would let out a shriek to his horse, who surged forward in a brisk trot, the farmer's wife all the while darting defiant glances at their competitor. When the farmer had had his fun he slowed down enough to say : "General, you've got a good one there", before going on his way.[289]

Julia was occasionally persuaded to go in her husband's buggy, as she had done in Detroit years before with the redoubtable "Nellie Bly" under harness. Although she was the only person who had a realistic chance of getting Grant to curb his pace, Mrs. G. 's sensible approach to driving was at odds with her husband's love of speed. More than once she made him stop and turn back, such was her unease at the flying pace. When she got off, Grant would then set off on his own, attaining speeds that had onlookers convinced his team was running away with him.[290] With his favourite slouch or rusty silk hat pulled well down on his head, nearly obscuring his vision, he would lean forward in the buggy until his shoulders were flush with the horse's tail. His trotters were trained to his voice and merely needed a few words from their driver to go forward .[291] A cruising speed of twenty-five miles an hour and more was commonplace.

According to popular wisdom, the president received a dressing-down and a $20 speeding fine from a policeman called West on Washington's Vermont Avenue. Having been detained at the White House on official business longer than expected, Grant was trying to make it to the speedway before the other horsemen had gone home. The officer was new to the area and didn't at first recognise the man he had

---

[288] George Childs, *Recollections*. Page 103. J. B. Lippincott Co. 1890.

[289] George Shrady, *The Last days of General Grant*. Page 22-23. Privately published.

[290] Ishbel Ross, *The General's Wife* . Page 215. Dodd, Mead and Co.

[291] W.H. Crook, *Memories of the White House*. Page 91-2. Little, Brown and Co. 1911.

booked. But Grant paid the fine without a murmur. [292] Julia had her own pair of carriage horses, "Major" and "General" , known for their steady behaviour under harness.[293] On fine afternoons the White House coachman would drive her out in the landau over the country roads near the capital, accompanied by her children or friends. [294]

In 1870, a year into Grant's presidency , a Washington newspaper gave a detailed account of the well appointed stables at the White House and the horses housed there, now numbering eleven. The complex was located at the south west corner of the garden, two hundred yards from the navy department . It was a two-storey red brick building with a mansard roof and had an extension built on the north end for foals and stallions. From this it is clear that a breeding programme was already well under way. All the stalls were equipped with oval windows large enough to admit the horses' heads which were reported to be "perpetually peering out at the neighbours" . [295]

An impressive carriage house stood in the centre of the main building, measuring fifteen feet by forty . It housed among other things Grant's great Brewster carriage that was pulled by his four in hand. Its gleaming black exterior was set off by a red stripe on its flank and silver lanterns on each side of the box, while the inside was cushioned with navy blue broadcloth . It looked every inch the $1,200 that Grant shelled out for it. Other vehicles housed there were a landau ,(the forerunner of the convertible), a barouche ,(lighter and lower than the landau and all the rage in Europe), and a phaeton for the children ,(a light two-seated boxless carriage. [296] (In 1909, President Taft converted the by then dilapidated stables into a garage for his interesting collection of early cars. The building was torn down completely in 1911.)

The state provided Grant with a carriage driver and groom . But the horses and carriages had to be paid for out of his private purse. The whole area was said to have been "as clean as a new pin". Some familiar names were listed among the

---

[292] Margaret Truman Margaret, *White House Pets.* Page 130.

[293] Ishbel Ross, *The General's Wife* . Page 281. Dodd, Mead and Co.

[294] Col. W. H. Crook, *Memories of the White House* . Page 90. Little, Brown and Co. 1911.

[295] *Colman's Rural World.* 1870. Nov 19th , Vol. 25, No. 34, page 266.

[296] Ishbel Ross, *The General's Wife.* Page 215. Dodd,Mead and Co.

stable occupants in the 1870 review. [297] There was "Jeff Davis" ,"Egypt" and "Cincinnati" . There was also "St. Louis" ("Cincinnati's" dark bay mate under carriage);and "Mary" and "Jennie" , described as one of the president's favourite driving teams, though seldom used. "Jennie" was also a saddle horse for Grant's daughter Nellie . Then there were three fillies: "Rebecca " (daughter of "Addie"), "Loretto " (daughter of "Jennie") and "Julia" (a black mare out of the thoroughbred, "Washington "). Finally there was a stallion foal of "Jennie's" , not named (possibly "Logan"). The newspaper didn't make reference to the eleventh horse, which was probably the Shetland , "Little Rebel" , known to have taken up residence in the White House for Jesse to ride, but perhaps overlooked because of his size.

While living at the White House, Grant would rise at about seven, accompany Mrs Grant to breakfast and work until about three. When he was at liberty after his day's work, he usually headed to the stables. He drove out himself nearly every day in his racing sulky or the slightly heavier four high wheeler - both light, precarious vehicles with iron wheels over five feet in diameter, that rattled loudly over the street cobblestones, left the driver nearly hovering over the tail of his horse, and also had the disconcerting habit of skidding on corners.

The shift from saddle to sulky after the war was a natural one for Grant. He had enjoyed driving a horse since childhood. There was the challenge of keeping the horse within the gait while urging him to trot at his fastest. Sometimes he would wait in the portico for White House carriage driver, Albert Hawkins, to come round with the buggy. Hawkins wasn't always on time but Grant never complained. He would patiently smoke and pace slowly up and down until he arrived. [298] Devoted as he was to the horses, Hawkins could do little wrong in Grant's eyes. He had come to the White House from military headquarters on I Street and was a first rate coachman. According to young Jesse, Albert could still the restlessness of a four in hand at will, almost by magic. He had to put this skill to the test many times, most notably when Buck Grant took it into his head one afternoon to crack the whip on top of the carriage, nearly causing a disastrous runaway. "That was thoughtless ",

---

[297] *Colman's Rural World.* 1870. Nov 19th , Vol. 25, No. 34, page 266.

[298] Thomas F. Pendel, *Thirty Six Years in the White House.* Page 73. Neale Publishing Co. 1902.

was Grant's only remark to his son, yet the words were as powerful to the boy as a severe chiding. [299]

Both "Egypt" and "Cincinnati" were driven to carriage from the executive mansion. "Cincinnati" frequently pulled the president's vehicle together with his mate ,"St. Louis". And Grant used him to pull his daughter's carriage on the two bleak, chilly days of his inauguration in March 1869 and 1873. In his first year in the White House, an equestrian statue was commissioned by young Washington businessman, Alexander R. Shepherd, who played a huge part in reshaping the city's appearance through the Board of Works. Grant chose "Cincinnati" as the "most appropriate horse for the purpose" . [300] For nearly a month the president had him tacked up and rode out to pose for the sculptor. Today the statue stands in front of the treasury building.

The most famous equestrian sculpture of Grant was finished much later in the late 1920s. If it took Grant four years to win the war, it took sculptor Henry Shrady twenty years to complete the sixty-five foot statue commemorating the feat. Situated in the Mall in Washington D.C., the enormous work depicts Grant lounging with loose reins on an alert looking horse, flanked by cavalry and artillery on the base below. The sculptor wanted to capture one of Grant's most famous attributes - poise in the midst of battle. Shrady was the son of the physician who attended Grant in the final months before his death, which gave him a uniquely perspective on the general. Since "Cincinnati" was long dead as Shrady worked on the piece, the sculptor tried to find a model that would resemble Grant's most famous battle charger. It was said he looked at three hundred horses before finally deciding on a New York police horse for the job.

"Cincinnati" and "Egypt" were particular favourites of Albert Hawkins. To Jesse Grant's young mind, the coachman never seemed to leave the stables. Hawkins, a tall, powerfully built man , had a strange ritual of holding a sugar lump between his lips and calling each horse by name to walk out of its stall and collect his treat. [301] "Jeff Davis" was no favourite of Hawkins, or of anybody else for that matter, with the exception perhaps of Grant or John Rawlins . In the year before his

---

[299] C.B. Galbreath, *Ohio Archaeological and Historica*l . Vol. 31. "Centennial Anniversary of the Birth of Ulysses S. Grant", Page 286. Accessed via *openlibrary.org*, http://www.archive.org/.

[300] John Y. Simon, ed. *Papers of Ulysses S. Grant* . Vol. 20. Letter of Grant to Alexander R. Shepherd. Date ? Southern Illinois Univ. Press.

[301] Jesse Root Grant, *In the Days of My Father*. Page 62. Harper and Bros. 1925.

death in 1869, Rawlins, then dangerously ill with consumption,would take a daily ride around Washington on the comfortable "Jeff" for the sake of his health, though it did him little good.

Photographs taken of "Jeff" in the field at Cold Harbour in 1864 reveal a very compact little horse with a naughty pony face, a forelock like a cow's lick, large eyes (what commentators described as hawk-like) and alert ears. In fact "Jeff's" character was far from gentle. Although he was often euphemistically referred to as spirited, he was in reality a notorious kicker and biter. Many of the stable staff in the White House were afraid to approach him and would give him his feed from the stall next door. If he heard Grant's voice in the stable , "Little Jeff" would throw his ears flat back on his head and pace his box restlessly until the general came up and gave him his attention. Frequently the desperate hands would try to imitate Grant's voice in order to pacify "Jeff", but the little horse was never fooled. [302] In spite of his earlier origins as one of Joe Davis 's carriage horse, Grant considered "Jeff" to be really only suitable as a saddle horse. This may have been down to his size, fourteen hands, which would have made it difficult to find a good match for him. Or there may have been other reasons, perhaps relating to temperament or the fact that "Jeff" was a natural pacer.

With his comfortable gait and small size, "Jeff" was an ideal transition horse for Jesse Grant to ride when he became too big for the Shetland ,"Little Rebel" . Putting his past adventure at City Point behind him, Jesse took to riding him regularly over the rolling lands to the south of the executive mansion, even to the point of being late to church on Thanksgiving Day. [303] "Jeff " still managed to get the better of Jesse, however, bucking him off one day during a morning ride near the White House. Through the window Grant caught a glimpse of the naughty pony jogging back to the stable on his own. When father and son met in the vestibule, Grant pretended not to know what had happened. "Where's Jeff ?" he asked as Jesse approached on foot. When he heard his dust-covered son's excuses, he enjoyed a hearty laugh at the boy's expense. Whether it was Adam Badeau , Daniel Ammen or his son Jesse, nothing amused him more than someone coming a cropper on a horse. [304]

---

[302] *Chicago Tribune*, Aug 9 1885 , page 20.

[303] John Y. Simon, ed. , *Papers of Ulysses S. Grant* . Vol 21. Grant to Ulysses Jnr. Nov 24th , 1870. Southern Illinois Univ. Press.

[304] Thomas F. Pendel, *Thirty Six Years in the White House* . Page 68 . Neale Publishing Co. 1902.

Chapter 19

*D*exter

It is a glorious day on August 14th 1869, five months after Grant's inauguration. Prominent horse fancier, Robert Bonner, invites the new president to drive his famous horse, "Dexter", at the Buffalo track. The occasion was recorded in the Currier and Ives lithographs of artist, John W. Ehninger . The date was well chosen. Two years before to the day the same horse had made his famous world record on the same track under boy wonder reinman, Budd Doble, "whose catarrhal name so fills the nasal trump of fame". [305] Back then it had also been a fine day, the track had been perfect and the crowd big. Doble had just inherited his new star from his regular reinman, Hiram Woodruff , and he was nervous. His main worry was to get "Dexter" passed the first turn as the horse was liable to break there through too much ambition .(He always liked to go at the top of his speed.) All the pre-race publicity had left the crowd expecting something special. Doble didn't carry a watch. He had to gauge the time himself, which he did to perfection on the second heat. The spectators went wild when a time of 2.17 ¼ was posted. Scores of them rushed onto the track to surround the young driver who had written himself and

---

[305] *Atlantic Monthly,* Vol. 38, issue 225. July 1876. Page 44-8.. "How the Old Horse Won the Bet" poem by Oliver Wendel Holmes.

"Dexter" into the history books. There was a further surprise for Budd Doble when an announcement came from the judge's stand that "Dexter" had been sold to Robert Bonner for $33,000. [306]

"Dexter's" new owner had left the north east of Ireland virtually penniless in the 1830's. He learned the printing trade in America and gained something of a reputation for the speed at which he could type set - 1700 ems an hour. [307] His ambitions took him to New York where he bought a modest publication called *The Ledger* in the 1850's. He turned it into one of the most popular weekly story papers of the era, with its very modern mix of romantic fiction, fashion and humour aimed largely at women. Bonner's novel approach to publishing and his flair for publicity gained *The Ledger* a circulation of well over a quarter of a million by the 1870s, making him a fortune. General Grant was the new linchpin in Bonner's publicity wheel . The newspaperman had been an enthusiastic supporter of Grant's presidency, encouraging the general to regard the office as a glittering prize for a job well done. "Perhaps you may look upon the presidency in the same light as I look upon "Dexter"", Bonner suggested in a letter to Grant in 1867. [308] Grant, who was more inclined to look on the presidency as a millstone round his neck , may well have smiled at the comparison.

Both men had harboured the same passion for fast horses since youth. But unlike Grant, Bonner's riches enabled him to buy the best and do exactly what he wanted with them. Like many rich men of his era, he had been encouraged by his doctor to take to road driving for the good of his health. His horses were guaranteed a life of luxury. Many owners sold him their priceless trotters for this reason alone. The record prices he was prepared to pay also helped to keep the market high, even during the recession years of the mid 1870s . Diseases of the hoof and shoeing were his life's study and his library contained one of the largest collections of veterinary books . Spectators would often congregate around the gates of Central Park just to

---

[306] John Splan, *Life with the Trotters*. Page 407-8.

[307] Matthew Hale Smith, *Sunshine and Shadow in New York*. Page 605.

[308] John Y. Simon, ed. *The Papers of Ulysses S. Grant*. Vol. 18. Page 272. Reference to letter from Bonner to Grant Nov. 29th 1867.

see the splendour of his teams, which strode out from his luxurious stables at Twenty-Seventh Street. [309]

After his sale for a record $33,000, "Dexter" was reserved for Bonner's personal use on the roads. When his original owner tried to buy him back for twice that amount in order to entice him onto the track once more, Bonner turned down the offer. The fact that he was a gelding with no breeding value (he had been too wild to keep as a stallion) puts the enormity of his price tag in context. Up until then "Dexter" had won thirty-four out of thirty-five races, only conceding to the celebrated "Ethan Allen" in a head to head duel in June 1867. Many horsemen believed that he hadn't reached his full potential when Bonner retired him. The gelding, whose face was distinguished by an unusual white rim around one eye, had a formidable reputation and used to run at people in his stall. But those who knew him well said that this was only bluster and that he could be kind underneath it all.

Within trotting circles it was believed that Grant had tried unsuccessfully to persuade the terse Ulsterman to sell him the gelding . But "Dexter" wasn't for sale, not even to the general. Instead Grant made do with driving the people's hero in Central Park or at Bonner's tanbark training track on 27th Street, during the many occasions that the Ulsterman invited him to take the ribbons. [310] In spite of his fame and prestige, "Dexter" was far from easy to drive . He always had problems with his mouth which made him a hard puller. And that coupled with his ambitious nature, often led to an unpleasant tug of war. ("Dexter" remained in Bonner's stable until his death in 1888.)

The 1870s marked the golden age of the trotter, as the wonderful descendants of "Hambletonian" began to show their class. Harness racing reflected the spirit of the times, with the training methods of Hiram Woodruff becoming the yardstick of excellence to which every driver and trainer aspired. A buggy with a matching pair of fine, fast Hambletonians was the ultimate status symbol. The popularity of the harness racer had far-reaching social implications, even influencing city demographics. It enabled the wealthy owner to live in the countryside and have his business in town.

For the competitive there was a "grand circuit" of sixty racetracks up and running by 1872 . The Fashion Course Philadelphia , Morristown New Jersey, Riverside Park Boston , East Aurora Buffalo, and Union Course Long Island to

---

[309] Matthew Hale Smith, *Twenty Years in Wall Street among the Bulls and the Bears*. Page 225.

[310] Philip A. Pines, *The Complete Book of Harness Racing*. Page 102.

name a few. Races in harness were usually a mile long (or two miles if it was a wagon), with the best of three out of five heats. Purses of several thousand dollars went to the winner. The crowds attending these meets were noisy and uninhibited, often hooting with derision if the times weren't fast or the judges' decisions weren't to their liking.

Typically famous trotters carried the names of people that were popular or famous: an interesting mix of Civil War heroes, robber barons, and the popular reinmen who drove the buggies. While Jay Gould bought up railroad after railroad across the country, his four-legged equivalent was posting a record time for a breeding stallion of 2.21 ½ on the turf, and commanding a stud fee of $200. General Grant's namesake on the track was an impressive chestnut stallion with a white strip on his face, whose fastest time at the Rochester track was half a second better than "Jay Gould's ".[311] "Phil Sheridan" and "General Sherman" won many battles on the turf, while "General Butler" was a good horse whose career was overshadowed by the murder of his driver on the track in Chicago in 1866.[312]

Because of his equestrian interests, Grant was invited to be guest of honour at what the papers called the "social event of all time". This was the lavish launch of Leonard Jerome's racetrack at Bathgate on September 25th 1866. It was the first flat race to be held in New York and paved the way for the inaugural Belmont Stakes the following year. From the vast grandstand, Grant would have had the great satisfaction of seeing "Cincinnati's" half brother, "Kentucky ", outpace the field to win the historic race comfortably.

But on the whole Grant, like Robert Bonner, had an ambivalent attitude to professional horse racing. George Childs noted he could seldom be induced to visit the Monmouth course with its gothic grandstand near his cottage at Long Branch. He preferred the more prosaic pleasures of county fairs. Privately Grant thought there was an element of ruthlessness in the racing business that he couldn't quite square with his love of horses. But then he was always more interested in the interaction with a horse and the personal thrill of driving a fast one. If he did go to race meets, they were usually feature events or private affairs among his new wealthy breeder and owner friends, because he could participate. So frequent were his appearances at these gatherings that it was nearly more newsworthy if he didn't

---

[311] W.H. Gogher, *Fasig's Tales of Turf and Memoir*. Page 41. Also John Wallace, *American Trotting Register*. Page 235 and 302.

[312] *Chicago Tribune*, Sep 24th 1866. Page 4.

turn up. A newspaper heading on the Baltimore horse fair in 1866 simply read : " The horse fair - Dexter wins- General Grant not present."[313]

A popular location for informal road duels was Harlem Lane, to the northwest of Central Park, which followed a straight and flat path for three quarters of a mile . Trotting men just called it "the road". Club houses sprang up along the route to supply tying up sheds and other facilities for the steaming horses after the races. The popularity of "the road" might have suggested that it had a good smooth surface, but this wasn't true. In spite of efforts to keep it in good order, the going was described as deep at best . (In wet weather it was a pitted, cratered mess.)But the duels of Harlem Lane were as competitive as any on the race track. And the sounds of the road were unforgettable as the drivers urged their horses on with their own individual yells and whistles.

When the lane spread out into open meadow to the north, the pace of the horses became more furious. This was not a pastime for the fainthearted. Contemporary equestrian artists like John Cameron portrayed many of these scenes. His lithographs convey a sense of elegant chaos, with scores of horses trotting flat out and in either direction, within an inch of each other. It mirrored only too well that other game of skill and chance being played out on nearby Wall Street. Many prominent businessmen dabbled in high stake finance in the morning , then took the reins behind their Hambletonians in the afternoon, especially Wednesdays and Fridays . It was said that not even an imminent great corner in the Street could generate the same excitement as the arrival of a new trotter on the Road. [314]

On a typical day at Harlem Lane onlookers could observe Commodore Vanderbilt, with or without tumbler of gin in hand, sitting behind his favourite roadster "Post Boy", as he raced flat out against the team of Wall Street doyen, Russell Sage. Many a time the mischievous Sage would goad the railway baron into dueling on the road for a trifling bet. With his hands visibly calloused from holding reins without gloves, Sage was frequently to be seen trotting his own team vigorously through Central Park. He was the subject of uncharitable remarks from bystanders, for, in contrast to the gleaming turnout of the other carriages, his tack and harness were renowned for their shabbiness, while his own costume was scarecrow-like. Despite this , Sage was fanatical about his stable of seven fast horses, located on West 44th Street.

---

[313] *New York Times*, Nov. 15th 1866. Page 1.

[314] Matthew Hale Smith, *Sunshine and Shadow in New York*. Page 531.

Best of all were the contests on the lane between "Dexter" and any gentleman who had the nerve to race against him. One such was railway speculator, Jay Gould . Although Gould was happier tending orchids than driving horses, the fashion of the time made it almost obligatory for the rich and successful to own a fast trotter . Robert Bonner wasn't a betting man and he never used "Dexter" for profit. He insisted his opponent deposit $10,000 in advance of the race to be given to charity. His other stipulation was that the gentleman must drive the contender himself . Great excitement and publicity would accompany these contests, as crowds cheered on the participants from the gates of Central Park or the top floors of adjacent taverns and hotels like "Harry Berthol's". Jay Gould duly pitted his stallion "Copperdust" against the king of the trotters one afternoon to a predictable result. It was one of the few times that Gould had to part with his money.[315]

The lengthy summers spent at Long Branch gave Grant access to the men who dominated his favourite pastime in New York - the "sealskin brigade" who indulged their passion for harness racing with bottomless purses. At this time Grant's acquisition of wealthy friends was marked, and was inextricably linked to his equestrian interests. The exciting, glamorous and insular pastime of trotting fast on the ever-improving roads of the eastern cities forged strong bonds between these men.

Jesse Root Grant's son valued the company of people who possessed the midas touch, possibly because the knack eluded him. Increasingly he numbered among his friends many figures who shaped the financial landscape of America, in an era when patriotism without profits was, to quote Russell Sage, like "a horse without a rider. "[316] Grant became acquainted with the celebrated entrepreneur Cyrus Field, the "locomotive in trousers".[317] He acquired friends among the merchants of Philadelphia - publisher George Childs, and through him the self-effacing but influential Anthony Drexel . The latter was a favourite with Grant's coachman since he would give out $20 tips each time he visited the White House. He became especially friendly with another Philadelphia businessman, the genial Adolph Borie, whose passion for horseflesh was matched only by his enthusiasm for the card table. Borie was to receive a special gift from Grant in the form of two of

---

[315] Matt Braun, *Hickok and Cody*. Page 195.

[316] Paul Sarnoff, *Russell Sage: The Money King*. Page 66.

[317] Henry Clews, *Twenty Eight Years in Wall Street*. Page 659.

his own fast carriage horses, together with an early art work: "An Indian trading", painted while he was a cadet at West Point.

Extreme wealth seemed to lie heavily on the shoulders of William Vanderbilt. Many a time he would cast a green eye at his comrade of the road, Robert Bonner, envying him his "poverty". But one of the few genuine pleasures "Billy's" riches gave him was an endless opportunity to own the best trotters in the country. [318]Dismissed as a "blatherskite" by his formidable sharp-tongued father, the Commodore, Vanderbilt's early years had been a struggle in spite of enormous wealth. Like Grant, he had dabbled in agriculture as a young man - selling his hay to the Federal cavalry stationed near Staten Island during the war. But behind a horse, the plodding, ruddy-faced magnate was transformed into a man of speed and grace. And gone was his taciturn manner when the subject being discussed was "horse". According to banker Henry Clews he could then outdo the celebrated eloquence of Chauncey Depew. [319]

In 1879 Vanderbilt paid $21,000 for a weedy little chestnut mare called "Maud S.", bred at Woodburn Farm, Kentucky. She made 2.10 ¾ in Chicago and 2.10 ¼ at Rochester during the 1880 and 1881 seasons - both world records. Since no other trotter could hold a candle to her on the track, Vanderbilt finished her racing career on a high note and reserved her for his own use on the road. In June of 1883 he achieved a personal best, doing a mile behind her in a staggering 2.15 ½. - faster than "Dexter" at his peak . "Not bad for an amateur", Vanderbilt remarked with understandable delight. [320]

Grant took the chance to take the ribbons behind Maud at the invitation of her giant-whiskered owner. He declared her the best mare he had ever driven. It was a sound assessment. The month of his death she went back to the track to break the 2.10 barrier he always predicted , doing a mile in 2.08 ¾ at the Cleveland track to shouts of "lift her! Come on!" from excited spectators. Her regular trainer who steered her that day, William Bair, for whom she had a special affection , maintained that Maud always sensed the big occasion and kept her best performances for a large crowd and an electric atmosphere on the track. To mark her world record

---

[318] Arthur T. Vanderbilt 11,*The Fall of the House of Vanderbilt* . Page 130.

[319] Henry Clews, *Twenty Eight Years in Wall Street.* Page 367.

[320] Arthur T. Vanderbilt 11,T*he Fall of the House of Vanderbilt* . Page 130.

achievement, the course directors had a golden horseshoe hung over the entrance arch with the simple message: "Maud S. ,2;08 ¾." [321]

Purchased then by Robert Bonner for twice her original price ,"Maud" , like "Dexter", was retired to a life of blissful comfort at the newspaperman's stable, where she was known as a voracious eater. Indeed she was the ultimate pampered trotter of the Gilded Age. Her groom of eight years, an elderly man called Charles Grant ,was her constant companion both in and out of the stable and even slept beside her stall. Because of her hoof problems, Bonner instructed his farrier to shoe her twice a week, which amused many in the trotting fraternity. "Maud" remained a household name , famed the world over, with her reign as the fastest horse in America lasting eleven years. Being a daughter of Kentucky she also made harness racing more popular in the south. (Bonner tried unsuccessfully to get her in foal but she died without issue in 1901 at the age of twenty-seven). In subsequent years her record would be lowered, but this was largely the result of replacing the high-wheeled racing sulky with the new bicycle tire model. No horses would ever match the class and renown of the trotters of Grant's era . Neither would the excitement that surrounded the lowering of their racing times ever be seen again.

The "sealskin brigade" were always on the lookout for a way of enhancing the speed and soundness of their trotters. They acted as a strong catalyst for improvements in stable management. With so much money and prestige at stake in the field of shoeing such valuable horseflesh, some intense and often public rivalries grew up among prominent farriers of the period. As Robert Bonner's personal farrier, David Roberge generated his fair share of envy. Roberge became a master in the art of balancing the hoof and he developed a variety of remedial shoes to deal with various causes of lameness. Methods of shoeing a horse that might seem extreme today were routinely put to the test in this era. Bonner and Roberge together developed the rolling motion shoe, the grab shoe, the rocking bar shoe and the hoof expander to treat various hoof problems. Roberge's book on hoof balance is still in print today.

One of the bitterest opponents of Roberge's methods was fellow Canadian , Alexander Dunbar - a radical, largely self-taught farrier who had once been employed by Bonner. Dunbar treated many of Grant's trotters, in one case giving great relief to a severely wrenched ankle suffered by "Cincinnati" in February 1871.

---

[321] W H. Gogher, *Fasig's Tales of the Turf and Memoir*. Pages 83-4.

[322] Dunbar's own book, published in 1871, was supposedly a treatise on the diseases of the horse's foot, but it read more like an attack on David Roberge . A particular bone of contention was Roberge's patented "rolling motion shoe", higher in the heel than the toe. In his book, Dunbar challenged Bonner to put high heels on his own boots, and walk over cobblestones and wet clay and then see how he liked it. According to Dunbar, Bonner had enthusiastically recommended the rolling motion shoes to Grant, claiming that "Dexter" and others had achieved their top speeds when wearing them . (In fact they were only used to alleviate navicular [323]) Any endorsement from the general was a powerful advertisement and Dunbar was quick to exploit Grant's name to bolster his theories. He maintained that Grant experimented with Roberge's shoes on some of his fast horses for a short while, but was unimpressed with the outcome and had them taken off within a few days to be replaced by the more conventional "burden" shoe. [324]

Although he could hardly compete financially with his new friends, Grant did his best where horses were concerned. Letters to his farm manager contain the names of many of the stallions that he was planning to breed from: "Jay Gould" ,"Messenger Duroc", "Kentucky Prince" ,and "Iron Duke" - some of the most prominent stallions of the period. A popular breeder known to Grant was Alden Goldsmith of Orange County , New York : an excellent judge of a horse who had stood many stallion foals of "Hambletonian" . Grant was to bring several of his mares to Goldsmith over the years. In his Walnut Grove parlour he could discuss all the latest theories on breeding , stable management, feeding, and diseases of the hoof.

Grant availed of the facilities of a much larger stud farm nearby owned by Charles Backman. Dubbed the "breeder's breeder", because of his indifference to producing colts for the race track, Backman was one of nature's gentlemen and a born salesman. Originally Stony Ford had been built as a hotel, and its generous rooms could be easily adapted to the entertainment of distinguished horse breeders like Grant . All the issues of the day and stories of legendary road duels would have been aired over a cigar or two with kindred spirits in Stony Ford's famous smoking

---

[322] Alexander Dunbar, *A Treatise on the Diseases Incident to the Horse.* Page 105. Quoted letter of David McAuley to Turf, Field and Farm.

[323] David Roberge, *The Foot of the Horse*. 1894, fig. 29.

[324] Alexander Dunbar, *Treatise on the Diseases Incident to the Horse.* Page. 49.

room : the thorny subject of hopples, whether a Frazier built sulky was better than a Toomey, the new system of feeding a trotter four times a day, whether it was right to train a colt to race. On the last subject, Backman was an advocate of discovering speed early in a trotter's life, unlike many breeders of his day. It was evidently a practice which Grant also favoured since many of his mares were already working in harness at two years of age.

At his farm, Backman had a peculiar loyalty to one stallion in particular . "Messenger Duroc", an unusually large, homely-looking son of "Rysdyk's Hambletonian", was tipped as a worthy successor to his distinguished father. "Duroc" was highly inbred, having the same blood on both dam and sire side. It would appear that his size, over sixteen hands, seemed to outweigh his other flaws, which included a pronounced ewe neck and gummy legs. Backman supported him religiously throughout his long stud career at Stony Ford from 1869 to 1893, mating him to the choicest brood mares available, including those belonging to Grant. But in the long run he proved to be a dismal failure as a speed getter.

It was through Robert Bonner that Grant came to know about another stud farm, this time in the Blue Grass region. But he had known its owner from an earlier time. General W. T. Withers, chief of rebel field artillery at the battle of Champion's Hill, was a gallant old adversary. Although plagued with a nasty war injury that eventually killed him, Withers managed to turn his modest Fairlawn Farm at Lexington into the best harness stock farm in America, mainly through his adroit selection of stallions and an unerring Bonneresque feel for publicity. Starting in the early 1870s, when to quote Withers himself, the breeding of trotters was considered an occupation unfit for a southern gentleman, the enterprise was located just outside the city and was connected to all of its major hotels and railway station via the telegraph , the omnibus or the cab. Fairlawn boasted two entrances, one off North Broadway, the other from Limestone Street. In Wallace's Trotting Register of 1885 no less than eighty-six stallions were out of Wither's stable. The general's price list makes interesting reading today. Breaking and driving was $25 a month. Feeding from October to June was $10 a month. Grass livery $2.50 a month. Mares kept at $1.50 a week during the season.[325] Unlike Charles Backman, he was no advocate of early training and didn't let a colt see a harness before the age of four.

There is no evidence from Grant's farm letters that he had any personal theories on breeding. No doubt he was advised by breeders like Goldsmith and Backman, following the fashion of the day, of "cross and outcross". Most of Grant's

---

[325] William T Withers, *Fairlawn Stock Farm Catalogue*, Fifteenth ed. 1889. Page 4.

foals were crosses. Their names were a giveaway: "Basham" for example. And both his principal stallions, "Claymore" and "Young Hambletonian" ,were themselves the products of crossing. Both "Dexter" and the stallion "Jay Gould" were products of the so-called "golden cross" that Grant would have been familiar with, and would have tried to copy. In this system daughters of the "American Star" stallion were bred to Hambletonians. What the "Stars" lacked in the legs they made up for in courage, while the Hambletonian /Messenger line gave the "Stars" strength and bone.

    One of the stranger features of Grant's farm policy was that if the mares didn't promise speed they were used for breeding, while the ones that did were reserved for training. His letters also reveal that he was not averse to adding race horse blood to his stock. "Legal Tender", "Virginia" ,"Belle of Tennessee" and "Sparkle" were all thoroughbreds. As the years went by Grant shifted his attention from his own stallions to the mares, preferring to take them to outside sires with proven form rather than his own stock.

But Grant's popularity as the people's hero wasn't as enduring as "Dexter's" . In his difficult dealings with the press, the president chose "horse" as his official hobby. [326] And, in the manner of some of his wartime "blinds", such talk allowed him to deflect many unwelcome questions. This ruse didn't always work though. By 1872, eyebrows were being raised in press circles at the value and quantity of the president's bloodstock. There were also allegations that his horses were shod at government expense . Increasingly Grant's harmless equestrian pastime, conducted amongst the wealthiest in society, came to be seen as a sign of extravagance. It proved that the president had lost touch with the common people. Grant dealt with these charges by playing down the value of his horses, giving them ridiculously slow speeds. He dismissed the *New York Times* claim that he had $70,000 worth of horse flesh and that each could trot a mile in three minutes with the slightly disingenuous remark : "…..only one of them can travel in less than five minutes. She might possibly do it in four, but I have never tried." [327] According to Julia's younger sister

---

[326] William T. Sherman, *Personal Memoirs of William Tecumseh Sherman* .Page 785.

[327] *New York Times*. Oct 7th, 1872.

From Cincinnati to the Colorado Ranger

Emma, the president's use of his four in hand as an official carriage invited more criticism because he "used two horses more than others thought necessary".[328]

By sending out some of his stock to his Missouri farm he could avoid much of this unhealthy attention. The tranquil comings and goings of the bloodstock were in marked contrast to the turbulent times for Grant back in Washington - with ongoing reconstruction problems, the threat of another war, Jay Gould's aggressive attempts to corner the gold market, faction fighting within the Republican Party, and not least the endless lobbying for posts and favours by friends and ex-friends alike. It is no wonder Grant returned to the farm frequently, at least in his thoughts if nothing else.

Transport of the bloodstock from Washington to St. Louis via Cincinnati took nearly a week, at a cost of $33 per horse. The president always took pains to ensure the safe arrival of his horses to the west, sending his groom Richard Curtin or coachman Albert Hawkins down with them, and wiring Charles Ford to help keep them secure until his farm manager picked them up. But if Grant thought that all was well down on the farm he was mistaken.

---

[328] *Washington Sunday Star*. Mar, 1917.

From Cincinnati to the Colorado Ranger

Chapter 20

*Y*oung Hambletonian

It is in Grant's farm letters that the stories of his horses unfold. The same names crop up time and again, allowing a picture to emerge of their traits. Grant spoke of them almost as if they were people, and it is clear that he was well aware of their individual characteristics. He took a personal hand in naming them too, with some thought going into the process. He was never without a mare called "Julia" in his stables from the close of the war until the end of his life. An Ethan Allen colt at the farm had been called "Expectation", but Grant instructed the name to be changed to "Bob Acres", because it was the name of the breeder, a character in a popular Sheridan play, and it also "sounded well". [329]

"Mary ",who was mentioned in the *Rural World* article about the White House stables in 1870, had given out in the front legs by 1872. Now fourteen years of age, she was sent west in May of that year, into the care of Charles Ford. Grant thought that the farrier at Jefferson Barracks, John Kiernan , might be able to help, presumably by the use of corrective shoeing. Kiernan was one of the first blacksmiths to have been entrusted with the knowledge of Alexander Dunbar's

---

[329] John Y. Simon, ed. P*apers of Ulysses S. Grant*. Vol. 26.1875. July 3rd. Letter to Nat Carlin.

revolutionary method for treating lameness. Fond of the paring knife, Dunbar was reputed to have rescued the careers of both "Rysdyk's Hambletonian" and "Dexter" by his treatment of their contracted hooves. Grant was interested in all innovations that promoted the good of the horse, once he was satisfied that they had practical merit. He endorsed Dunbar's methods, although they seemed extreme and flew in the face of traditional farriery. Dunbar claimed that some of the general's other trotters had been successfully treated for lameness by his system, which involved the widening of the heel so as to take pressure off the tendons of the leg. [330] Grant also made several recommendations to the U.S. cavalry that they adopt the system, since the money saved in prolonging the animal's usefulness would more than make up for Dunbar's extravagant fees.[331] This caused some disquiet among certain members of Congress who tended to view Dunbar as an ignorant charlatan. [332]

In spite of the attention given to her at St. Louis ,Mary never pulled the president's buggy again . Later Grant tried to get her in foal but gave up after several costly attempts. Instead she settled down to semi-retirement in the form of some light farm work at Gravois.

"Jennie" ,"Mary's" carriage mate, had been sent west in 1871 and was a popular brood mare, perhaps because in her heyday she had been faster than "Mary" by ten seconds, doing a mile in 2.30. "Jennie" was bred to all the Grant stallions in addition to some other stallions of note, notably the large bay, "Messenger Duroc", who passed on little else to his colts except a tendency toward brittle and sore feet , and a distinctive grey tinge to their back legs which was his hallmark . [333] "Jennie" proved very fertile and the farm at White Haven abounded with her foals. Even as late as 1875,when she was eighteen, Grant expressed a wish to breed more foals from her.

"Rebecca" (Becky) was the full sister of Grant's own bred stallion, "Young Hambletonian" , but was always more promising in terms of speed. "Becky" was sent east in the spring of 1873 to be bred to "Messenger Duroc" at Charles Backman's stud. Grant was anxious to get a stallion colt out of her to put on the farm. But she produced a filly instead. Backman then offered Grant one of his own

---

[330] Alexander Dunbar, *Treatise on Diseases Incident to the Horse*. Page 29-35.

[331] Ibid, letter of USG to E. M. Stanton, June 29th 1867 , page 147-148.

[332] James Parton, *Atlantic Monthly.* "Log-Rolling at Washington" Vol. 24, Issue 143. Page 370.

[333] Ken McCarr, *The Kentucky Harness Horse*. Page 11.

colts by "Messenger Duroc" as a substitute in the fall of 1874, which he accepted. It is not known whether this colt ever arrived at White Haven.

The mouse-coloured mare, "Beauty", was foaled in 1869 out of the famous Morgan, "Ethan Allen". For this reason Grant prized her highly as a brood mare. But an angry, badly-aimed kick from an impatient stable hand at White Haven caused her to miscarry her foal. Despite the risk of failure, Grant advised his farm manager to try her again in 1874. Luckily she resumed her breeding career without incident, producing several colts by Grant's other stallion, "Claymore".

"Topsey" had been presented as a gift from the Russian ambassador to Washington in 1867. She was a giant of a horse at seventeen hands, and became a favourite brood mare. What Grant appeared to like about her was her size, for he was always partial to large horses and she had the potential to give greater bone and bulk to his stock. One of "Topsey's" colts, "Cyntrella", showed such potential that she was put in training with Budd Doble - the most celebrated reinman in America since he had driven "Dexter" into the record books. Tragically, "Cyntrella" was burned in a fire at Doble's barn in New Jersey, and her potential was never realised. [334]

On the rare occasions that Grant was able to visit St. Louis, he was never left alone. Instead there were the usual round of inspections, tours and receptions, where he was entertained on a grand scale. Grant loved to take in the October St. Louis fair, held on a remote stretch of land between Grand Avenue and the Natural Bridge Plank Road. The organisers of the event warmly encouraged his participation as it was a huge crowd puller, although Grant frequently asked for a low-key presence without any fuss. But patronage and corruption seemed to dog the president wherever he went, even at the fair. If his animals ever entered a class and won he could never know whether they had earned their premium or were favoured because they belonged to General Grant.

In 1874 Grant entered two stallions, "Claymore" and "Young Hambletonian" at the fair. The same horses had also been entered in 1871 when they were very young, but without success. "Claymore" was a dark bay colour and stood fifteen hands and a third high. He had been purchased as a breeding stallion from the prominent breeder M. H. Sanford in the 1860s. "Claymore" was considered an extremely good mover, and since Grant was attracted by action as much as by speed, he was quick to breed him to nearly all his mares, using him more often than "Young Hambletonian". As his name suggests, "Claymore" was of Henry Clay stock on his

---

[334] *St Louis Globe Democrat*, Oct 1st, 1875.

mother's side, though his sire was the Hambletonian "Peacemaker",owned by Civil War veteran, General B. F. Tracy of Owega . The Clays were very much out of vogue with the sealskin brigade, with Robert Bonner describing Clay blood as "sawdust in the trotter." [335] Evidently Grant didn't think so.

Standing beside "Claymore" at the fairground was the bright chestnut coloured, white-faced "Young Hambletonian", foaled in 1868 out of Grant's beloved Morgan carriage horse, "Addie" . His sire had been "Iron Duke", son of "Hambletonian". He was slightly smaller than "Claymore" at fifteen hands.

Competition was particularly stiff in 1874 with between twelve and fifteen of the best horses in the country assembled for the trotters in harness class, many of them from as far afield as Kentucky . A journalist working for a St. Louis newspaper, Charles Gonter, accompanied the president as he surveyed the opposition. Both men agreed, perhaps reluctantly, that the Kentucky stock outclassed Grant's two contenders. But the judges couldn't quite make up their minds. Eventually the casting vote was given to volunteer officer, General John McDonald, then internal revenue supervisor of the state. He gave first premium to "Young Hambletonian". Grant wasn't fooled. According to the journalist, he "flushed, took his cigar out of his mouth, threw it on the ground and said in a low voice: "this is an outrage" ". Grant had long wished his stallion to do well at the St. Louis fair. But the manner of his winning displeased him. [336]

The St. Louis "Whiskey Ring" went into operation in September 1871. With some of Grant's close Washington aides involved, its aim was to raise funds for the president's re-election to a second term. The colourful, unpolished John McDonald was the main link with the president in Missouri, keeping in with Grant in large measure through his clever catering to his major weakness for horses. McDonald quickly stepped in to supply Grant with free carriage horses when his stocks were running down in the early 1870s, particularly after the death of Charles Ford in 1873. During the president's October visit to the fair in 1874, McDonald put his fast team at his disposal. Grant decided to try the horses out by driving them from the Lindell Hotel to White Haven down the familiar old Gravois road. Accompanied by Adolph Borie, he set off in the buggy. McDonald had advised him that he might need to use the whip to attain any kind of speed. But Grant was surprised to find that when he drew the lines the team went like a shot out of a gun, leaving Borie clinging

---

[335] Philip A. Pines, *The Complete Book of Harness Racing*. Page 98.

[336] Walter B. Stevens, *Grant in St. Louis*. Page 112. The Franklin Club 1916. Republished Applewood Books, 21 Feb 2008. Accessed via Google Books. Jan. 24, 2012.

to his seat for dear life. Grant took great pleasure in using the team for the rest of his visit, even appearing at their stables before they were hitched up. During the week he made McDonald an offer of $1000 for them. Instead "Mack" insisted on giving them as a gift when he returned to the White House .[337]

The Hambletonian line wasn't completely dominant at Grant's stud farm. There was an extensive collection of Morgan stock too. "Addie" ,"Young Hambletonian's" dam, was out of the Morgan, "Vermont Black Hawk" . There was also the Knox mare mentioned in one of Grant's farm letters, evidently out of the famous Morgan stallion "General Knox" (affectionately known as "Slasher"). "Ethan Allen" was recognised by all horsemen at the time as a beautifully built little stallion with a near perfect action and an unusually friendly temperament. He had been one of the few horses to beat "Dexter" in a best of five race on Long Island, June 1867.(Although it wasn't a true contest as the gregarious "Ethan" couldn't do without company and had to have a mate in harness). "Ethan's" form and appearance made him particularly attractive to breeders, and between 1873 and 1875, several of his colts turned up in White Haven, including "Beauty" and "Bob Acres", (who went on to achieve a time of 2.28 ½ at Cincinnati in September 1882.) [338] Grant would have had to send his mares all the way to Kansas to breed with "Ethan Allen" , for a fee of $500 at Sprague and Akers Stud Farm .

This meant that three major trotting bloodlines - the Clays(or Bashaws),the Hambletonians and the Morgans - were represented among the president's stock. The Morgans with their great temperaments and high stepping trot, contrasted with the long-striding and often difficult Hambletonians. The Clays had a medium stride, in between that of the two others but they weren't tough. Possibly Grant thought of producing a hybrid that would enhance the speed, movement and quality of his trotters.

What Grant envisaged for White Haven was really an elite type of farming, requiring a high degree of specialisation. William Elrod may have been unsuited to this sort of specialisation. There is little to suggest in his background that he had any stud farm skills, although initially Grant seemed to give him a free hand in choosing which stallions to mate with his mares. It would have been difficult for Elrod to fill the role of manager of such a highly strung stable and without doubt there would

---

[337] General John McDonald, *Secrets of the Whiskey Ring*. Page 316. Belford,Clark & Co. 1880. Accessed via Google Books , February 9th 2012.

[338] J.H. Wallace, *Wallace's American Trotting Register*. Vol. 5. Page 423.

have been many handling challenges associated with these sharp and turbulent animals. Grant's letters give some clues that he was dissatisfied with the work of his farm manager. There is a tendency to repeat the same instructions over several letters, as if the writer didn't fully trust Elrod's willingness to carry them out. [339] Grant frequently had to emphasise that the horses he was sending out to the farm were not to do heavy farm work. He would give a detailed history of their pedigrees to stress the point. Had Elrod been a good stockman, Grant would not have needed to spell this out to him. One of the general's main grievances during this period was that Elrod didn't write to him very often to give news of his stock ,which he always enjoyed hearing about . [340]

But William Elrod faced a tall order at White Haven. The diverse nature of the farm, with strawberry, cereal and even wine grape production, meant that he would have had to spread his time very thinly. Elrod's distant employer changed his mind about a lot of things including which type of grape he wanted to cultivate. This must have been frustrating . Grant was under pressure to make the place pay. He was by no means a wealthy man, and his expenses were enormous, largely because of his bloodstock . But it would have been unusual for a busy stud farm, as White Haven effectively was at that time, to be engaged in such varied agricultural activities. And the breeding programme at the farm seemed surprisingly intensive, with nearly thirty brood mares and several resident stallions to attend to, not to mention the foals .

Given that the president had little personal involvement with the farm, it is difficult to explain why the breeding programme became as frenetic as it did. Grant was generous with his horses and many of the bloodstock produced at the St. Louis farm went as gifts to friends and dignitaries, so this may have been one of the motivations. He also liked to have friends bring their mares to the farm to be covered, and he would often charge them nothing. [341] The old cavalry general of the Indian Wars, William Harney, brought over at least one racing stallion, a relation of "Lexington", that was to be trained and prepared for the track. Grant may have been hoping to breed something special out of his own stock that would make a genuine impact on the American carriage horse . He predicted that the era of the 2.10 trotter was at hand, and in a letter to Robert Bonner he remarked, albeit jokingly, that an

---

[339] John Y. Simon, ed.,*Papers of Ulysses S. Grant.* April 2nd 1868. Oct 23rd 1870. Letters to William Elrod.

[340] Ibid, Letter to Elrod,June 23rd 1871.

[341] Ibid, Letter to Elrod. May 11th 1873.

animal with such speed might come from his own St. Louis stock. [342] However it is somewhat ironic that with all the horses being produced at White Haven, Grant frequently had to borrow carriage horses from Charles Ford or from local livery stables during his visits west.

In February 1873 a fire destroyed "Wish-Ton-Wish", (the Dents' villa in the woods of White Haven),leaving the president without a residence on the estate. From now on he would have to stay at hotels whenever he visited St. Louis. Elrod's departure from Grant's payroll later that year may have been due to the fire. But no doubt there were other grounds for dissatisfaction. The road in the estate not straightened. The fence not built. The timber that was never cleared away.

The press rumour mill was seldom out of action when it came to Grant's stable. In 1871, news reached the president from a third party (on foot of a piece in the press) that some of his stock at the farm was in poor condition. It had been a bad year for the White House stable . A disease had begun to undermine some of the stock there also. It started harmlessly enough as a small sore on the horse's back which caused the hair to fall out. But the sore soon spread over the top of the animal and death would result after a few days . The president's veterinary surgeon, Dr Braley , had no answer . Then one of his two year old driving mares, " Little Orphan", had put her leg through the iron foot rest of the sulky causing a nasty ulcer which then became infected. While "Little Orphan" recovered herself, she passed on the infection to one of her companions in the field who died. [343]

With all this happening in Washington , Grant wrote a rather fretful letter to Elrod, expressing his distress should the allegations about the state of affairs in St. Louis be true, and re-emphasising his close personal ties to the breeding stock: "Young Hambletonian was foaled mine from a fast mare which I owned until she died two years ago, and for which I would not have taken $5,000.00". [344] The fast mare mentioned was his beloved "Addie", one of the first he was to acquire after the war, and described always as "fast and stylish" with a "high carriage" characteristic of the Morgans . She was Grant's favourite colour: dark bay - "not a white spot on her", and a full sister to "one of the best stallions in Massachusetts ". Addie apparently died from consuming some poisonous vegetable matter in the pasture a few years earlier, and the loss seemed to weigh heavily on Grant.

---

[342] *New York Ledger*, Aug 6, 1885. Letter from Grant to Robert Bonner, Mar 30th 1868.

[343] Alexander Dunbar, *A Treatise on the Diseases Incident to the Horse* . Page 149-151.

[344] John Y .Simon, ed. P*apers of Ulysses S. Grant.* Letter to Elrod, July 30th 1871.

The departure of William Elrod from White Haven in 1873 lead to the appointment of Nathaniel Carlin to the caretaker post .Carlin had come warmly recommended by Charles Ford, for whom he had worked. But there is a suggestion that Carlin may not have enjoyed good health, because he had found the work at Adam's a little too heavy and was looking for something less demanding.[345] The new manager must have been good with horses - Ford would never have recommended him for the job otherwise - and some of Grant's letters imply that Carlin was engaged in the training and breaking of his colts. Grant's letters to the farm became more upbeat as he proudly set out the pedigrees and backgrounds of his various horses to his new caretaker. [346] If anything the breeding programme became more ambitious than ever under the new supervisor. Carlin frequently urged Grant to purchase more brood mares and Grant's letters to the farm are filled with new names, including a new stallion for the farm, the "Ethan Allen" bred "Bay Star". Carlin's enthusiasm for horseflesh was at the expense of the farm's finances however and he never made it pay. He was sloppy about things such as receipts and expenses . And in time he would write less and less to Grant in the east about the stock , just like William Elrod.

---

[345] Ibid, Vol 22. Oct 27th 1873. Ford gives Carlin a glowing reference.

[346] Ibid, Vol. 25. March 8th 1874. Letter to Nat Carlin.

Chapter 21

*L*ogan

If none of Grant's Hambletonian foals had inherited the notoriously fierce temperament of the infamous "Abdallah" ,"Young Hambletonian's" great grandsire, Grant would have been a lucky horse breeder indeed. The harrowing details of this tough and spirited stallion's life were the stuff of legend among trotting men. Twenty years after his death he was still remembered as the horse that died standing up in a deserted beach shanty at the age of thirty-three, having dug relentlessly into the sand with his fore feet. [347] Though he sired the most amazing trotters in the United States, "Abdallah" could never be broken to harness himself and most of his grooms were terrified of him. His appearance was far from beautiful . Alden Goldsmith had seen him in his latter years and described the sight as grotesque. His ears were distinctive : as pointed as pencils. Many of Grant's Hambletonian colts would have shown this unique characteristic, because it tended to be passed on.

But "pencil ears" were the least of "Abdallah's" great legacy. That was toughness. Unlike the Clays, his colts could stand up to very early training and a certain amount of misuse. But this toughness came at a price, for they were as "wild

---

[347] John Hervey, *The American Trotter*. Page 55-6.

and playful as kittens." [348] At least one of the first colts to be bred by Grant from his own stallion ("Young Hambletonian") and mare (probably "Jennie") proved to be vicious and unsuitable as a carriage horse. Grant had earmarked the colt ,"Logan", as a gift for one of his closest friends -   card player, horse fancier ,and future traveling companion, Adolph Borie. But in a letter to Borie in 1873, Grant expressed his disappointment at having to send another horse in "Logan's" place , and not one of his breeding. [349] Instead he said he would send the colt to his son to use as a saddle horse . Fred Grant must still have been taking his father's equestrian cast-offs as he had done during the war. Now a second lieutenant in the U.S. cavalry, Fred became a member of the Yellowstone expedition that year and the unpopular "Logan" may have wound up back in Grant's possession , as is suggested in a letter the following month. [350]   Jesse Grant referred to the arrival of a beautiful but capricious horse at Long Branch around the time that Fred was stationed in "Indian country".[351]

"Logan" seems to have been an unlucky individual . In addition to temperament problems, he suffered from a bout of founder (laminitis) at the farm sometime in 1871 . Grant was clearly up to scratch on the latest theories associated with the condition , no doubt having discussed such topics with the likes of Robert Bonner, a great authority on ailments of the hoof. In a letter to Elrod he pin-pointed diet as the reason - in particular the colt's exposure to overly rich clover hay at the farm. This was an interesting viewpoint because traditional books of the period, like for instance Fancher's *American Farrier and Horse Trainer*,(1867) held that founder was the result of exposing a very warm horse to sudden cold air or cold water.

Other factors may have contributed to "Logan's" condition. Insufficient exercise would be suspected, given William Elrod's feckless approach to the yard. "Logan" had featured prominently in Grant's letters up to this time and clearly a good deal of thought had gone into his future. But his owner's well- meaning hopes for his horses were often at odds with their fate. It is known that he had sent "Logan" to Charles Ford's stable during the winter of 1871 at his own expense. He may have wanted the colt placed in the hands of someone he trusted more than Elrod, or at least removed from the environs of White Haven. Grant freely invited

---

[348] Hiram Woodruff, *The Trotting Horse of America*. Page 73.

[349] John Y. Simon, *Papers of Ulysses S. Grant*. Vol. 24. Letter to A. E. Borie , April 13th, , 1873.

[350] Ibid. Grant to Fred, May 25th, 1873.

[351] Jesse Root Grant, *In the Days of my Father*. Page 93.

Nat Carlin, then Charles Ford's employee, to use "Logan" as a saddle horse during his stay at Ford's. So Grant may have been engineering a regular exercise regime for the horse .

"Logan" recovered from the condition and Grant stated that he would send for him the following Spring, and have him brought up to the White House, where his training as a carriage horse would begin. The president liked to take a hand in this training. A letter to Borie on the subject of two colts he was sending out, reveals a hands-on approach.

> I would advise…..that you let your man drive them twenty to thirty miles a day for three or four days to-gether, either to a light carriage or a buggy, after which no doubt they will be as steady as old horses. They are very gentle as it is but a little coltish .I drove them ten miles last evening in one hour and although too fleshy for hard driving scarcely a hair was turned on them. [352]

In spite of all the measures taken to give "Logan" a good start, he proved to be uncooperative in his training under harness. "Logan's" many problems perhaps exposed the challenges and shortcomings of the stud farm at White Haven. There were issues relating to the patient handling of highly strung young horses, and the exercising of them. There were problems to do with the use of appropriate fodder and its storage. For instance storage of the hay over the horse stalls in the Grant barn may have been detrimental. This simple convenience, which was the accepted norm of the day, could even have been Grant's undoing as a breeder of fast trotters. Any sweat or condensation coming from the horses below would have risen up and dampened the fodder overhead, leading to the growth of mould and fungal spores. This would not have told in an ordinary farm horse; but in a fast trotter, whose wind is everything , it may have been a significant drawback . In 1875 Grant wrote to Nat Carlin informing him that two of the horses sent to him had inexplicably broken down in wind without much exertion. [353]

While Charles Ford was alive Grant always had a trusted informant in the west who could keep him abreast of the situation at the Gravois. This link was probably vital to his continued involvement with the farm, in spite of his absence. But the death of Ford in October 1873 changed all this. The constant rumour-

---

[352] John Y. Simon, ed. *Papers of Ulysses S. Grant*. Vol. 24. April 15th , 1873. Grant to Borie.

[353] Ibid. Vol. 26. Grant to Carlin 1875.

mongering of the press would have done little to soothe Grant's mind either. Again in 1874, a report appeared in the *St. Louis Democrat* claiming that disease had broken out among the horses at the farm, taking the life of at least one filly. [354] The piece prompted the farrier at Jefferson Barracks to write a letter to Grant refuting the allegations.

But by the middle of 1875, Grant seemed deeply disillusioned with his farming enterprise. The depth of this disenchantment can be gauged in the tone of his letter to Nat Carlin of July 3rd 1875. "Logan's" father, "Young Hambletonian" , was seven now and no doubt getting more full of himself with every passing year."You may also sell Hambletonian or exchange him for brood mares if you have a chance. Get rid of him." [355]

It would have been unthinkable for Grant to have spoken like this of his chestnut stallion a few short years before. Back then "Young Hambletonian" had promised great speed and Grant wanted him as a poster horse for his stock . From the tender age of two, Grant bred him to most of his own mares. But his fastest recorded time was a modest mile in 2.40 minutes. Ultimately he may have been a disappointment, with his foals failing to show potential or size and at least one of them proving to be vicious. Outwardly ,though, Grant continued to be loyal to the stallion, promoting him to friends like Ned Beale, who was about to try bloodstock farming himself .

The emergence of the Whiskey Ring scandal in St. Louis in the mid 1870s finished Grant's rural dream, depriving him of ever using the farm as a peaceful place of retirement after the eight fraught years in the White House. But even without the scandal it is unlikely Grant would ever have returned to live at Carondolet . White Haven was a place he could daydream about and escape to in his mind, as long as responsibilities kept him elsewhere. When those duties showed signs of abating, and he was potentially free to return, the rural idyll somehow lost its appeal. It would have been like turning back on the road, revisiting a past that both he and Julia had long outgrown - whether they liked it or not. White Haven had always been an expensive drain on the president's funds. Grant's son, Jesse, maintained that his father never sold a horse in his life. And while that statement wasn't factually true, the spirit of it was. Grant seemed reluctant to sell any of his stock, which would have given him some income. For instance he continued to breed mares that didn't promise speed instead of selling them on. And his old and

---

[354] *St.Louis Democrat*. July 31st 1874.

[355] John Y. Simon, ed. *Papers of Ulysses S. Grant*. Vol. 26. July 3rd , 1875. Letter to Carlin.

decrepit stock remained with him for as long as they could eat grass. Between 1868 and 1875, Grant's written directions regarding the sale of colts on his farm are scant.

The final auctioning off of the stock at the end of September, 1875 must have been a sad occasion. Despite Grant's desire to be free of the financial burden, it was really the end of a long-held dream. Although he was there or there abouts, Grant lacked that element of luck as a breeder that would have made all the difference. None of his trotters appear in the ancestry of the winning standardbreds of today.[356] Perhaps it wasn't surprising. Grant bred for stock purposes and for the road, never for the track. His intense loyalty to Charles Backman's large stallion, "Messenger Duroc", may have cost him dear also. His lack of personal supervision at the farm, together with his inability to find a suitable and conscientious farm manager, would also have counted against the chances of success.

The sale at the farm attracted a great deal of attention in St. Louis as curious members of the press and public rode out in their droves to White Haven, causing traffic jams on the Gravois road . Thirty-nine horses and two mules went under the hammer that afternoon. The knock down prices agreed on were a source of bewilderment to the newspapers . "For a song" was the popular heading in virtually all the local papers covering the story. Although the country was in recession since the banking failures of 1873, it was felt that not even the depressed state of the market could explain it. That the mules fetched higher prices than most of the trotters would have been a further source of disappointment.

Grant didn't attend the auction, but many of his old associates in St. Louis did, and were perhaps acting on his behalf. Fent Long, his farm agent was there, as was H. C. Wright, who had ground grain for Grant in the 1850s and had sent a mare to the farm as recently as 1873. Elias W. Fox, one time customs surveyor in the city and well known to Grant, bought "Young Hambletonian" for $300 along with two untrained colts. "Jennie", one of Grant's favourite brood mares, was knocked down to C.A. Farris for $58. The unusual "Topsey", the gift from Russia , went to the bid of Justice Cunningham for $60. There was great interest in the sale of the mare, "Vicksburg ", whom Grant had briefly ridden as a spare horse during the Mississippi campaign. She was a good age now, but many were still surprised at her docile

---

[356] Philip A. Pines, *The Complete Book of Harness Racing.* Page 259.

appearance. She went for $56 to H. D. Hatch. [357] The hay from the barn was also sold though at a poor price, since much of it was reported to have been damaged. [358]

Many of the president's other horses enjoyed more interesting fates. Grant didn't sell the incomparable "Butcher Boy" . Like "Jack" before him, he went as a gift to his old business advisor in Chicago, J. R. Jones, to hack about with in Jones's old age. Unfortunately Jones didn't think he was quite old enough to potter about at home with Grant's carriage horses, although he did a certain amount of boasting about the fact . [359] The following year the president rescinded his appointment as Collector of the Port of Chicago , a move which sundered their friendship.

The good moving stallion, "Claymore" was presented to the skilled and progressive one-time governor of Colorado, Alexander Cameron Hunt. The gift caught the notice of the *New York Times*. But the value put on the stallion by the newspaper, $4,000, was in contrast to the modest sums fetched by the other stock at the St. Louis auction. "Claymore" was the first of Grant's stock to go to Colorado, beginning an association with the state that would go further in the next decades. Hunt must have been enthusiastic about the gift as Grant wrote a letter to his legal representative in St. Louis, Judge Long, requesting information on "Claymore's" pedigree for his new owner. [360] Hunt sent the horse to his ranch on the picturesque lands between Denver and Colorado Springs . Like Grant, the ex-governor quickly became "horse poor" from his bloodstock activities and the ranch was sold on soon after.

In 1880, the president's saddle horse, "Legal Tender", now standing in Kentucky , was acquired by the pioneering Kansas stockholder Wilbur E. Campbell . In an early experiment to improve the quality of the native cow horses, Campbell mated the stallion with up to fifty of the best Indian ponies. The experiment wasn't entirely successful, as many of the resulting colts turned out to be too highly strung for the job. Campbell then turned his attention to the breeding of driving horses. He mated some of the mares out of "Legal Tender" with a son of "Electioneer" bought

---

[357] *St. Louis Globe Democrat.* Oct 1st, 1875.

[358] *New York Times* , Oct 4th, 1875. page 2.

[359] William Mcfeely, *Grant*. Page 399.

[360] John Y. Simon, ed, *The Papers of Ulysses S. Grant.* Vol. 26. Letter to Judge Long. Oct 15th 1875.

from Leland Stanford's Palo Alto stock farm. This time the result was a great success. [361]

Eight horses from the St. Louis auction went back east to Grant. [362] But much of the breeding stock ultimately ended up in the Washington farm of his friend General Ned Beale . "Ash Hill" was then a beautiful thousand acre estate, situated just ten miles outside the capital. Its facilities were superb, with two training tracks within its limits. In subsequent years, Buffalo Bill Cody would keep his animals there after the show season. The timing was right. Beale had purchased the farm in 1875 just as Grant was winding down his at St. Louis. A month before the sale of his stock, Grant wrote to Beale from the Branch, offering him the pick of the stock at his own price. "Young Hambletonian" ,in particular, was promoted in the letter, so Grant was obviously hopeful that Beale would take him, although that does not appear to have happened . The plan allowed the president to see his horses whenever he wanted . The following April, Grant was the guest of Ned Beale at Decatur House, just opposite Lafayette Square. He was eager to drive out to Ash Hill, undoubtedly so that he could look at the stock. When Grant vacated the White House in 1877, he would stay with Beale at Decatur House on visits to Washington . In this way he could always see his horses. Breeding from the president's stock continued at the farm. For his efforts Beale was rewarded with the plum job of minister for Austria, where he became an avid advocate of the country's agricultural practices. [363]

Old names cropped up in Grant's correspondence around this time, notably in a letter to his friend Elihu Washburne, who shared an interest in driving. Grant informed Washburne that "Old Bucephelus" (undoubtedly "Cincinnati") had begun to assert his running pedigree in his latter years at the White House, becoming rather dangerous to drive and needing an increasingly stronger bit to be held. [364] "Cincinnati" stayed in the White House until shortly before Grant's departure in 1877. Still mindful of the dying wish of Mr Grant of St Louis that he should never

---

[361] C. W. McCampbell , *Kansas State Hist. Soc.* Aug 1948, Vol, XVL. No. 3. Aug 1948.

[362] John Y. Simon, ed. *The Papers of Ulysses S. Grant.* Vol 26. Letter to Judge John F. Long. Oct 15th 1875.

[363] Gerald Thompson, *Edward F. Beale and the American West.* Page 206-207.

[364] John Y. Simon, ed. *The Papers of Ulysses S. Grant.* Vol. 26. Letter to Elihu Washburne, Aug 23rd , 1875.

be allowed to fall into the hands of anyone who might ill-treat him, the president found a suitable place of retirement for the great horse at the Maryland estate of Daniel Ammen. Peacetime always proved more dangerous for war horses like "Cincinnati" and "Traveller" than the days of battle. In September of 1878, the horse that had seen out the entire Virginia campaign was found with a broken foreleg in the pasture, and had to be destroyed. He was twenty- one years of age. [365]

---

[365] Theo Rodenbough, *Pictorial History of the Civil War. The Cavalry.* Page 298 . Also Frazer and Robert Hunt, *Horses and Heroes*. Page 129, (though here the date given for his death was 1874.)

Chapter 22

Leopard and Linden Tree

The possibility of being free to indulge in a lengthy spell of travel - taking the ultimate escape from the stifling world of Washington politics - must have been on Grant's mind for many years. Now free from office ,and with the farm rented out and the bloodstock dispersed into good hands, it was time to act . In 1877, Ulysses and Julia got together all the money they owned and set out on an unprecedented tour of the world. Grant's inherent restlessness and pure love of travel lead to an itinerary that lasted over two years.

America's most patriotic of citizens was in his element abroad, taking a unique opportunity to broaden his knowledge of international affairs, and to build bridges with many old foreign powers on behalf of the new emerging one . Although the Grants were travelling in a private capacity they were surprised to find that the general's reputation was as towering abroad as in the United States. There was often a huge fuss made of them wherever they went, marring the experience somewhat for Grant, though perhaps Julia felt differently. When the ex-president was free to do so, he liked nothing better than to wander the streets of the many places he visited, people watching. [366] His travels only reinforced his strongly-held view that America was the best place of all to get ahead in life. [367]

Characteristically, the Grants avoided retracing their steps wherever they went. More remarkable still was the mode of transport chosen, especially in the Middle East. Sometimes they journeyed on the back of a horse, camel, elephant or donkey to their destinations, experiencing the sort of physical risks that few VIPs would have braved. While in Egypt, Grant subjected Julia to some good-natured ribbing about how she rode her donkey. In a letter to Fred he joked :

> ..your ma balances on a donkey very well when she has an Arab on each side to hold her and me to lead the donkey. Yesterday , however, she got a little out of balance twice, but claims that the saddle turned. Of course it did. How could it have done otherwise with 185lbs. in a stirrup on one side and the donkey only weighing 125 pounds. But she rides a donkey very well on the whole. [368]

During their stay in the Holy Land, the Grants set off in an open wagon from Jaffa to Jerusalem - a distance of forty miles - overnighting in the town of Ramleh . When they moved off the following day, they were met by an escort of Turkish cavalry. Mindful of Grant's fondness for horses, one of the officers produced a beautiful Arab stallion for the ex-president to ride. Despite declining fitness, Grant had lost none of his enthusiasm for the saddle. Besides, the road had become increasingly rocky and treacherous, making travelling by wagon a truly bone-jangling experience. The best way to travel now was on horseback. But when Grant climbed into the saddle the stallion reared up without warning, giving him no choice but to roll off. Jesse Grant, who had accompanied his parents during the journey, recalled how the Turkish officer sprang forward with his gun to give the horse the bullet. Only Grant's quick intervention saved the animal from execution. Without any fuss he remounted. This time there was no trouble and they continued on their journey. [369]

The Americans got as far as Koleniyah ,where a large company of Turkish cavalry were waiting to escort them to Jerusalem . Mrs Grant had her own problems

---

[366] Adam Badeau, *Grant in Peace*. Page 301-302.

[367] George Childs, *Recollections*. Page 135. (Quote taken from Grant's Independence Hall Speech ,Philadelphia Dec. 12 1879.)

[368] Ishbel Eoss, *The General's Wife*. Page 261-2.

[369] Jesse Root Grant, *In the Days of my Father*. Page 281.

to deal with. The cavalry had brought horses for everyone to ride, and Julia almost passed out when she caught sight of the horse that her hosts had selected for her - a huge, grey, fuming stallion that would scarcely let anyone near him. [370] It had been many a year since she had thundered over the undulating hills of White Haven on her part Arab," Psyche".

Julia used every trick she knew to delay getting on the horse's back, a ruse which didn't escape Grant's notice. "Do hurry up and get on, Julia ", he said impatiently. This irritated her so much that she privately hoped the stallion would bolt there and then and throw her over a precipice so that he would have to eat his words! [371] In spite of her forebodings, the subsequent journey passed without incident, although every so often she noted the stallion turning round to gaze at her with what looked like an air of amusement.

No doubt Grant had quietly concluded that his wife's riding ability was more than equal to the task. But the damage was done. Julia was furious. Silently she fumed at the back of the cavalcade as Grant rode up at the front, much as he had done throughout the war. Everything went well until they had to cross the high waters of the Ajalon River. Again Julia became apprehensive, but her hero of Gravois Creek had already heedlessly crossed the waters and was now far ahead of her, seemingly unconcerned for her safety. Noting her hesitancy, a young Turkish officer riding beside her came to her rescue and he lead the skittish horse down the bank and through the water.

A great crowd together with one of Grant's greatest dreads, a military band, had gathered to meet the cavalcade as they approached Jerusalem. When they reached their destination, the practical Julia wasted no time in swapping her grey stallion for one of the Pasha's donkeys. Now she could go on her way, if not in comfort, then at least in relative safety. Grant however was delighted with the opportunity to ride yet another Arab stallion, this time the Pasha's own - his face almost entirely encased in elaborate gold embroidery.

Grant had been fascinated by the toughness and stamina of the horses he encountered on his journeys in the Holy Land. Sultan Abdul Hammid II, the ruler of the Ottoman empire, was well aware of the ex-president's special passion. Anxious to court America's favour, the sultan had the idea of making some gesture of goodwill to one of its most loved citizens. When Grant arrived in Constantinople an

---

[370] John Y. Simon, ed., *The Personal Memoirs of Julia Dent Grant*. Page 233.

[371] Ibid, page 233.

invitation was sent out at once to visit the royal stables at Ayazaga with its valuable Arab stallions - many with pedigrees stretching back before the time of Mohammed . Jesse Grant accompanied his father on the visit along with a high-ranking Turkish official and the American consul. Contrary to popular belief, the sultan wasn't present himself at the time - he was still in a state of official mourning over recent Russian military victories in Turkey .[372]

The Turkish official invited Grant to name the two best horses in the stables. Ohio's most passionate horseman walked down the long, low-ceilinged aisle with stalls on both sides. The stalls were far from luxurious. The occupants spent their day standing on a plain stone floor without bedding or exercise, and were tied on either side of the face with a head collar. The hard conditions they endured were a tribute to their toughness.

Nearly seventy stallions were on show, most of them tribute gifts from Bedouin tribes. Even Jesse ,who was not one to be easily impressed, was overcome at the spectacle. After a thorough examination, Grant made his choice - a pair of bays. Grant always had a preference for bays, owing perhaps to his military background. In war they were a less obvious target for sharpshooters. The official said nothing at first . Perhaps the two chosen had not been true to type, or were too valuable. Finally he said: "any other two !". [373] Grant smiled and reviewed the group of horses once more. He picked out what he considered to be the next best stallions : two greys this time .

" They are yours General Grant by order of the Sultan !", the official declared . Grant was taken aback and declined the offer, citing his lack of suitable transport as an excuse. The well tutored official had an answer for him. The American man of war docked at Constantinople harbour could be cleared of its top deck guns and fitted out with stables. Ignorant of the ways of the Turkish court, Grant continued to refuse the sultan's offer until the American minister had a quiet word in his ear, warning him in no uncertain terms that he must not refuse the gift. It would be nothing short of a personal insult to a ruler whose every whim had been indulged from an early age. The minister offered to take charge of the matter and make the necessary arrangements. Thus Grant became the unwitting owner of two magnificent eastern stallions . He continued on his world tour as the two horses,

---

[372] Jesse Root Grant, *In the Days of My Father* . Page 291.

[373] Gene Smith, *Grant*. Page 611. (Attributed to the sultan but most likely uttered by his representative.)

complete with their unusual Turkish blankets and special horse shoes, were prepared to be put on board the steamer, the Norman Monarch.

After thirty-one days at sea, during which they were fed on honey and barley, the stallions arrived on American soil. At New Haven a crowd of five thousand well-wishers assembled and a band serenaded them to their stables. It was said that the Norman Monarch filled its empty top deck with American guns and ammunition before sailing back to Turkey. [374] 1878 was a significant year for Abdul Hamid on many fronts. Not only did he bestow two stallions on Ulysses Grant, but he also signed a treaty leading to an opening up of the empire and the promise of foreign investment and trade. The American gift did nothing to hurt these initiatives.

The two stallions were duly registered in the American jockey club stud book and the American Arab stud book. Their names were "Leopard" and "Linden Tree": a direct translation from their Turkish titles. "Leopard" was five years old and "Linden Tree" just four, although he looked considerably older than his stable mate because of the distinctive black rings (or kehilans) around his eyes. Both horses were small and compact, little over fourteen hands high. They received a luke-warm reception from papers like the *New York Times*. "Every effort to improve the home-born breed with these oriental coursers has proved a signal and complete failure", the paper warned. [375]

In spite of this, "Leopard" and "Linden Tree" were feted wherever they went. They were exhibited at fairs throughout the United States for three months by Philadelphia horse fancier, Major J. K. J. K. .Levitt. After this they wound up at the Virginia farm of Ned Beale. Ash Hill was to be their home for the next few years, becoming a magnet for souvenir hunters, who travelled surprisingly long distances in search of anything from strands of tail to hoof clippings. From the start "Leopard" won the hearts of anyone who came in contact with him, with his inquisitive and playful nature and graceful appearance. He enjoyed all the attention he received and never walked when he could dance. "Linden Tree" seemed more of an enigma - shyer by nature and plainer in appearance. He would stay at the back of his stall when spectators came near.

Meanwhile, back on European soil once more, Grant showed again that he'd lost none of his touch on horseback, although he hadn't ridden regularly for many years.

---

[374] Ben Hur, *Western Horseman*, May/June 1947. "General Grant's Arabians. ". Page 47.

[375] *New York Times*, June 3rd, 1879.

In Milan, he was invited to inspect the famous Bersaglieri Regiment of the Italian army. One of the witnesses there was Alfred M. Fuller, a captain with the U. S. Second Cavalry, who wrote about the occasion over a decade later. At the stables the young officers had arranged for Grant to ride a "suitable" mount that would be representative of the regiment's horses. The animal chosen was an immense bay blood horse, decked out in a brand new pigskin saddle. According to Fuller, it took three grooms just to hold the horse outside Grant's hotel while they waited for him to come down. When Grant did appear, it seems that some of the Italian officers were a trifle disappointed at the lack of dash in the appearance of the great man. Fuller continued:

> a more restless, wicked appearing animal I have seldom seen. I was in mortal fear that our general would be speedily thrown and crushed to death by the cruel hooves. From the sly winks and nudges that passed between these dandyish officers, it looked to me very much as if they had assigned to the general a young untameable horse that had never been ridden. My fears were somewhat removed when I saw general Grant's eyes light up with admiration as he gazed upon the horse. [376]

Witnesses observed that Grant had some difficulty getting up into the saddle and needed the help of two officers. But as soon as he was aboard his form grew tall, in spite of being dressed simply in plain black frock coat and trousers. "After a few futile plunges, the horse discovered that he had his master and started off in a gentle trot" said Fuller. "From that time on horse and rider were as one being." [377] It seems that Grant was reluctant to get off the horse once he had got his measure, spending many hours reviewing troops that afternoon. The Bersaglieri regiment were noted for performing everything at a run and Grant was only too happy to fall in with their traditions, galloping his horse for two hours to keep the troops on the move. Fuller observed that when the party returned at last to the hotel, Grant was as fresh as a daisy, while some of his fresh-faced escorts were showing discernible signs of fatigue.

Not surprisingly many of Grant's visits to European cities included several martial inspections. In Berlin, the Prussian army staged a grand review in his honour, and a cavalry horse was presented for him to ride. Grant had a bad cold that day, which the wet and bitter weather did nothing to improve. For once he declined

---

[376] Captain Alfred M. Fuller, "Grant's Horsemanship- an Incident". *McClure's Magazine*, April 1897. Page 501.

[377] Ibid. Page 501.

the invitation to inspect the troops on horseback , but enjoyed the experience from the ground nonetheless . Grant praised the control that the men exercised over their mounts, even when they were staging a show of mock confusion in the field. He noted the routine use of spurs in the Prussian ranks, something that, in his view ,the American cavalry would have benefited from enormously. [378] And as the stentorian commands rang out across the field, perhaps he was reminded of earlier days and remembered his riding instructor at West Point, old Hershberger.

---

[378] John Russell Young, *Around the World with General Grant*. edited Michael Feldman. Page 161.

Chapter 23

St Julien

The year 1879 was a significant one for those interested in the trotting horse. The National Association of Harness Horse Breeders met in New York to regularise the sport, laying down certain conditions for a horse to get on its register. The main requirement was that it should be capable of trotting a mile in at least 2.30 to harness, or 2.35 to wagon. It was a revolutionary move that paved the way for the foundation of the Standardbred.

The man who did most to unify trotters into a recognisable breed was one of the most divisive figures of the era. Though not a horseman himself, sports journalist John Wallace had no shortage of equestrian theories . He was the first to see the need to compile a trotting stud book in the late 1860s. Pedigrees of harness horses had never been formerly set down before then and a state of near chaos reigned . The project was a great success, financially and in every other sense, encouraging the "Muscatine philosopher" as Wallace was called, to produce several more publications throughout the 1870s. For the first time, stallions were assigned a number with the notorious "Abdallah" at the top of the list and "Rysdyk's Hambletonian" at number 10. Wallace, a pugnacious character, became a "terror to evil-doers in the realm of manufacturing fraudulent pedigrees" [379] He waged virtual

---

[379] John Hervey, *The American Trotter*. Page 280.

war on the breeders of Kentucky by his dismissive rejection of their own standard rules. Increasingly trotting stallions were lauded or rubbished depending on who they belonged to rather than their speed, as the trotting world split into several well-defined camps. Despite this, the adoption of the standard in 1879 provided great impetus for the sport, and sent blood stock values high in subsequent years .

That same year, Ulysses and Julia sailed back to the United States, landing in San Francisco Bay to a fabulous reception from a public that had followed their travels avidly in the newspapers, and had rediscovered their own affection by seeing the homage paid to the Grants by foreign nations. Worn out by the constant journeying, Julia was happier to be back in America than her husband. For Grant faced an uncertain career prospect and without a real home to go to.

On his arrival Grant was invited by the Golden Gate Fair District Association to serve as official timer at an important event . During the 1870s "Dexter's" trotting record had tumbled. "Goldsmith Maid" took the honours in 1872 with 2.16 ¾ and again in 1876 with 2.14 - on both occasions driven by Budd Doble. Then in 1878, reinman John Splan drove "Rarus" to 2.13 ¼.. Now an attempt was to be made in San Francisco to beat this record.

The man to do it was Grant's ambitious trotting friend from the east ,Orrin Hickok - known always as the "Talleyrand of the Turf ". Since he was a young boy at Ashtabula , Hickok had longed to make a career riding race horses. But his large stature made this impossible and he switched his considerable horsemanship to driving instead. He first made his reputation as a trainer and driver in Wisconsin,using a combination of tenacity and horse psychology to get the best out of his stable. He moved to New York in the early 1870s. His horses were so well turned out, so thoroughly trained and with such good mouths ,that they put even the teams of "Bonner of the Ledger" in the shade.

Hickok's "St. Julien" was an imposing dark bay horse with a big attitude who had once pulled a milk wagon. But he was about to give an exhibition of speed that had never been seen before . That afternoon, bathed in the late October sunshine of Oakland's mile-long track, the son of Alden Goldsmith's "Volunteer" did the distance in 2:12 ¾ under "Talleyrand's" determined hand. He went straight into the record books as Grant's hand held the official watch that recorded the time. [380] The general was as delighted with the record and reputedly threw his hat in the air . It was a wonderful homecoming . (St. Julien surpassed his own record the following year at Hartford Conn., coming in at 2.11 ¼.)

---

[380] Philip Pines, *The Complete Book of Harness Racing*. Page 282.

The home comers went on to spend a fascinating day at Palo Alto Ranch as the guests of Leland Stanford , who like many rich men had come to road driving on the advice of his doctor. Grant would have caught a glimpse of the future of the trotting horse there, with its "kindergarten" track and the scale of its operations. Three years earlier, Stanford had gone to Charles Backman at Stony Ford Farm and bought thirteen horses, most of them by "Messenger Duroc". One who wasn't by "Duroc" though would prove to be among the most successful stallions of the trotting world. But at the time of Grant's visit Stanford was just starting out on his experiment of breeding this stallion called "Electioneer" to Kentucky thoroughbred mares, some of whom were by "Lexington" . Like Grant, Stanford believed that speed should be developed early and that the infusion of thoroughbred blood in the trotter was a good move . He also believed that speed was born, not made, and was fascinated with the mechanics of gait. Indeed "Electioneer" had a most distinctive style of trotting, described as a smooth rolling wheel motion, that he passed on to most of his get. [381] Stanford thought that colts should be trained early but with short, sharp brushes of speed devoid of distance work. To test his theories he built his miniature trotting track in 1879,which no doubt he showed off to Grant during his visit. Demonstrating his scientific approach to studying the horse's gait, Stanford was the first to use sequence photography to capture the foot fall of a trotting horse, proving that the animal had all four feet off the ground at one point in the sequence. The experiment in 1878, using the skills of photographer Eadward Muybridge, cost him an enormous $40,000, and paved the way for moving pictures in California .

Together in the west for the first time in their lives, Ulysses and Julia took the opportunity to tour California extensively, seeing many of its natural wonders. Local "whips" queued up to drive their stagecoach at Yosemite , among them the well-known mountain driver, George Monroe , (killed by a wild mule a few years later). In twenty years of treacherous driving between Mariposa and Yosemite , the legendary Monroe had never injured a passenger or a horse. Thus he was an ideal choice to make the difficult journey into the valley. Noting that Monroe drove his six horses like a one in hand, Grant found the experience thrilling as he sat up on the box beside his driver. This was not the case for Julia, however, who tended to view these difficult stagecoach journeys with some dread.

On another excursion, Julia became convinced that the coach was actually running away. At a particularly dangerous bend the ground gave way, causing the coach to leave the road . The driver was skilled and managed to pull up the team

---

[381] John Hervey, *The American Trotter*. Page 126.

before any harm came to his passengers. But Julia had had enough. At the first opportunity she hopped out and refused to go any further. Nothing Grant or the driver said could persuade her to hop on board again. The situation was rescued by two passers-by in a buggy, who offered their vehicle to the Grants. With her husband now holding the reins, Julia had the unexpected pleasure of being driven over the most romantic landscape in the state by her own "Ulyss".[382]

Such incidents were more common than usual. The Methodist minister, Charles Fowler, heard that Grant's driver in Colorado "ran his horses down the mountain" to see if he could "stir his nerves" during a visit to the state. When asked if he had any recollection of this, the general typically replied that he was unconscious of any danger but remembered the horses pulling the coach as being the same span that had taken Sheridan, Sherman and himself to Denver a dozen years before.[383]

(Ten years earlier, during the intrigue-ridden summer of 1869, the Grants were the unwitting victims of a more muted conspiracy to achieve an unheard of record.[384] The president's visit to the White Mountains, New Hampshire, was just the spur needed by local whips to carry it off. The plot was planned with great precision and included the use of a cannon at Echo Lake to fire off three times after the coach had passed, while other whips acted as timers at various points on the journey. The eleven mile trip from Bethlehem to Profile House over near vertical hills was done in fifty-eight minutes, and was spoken about for years afterwards. True to his habit, the president had asked if he could sit up with the driver. As a result he arrived at the hotel covered in dust. The horses had made such a huge effort that they needed to be tended to for several hours afterwards. Grant thoroughly enjoyed the journey and was particularly impressed with the driver, Edmund Cox, whose team of six sorrel thoroughbreds was the pride of the Plymouth and Franconia line. That Christmas, he presented Cox with an elaborate pig-skin coach whip, now in the possession of the New Hampshire Historical Society.[385])

The Grants eventually returned east to a quiet, relaxing stay at Ned Beale's Decatur House in Washington. During the visit Grant was enthusiastic about driving

---

[382] John Y. Simon, ed., *The Personal Memoirs of Julia Dent Grant*. Page 309-10.

[383] Charles Henry Fowler, *Patriotic Orations*. Page 155.

[384] Alice Bartlett Stephens, "Coach Ride in the White Mountains", *The Granite Monthly*, Vol. 34. Page 95.

[385] Ibid. Page 112.

out to Beale's farm at Ash Hill to see the two stallions that Sultan Abdul had given him during his visit abroad. He very nearly missed them. The previous week a plot had been hatched by a blacksmith at the Beale estate to kidnap the horses and hold them for a ransom. But two of the men involved, Nolan and Rickar, lost courage and stole a group of chickens from the farm instead. Their plan was unravelled by the authorities when they were found to be selling the birds on the streets of Washington, where they were promptly arrested. [386]

How different "Leopard" and "Linden Tree" must have looked in the Virginia snow from their time in the royal stables at Ayazaga. Some of Grant's old breeding stock from St. Louis remained at Beale's estate as well. And they were still producing colts. Grant must have discussed with Beale the possibility of donating some of these fine horses to the Japanese emperor, whose court and country had so beguiled the general during his world tour. The following month, the papers were pleased to announce that Grant had made a present of three stallions to Emperor Meiji and the Japanese government. The first was "Barb", a four year old bay. The second was "Kingsley", a larger seven year old thoroughbred out of Saratoga Cup winner, "Harper's Longfellow". The trio was completed with "Black Hawk Jnr.", a jet black morgan trotter whose long luxurious tail nearly swept the ground. All were valued by the *New York Times* at $4,000. [387]

Although he was delighted to see them, Grant was aware that he would have little time or resources to devote to his horses over the coming months, particularly the Turkish stallions. It would be up to others to enjoy their qualities. He registered "Linden Tree" in the name of his son, Ulysses, and gave "Leopard" to Ned Beale as a gift. [388]

The two grey stallions soon attracted the attention of one of the most dedicated horse breeders of the era, Randolph Huntington. Having made a considerable amount of money in pharmaceuticals, Huntington, a native of Springfield Massachusetts, spent many years breeding trotters of the Henry Clay family. His interest in the Clays stemmed in part from a family connection with the old Henry Clay stallion of the Genosee Valley. But he had also spent long years observing the Clays as carriage horses in New York. Although they were much out of fashion among the trotting brigade - "sawdust in the trotter" according to Robert

---

[386] *Philadelphia Times*, Dec 27th, 1879.

[387] *The New York Times*, Feb. 2nd, 1880.

[388] Gerald Thompson, *Edward F. Beale and the American West*. Page 221.

Bonner - Huntington felt they had no equal. Now he was to turn his life's work to the dream of creating a new breed of light carriage horse, in the mould of Count Orloff's Russian horses . He wanted his creation to be unique to the United States and well suited to the native terrain. He dreamed that it would become a recognised American breed, the first of its kind, one that would be much sought after both domestically and overseas. Huntington believed that Arab blood was essential in achieving his goal. When General Grant's desert stallions arrived on his doorstep, he couldn't believe his luck. These were just the foundation sires he had been looking for. He corresponded with Grant about his interest in the stallions and discovered that the general too was taken with the idea of a national breed and was aware of the importance of primitive blood in the formation of a distinctive self-sustaining type.[389]

Huntington had an almost religious devotion to the Arab, referring to it as "God's horse". He described his first sighting of the two stallions at General Beale's farm in almost mystical terms, praising their perfect conformations with heaped superlatives. In one of the paddocks near the front lawn, Beale's groom, Addisson, put the two horses through their paces on the lunge line, sending Huntington into a state of rapture. Such was the balance and lightness of the Grant stallions, that they didn't even need protective boots as they moved. Huntington realised how valuable this clean movement could be if it was bred on.

The Massachusetts breeder wasted no time in seeking permission to send several of his choice Henry Clay mares, who were only three times removed from eastern blood, to be bred to "Linden" and "Leopard" . The resulting colts turned out to be impressive and surprisingly large. Their breeder dubbed them the Clay-Arab. Huntington was a great advocate of the old breeder's rule of out-crossing once and then breeding back by three close relatives, and he set about doing this.

No photographs exist of the Grant stallions. Instead Huntington commissioned artist Herbert Kitteridge to sketch them. His work comes very close to photographic representation. Although Huntington thought "Linden" superior to "Leopard" in his paces and conformation, the flashier "Leopard" always overshadowed his stable mate , taking first prize in the national horse show in Madison Square Garden in 1883 and 1884.

---

[389] Randolph Huntington, *General Grant's Arabian Horses, Leopard and Linden Tree, and their Sons Beale and Hegira.* Page 8.

Now that two new horses associated with Grant were achieving great prominence, the press were back in business. Their latest claims concerned the temperament of "Linden". According to the papers, "Linden was vicious". Reports came through that a milkman was suing Ulysses Jr. after the stallion broke loose at Salem in the Winter of 1881 and attacked his horse and wagon, causing serious injury. [390] (A jury awarded him $5,000 in damages in 1884.) Huntington did his best to dispel these rumours, claiming that none of "Linden's" progeny at his barn showed any signs of meanness. If anything, they were particularly easily broken and well mannered. [391]

But the most intriguing aspect of the Grant stallions concerned "Linden Tree's" pedigree - or lack of it. Although registered in the Arab stud book, it became apparent from "Linden's" conformation and way of going that he wasn't an Arab at all, but a Barb. Barbs had been mistaken for Arabs in the past. A similar mistake was made with the famous Godolphin, one of the foundation sires of the English thoroughbred. But American horse enthusiasts seemed dismayed that General Grant would choose the poor relation of eastern breeds when he was free to select any stallion at the sultan's exclusive stables. As a result, many versions of how and why "Linden Tree" ended up on the boat to America began to unfold - versions as numerous as the Tales of the Arabian Nights.

War veteran, Major C. A. Benton, who made a study of Arab horses in America, thought he had the answer to the mystery. Stationed in Constantinople not long after Grant's visit there, Major Benton tracked down the keeper of the intrigue-ridden court stables. He learned from this man that one of Grant's chosen stallions had injured his leg before he was due to sail. Fearing the wrath of the sultan, the keeper kept the injury secret and another horse, a Barb, was substituted because he bore a striking resemblance to the original. Another theory suggested that Grant picked "Leopard" and the sultan picked the "Linden". [392] But Jesse Grant's account of the visit made it clear that the sultan didn't attend the tour of the stables, so this is unlikely. In 1906 the Arab horse breeder, Homer Davenport, learned from the Turkish court interpreter, Alexander Gargiulo, that the sultan would never have dreamed of keeping a Barb at his stables in the first place, since he disliked the Barb

---

[390] *The New York Times,* June 6th, 1884. Page 5.

[391] Randolph Huntington, *General Grant's Arabian Horses, Leopard and Linden Tree, and their sons Beale and Hegira.* Page 14-15.

[392] Ben Hur, "General Grant's Arabians". *Western Horseman,* May/Jun, 1947. Page 48.

people and didn't care for their horses either. [393] In a further twist Mr. Gargiulo insisted that the sultan had picked out a black horse for the general after he left Constantinople . The interpreter said that he tried it out and found that it wasn't a suitable saddle horse. But rather than tell the truth, Gargiulo came up with a crafty ruse, telling the master of ceremonies at the stable that no American president ever rode a black horse! Another would have to be substituted. According to Gargiulo, this is how "Linden Tree" came to be chosen.

But perhaps it was no accident that Grant chose a Barb out of the sultan's seventy strong stable . It was always the definitive war horse of the east and had given the Henry Clay line its origins. "Linden's" breed might have been very appealing to someone with Grant's background in producing trotters. Though Grant had no time for Napoleon, he may well have admired the famous horse he rode in battle for fifteen years, the Barb "Marengo ". Major Benton's story, and that of interpreter Gargiulo, were probably elaborated to save Grant's reputation as a judge of horseflesh. On his visit to Ash Hill in 1880, Grant would have noticed if either of the stallions at Beale's farm had differed from the two he had picked out at the royal stables the year before. Yet there is no record that this most observant of men in horse matters ever commented on a difference, which is reasonable proof that "Linden" and "Leopard" had been his original choices.

Randolph Huntington must have known early on that "Linden Tree" was a Barb. In his book about the two stallions he slyly refers to "Linden" as belonging to the "Godolphin Arab" family. Yet officially he wouldn't entertain the notion that he was a Barb. He corresponded with the general in 1882 with a view to finding out more about the stallions' pedigrees. Grant wrote back but without the details Huntington wanted. He could only speak in general terms about the horses, concluding his letter by stating: "the fact of these horses being from the sultan's own private stables, and being a present from him as an appreciation of our country among the nations of the earth, is the best proof of the purity of their blood".
[394]Subsequent investigations by Huntington revealed that "Leopard" had been bred by a ruling member of the Bedouin Fid'an tribe. "Linden's" family tree remained delightfully obscure.

The incessant touring of the previous years may have cured Grant's restlessness. But when it ended he had little money left and no work to go to. A

---

[393] Homer Davenport, *My Quest of the Arabian Horse*. Page 21.

[394] Randolph Huntington, *General Grant's Arabian Horses, Leopard and Linden Tree etc.*.Page 16.

group of friends headed by George Childs donated a fund to Julia and Ulysses, so that they could buy a house in New York. They found a comfortable brownstone at Number 3, East 66th Street. The Empire City - centre of the trotting scene, home to most of the "sealskin brigade" and to the fortune seekers and makers of Wall Street - became the couple's home for the rest of their married lives. The house was near Central Park, which Grant used at every chance to drive his buggy. He was also able to drive out from the city to his summer cottage at "the Branch", a distance of twenty miles.

The New York that the Grants were returning to was an increasingly sprawling place of uncontrolled growth. Horse cars, omnibuses and carriages competed for limited space on teeming streets. There had been a noticeable shift in fashion during the couple's absence abroad. The new decade saw the popularity of the fast pacer decline as four in hands, tandems and dogcarts came to predominate on the ever congested roads.[395]

---

[395] Ishbel Ross, *The General's Wife*. Page 279.

Chapter 24

Silver

Grant now faced the eternal problem of all ex U. S. presidents - what to do after office. His haunting memories of the Isthmus of Panama had never faded, prompting him to revive his old idea of raising funds for a Nicaraguan canal in collaboration with Ned Beale and Daniel Ammen. But he blew hot and cold on the project and nothing came of it. Even in the early 1880s the lure of the railroad business was strong. He was invited to become president of the Mexican Southern Railroad Company, which aimed to build a track between Mexico and the Pacific. Grant always liked to think of himself as a businessman. But Julia's observation that "the Vicar of Wakefield's Moses was a financier beside him", was probably a more realistic analysis. [396] At his office, Number 2, Wall Street, room 6, Grant was already swimming with perfect eels. Sitting on the board of Mexican Southern were Jay Gould and Russell Sage. Indeed Grant was now a frequent guest at Sage's famous secluded buffet lunches on Broadway, where not even the waiters were admitted in case they overheard anything.

---

[396] John Y. Simon, ed., *The Personal Memoirs of Julia Dent Grant*. Page 72.

But in the short term, Ulysses had little prospect of earning an income out of his new presidency, and he looked around for something else. In 1881 his genial middle son, Buck, went into an investment business with one of the most promising young operators of Wall Street, Ferdinand Ward. Grant and his extended family invested their savings and assets in the firm . Here at last was a company that could look after his money. A close relation and a seemingly brilliant young financier that he liked and trusted were at the helm. Life seemed to be going well for him in New York. The money rolling in from his investments with Ward would be sure to support a good lifestyle. He was also much in demand at public dinners, which he had grown to almost enjoy. There was an open invitation from William Vanderbilt to drive his stable star, Maud S. whenever he liked. At his home on East Sixty Sixth Street he now had three good teams at his disposal, which he could exercise in Central Park or drive out to Long Branch. [397] Included in his stable was a favourite driving mare, "Silver", together with her two prized fillies. Grant had switched his attention to another stallion at Charles Backman's stud farm called "Kentucky Prince" - a lop-eared, chestnut horse related to "Lexington ", who was siring many standardbred champions. Both of "Silver's" fillies were out of "Kentucky Prince" .

Grant became close to Ferdinand Ward, regarding him more as a friend than a business associate . Everyone who met the young businessman remembered his magnetic and persuasive personality topped off by a disarmingly unassuming manner. [398] And no doubt he could "talk horse" with the best of them. But during a trip to the countryside, Grant inadvertently terrified the man who would soon ruin him. One day the two set out on a carriage ride at the young businessman's palatial residence in Connecticut , with the ex-president taking the reins of their two-seater buggy. The buggy was Ward's but the horses attached to it had been borrowed from Grant: two of the general's typically highly strung mares . Grant set off at his usual lick, with his somewhat cramped passenger needing all the strength in his arms to keep his hat on and remain in his seat at the same time. [399]

When they reached a nearby village, the team came by a burning house. The flames and confusion on the street sent the mares into orbit .As they reared and plunged wildly, Ward was sure that the carriage would overturn, and he would be

---

[397] Adam Badeau, *Grant in Peace*. Page 553.

[398] Henry Drew, *Twenty -Eight years in Wall Street*. Page 215.

[399] Ferdinand Ward, "Grant as I Knew Him", *New York Herald*, (magazine section) December 19, 1909, page 1-2.

pitched out and killed. Seeking reassurance , he darted a glance in the direction of his distinguished driver. Far from being fearful, Grant was actually enjoying the pandemonium, as there appeared to be a faint smile on his lips. Despite Ward's fears, the carriage didn't overturn and the pair reached their destination safely. Ward wasn't as bold behind a team of horses as when he was off speculating with other people's money. For once his legendary smoothness slipped. He crawled down from the buggy and tottered into the house. With his nerves all ajar from the journey, the great dissembler lost heavily at the planned poker game that night. But the incident left no mark on Grant who had an exceptionally good game. Grant hadn't known about Ward's peculiar business practices at the time. But if he had, he couldn't have arranged a more fitting trip.

On an icy Christmas in New York in 1883, Grant slipped on the pavement while handing his carriage driver a present. His left leg and hip, injured at New Orleans twenty years before, took the brunt of the impact. He never came out of his house a well man again. The finance company that he had invested all his savings in was a Ponzi scheme. Exploiting the Grant name to give cast-iron respectability to his activities, Ferdinand Ward used the firm's securities as collateral against multiple bank loans. The whole enterprise collapsed in May 1884, ruining Grant and his family in a way that somehow typified the age. It bankrupted the Mexican Southern Railroad and sent tremors through Wall Street. Share prices tumbled with many of Grant's wealthy friends losing heavily. (Ward served over six years in Sing Sing for his activities.[400]) Grant hadn't only to deal with the financial hardship of the bankruptcy. The scandal threatened his reputation, with insinuations of stupidity or even collusion.

At the start of the firm's troubles Grant had travelled to William Vanderbilt's mansion on Fifth Avenue to ask for a loan that he hoped would rescue the company. Ruthless in business, kindly in friendship, Vanderbilt handed over a cheque for $150,000 with no questions asked. Unfortunately the loan was swallowed up by the firm's enormous debts, leaving Grant no option but to sign over all his property, war memorabilia and gifts from abroad to the richest man in America as a matter of honour. By now William Vanderbilt's health was also failing. Unbeknown to his friends, a growing blindness in one eye had robbed him of the pleasure of driving his own teams, and to his great annoyance he had to employ the services of a driver for once . In August 1884, he let "Maud S. " , the queen of his stable, pass into the

---

[400] Ibid. Page 1.

hands of Robert Bonner , although the $40,000 he received for her was some consolation.

For the first time in nearly twenty-five years Grant became horseless, selling his remaining three teams and carriages and letting the groom go. The farm in St. Louis - the setting for Julia's idyllic childhood and Grant's ambitious stud farm activities - was sold for $60,000 to pay off some of the debts . As a favour, George Childs took Grant's favourite mare, "Silver", along with her valuable daughters ,"Julia" and "Ida". All three went to the publisher's residence, Wooton Mansion, Philadelphia . [401] No doubt Grant's eagerness to take up his friend's invitation to Philadelphia in the Spring of 1885 was prompted by a wish to see his mares once more. Sadly he never made the trip.

1884 continued on bleakly. Grant was diagnosed with cancer of the mouth. It was particularly ill-timed . The general never saw himself as a writer. Yet after the bankruptcy he doggedly set about putting pen to paper on his war experiences for *Century Magazine*, at $500 an article. The initial pieces evolved into a more extensive project with a book in mind. Now its author was unsure whether he could continue. Labouring under great pain and discomfort, Grant worked tirelessly on his articles at Long Branch and at East 66th Street. As the cancer progressed it took away his ability to eat and drink normally. He described the sensation of swallowing water to George Childs as being akin to molten lead passing down the throat. [402] Unable to sleep, he often worked on his writings instead late into the night.

For a change of air and a break from the work, he would go out for the occasional drive in Central Park with Fred or his Mexican friend, Mattias Romero. But he found his favourite diversion increasingly exhausting. Rugged up against a stiff autumnal breeze, he paid a last visit to Alden Goldsmith's Goshen barn in November . The sight of the fine Hambletonians in stable and paddock helped to take his mind off the pain in his mouth and throat. The offer of a simple treat of roast chestnuts had to be declined however ,until Goldsmith suggested mashing them up to form a soft paste. [403] As he looked out over Goldsmith's pasture, Grant enjoyed what he swore was going to be his last cigar.

---

[401] George Childs, *Recollections*. Page 94-5.

[402] Ibid. Page 113.

[403] Richard Goldhurst, *Many are the Hearts*. Page 148.

Just as the general's trials were beginning in 1884, Randolph Huntington, now a virtual recluse at his stud farm in Bloomfield New York, decided to write a book about "Leopard" and "Linden Tree". A key motivation for the work was his knowledge that the general had fallen ill, and he hoped that a book on the subject might lift his spirits. He also wanted to set the record straight and explain his theories about horse breeding. Huntington had been wounded by the prejudice of other breeders and horsemen against his support for Arab blood. The book gave him the opportunity to retaliate against their criticisms that, for example, his "Clay Arabs" were neither one thing nor the other , and that it was ludicrous to improve the trotting horse with a breed that liked nothing better than to gallop. The resulting work, *General Grant's Arabian Horses, Leopard and Linden Tree, and their Sons Beale and Hegira*, turned out to be one of the most extraordinary equestrian books ever written - an intense mixture of passion and bitterness - dedicated to "General Grant and his love of horses".

The terms of Grant's own book, negotiated with his publishers, "Century Magazine", were far from generous. Many years before, Mark Twain and Ulysses Grant had met at the White House when the author was petitioning on behalf of his father-in-law's business. It had been an awkward encounter, with Twain getting a taste of the coldness of manner that Grant often showed to those he didn't know.[404] Later at an army reunion banquet at Haverly's Theatre in Chicago 1879, the two men met again. This time an unlikely friendship developed, for Twain had been an ardent critic of the Grant administration . But they were both innate travellers and appreciated the power of rivers, one in particular. Before the war, Samuel Clemens had plied his beloved trade as a riverboat pilot. To Hannibal's famous son, it was the freest lifestyle on the planet, for the pilot was answerable to nobody . Yet perhaps Twain recognised that as a boy team driver in Ohio, Grant could well have surpassed that life of unparalleled independence, and at a younger age.

When the author saw Grant's plight, he stepped in. He was flabbergasted at how little *Century* was paying Grant for his work, arguing that any "unknown Comanche Indian " who decided to put pen to paper would have been offered as good a deal. [405] Recognising the true worth of the highest ranking general's account of the war, Twain offered an infinitely better deal with his own publishing company - one that would give Grant a realistic chance of clearing his debts. Twain' s Charles

---

[404] Mark Twain, *Autobiography*. Vol. 1. Page 13.

[405] Jean Edward *Smith,* Grant. Page 623.

Webster & Co. brought the classic *Memoirs* to print. The contract terms were seventy percent of the profits, allowing Grant to leave his family on a good financial footing. Twain was also able to provide encouragement as the memoirs were being written, reassuring a less than convinced Grant of the literary merits of the work.

To someone as active as Grant, who valued the freedom of the outdoors, the confinement of his last months was a trying ordeal. As he weakened he took the offer of a cottage at Mount McGregor, away from the stifling heat of New York. He left the city for good in Vanderbilt's private rail car, catching a glimpse of West Point from the train window. Now too weak to walk any distance, his only means of travel was a rickshaw, sometimes pulled by Fred but more usually by his valet, Harrison Tyrrell. It was his habit to refer dryly to his new mode of transport as " my horse ". [406] He would elaborate on the metaphor, declaring his last horse the safest he had ever ridden as it was unlikely to ever run away with him up the hill. [407]

Grant passed away surrounded by his family on July 23rd 1885 at the age of sixty-three. His funeral in New York posed a logistical nightmare for the man given the job of organising it, General Winfield Scott Hancock . How was he to get all the groups who wanted to march in the procession through within the hours of daylight? There was the issue of spectators and space for the carriages. In addition, the rising ground leading up to the proposed tomb site would be tiring for the marchers. Work got under way over a week before the funeral to roll and level 127th Street in order for it to bear the procession. Albert Hawkins asked to be allowed to drive the catafalque on the day . But his request was turned down by the family. [408] The hearse was eventually pulled by a span of twenty-four black horses, which would have been beyond the skill of even Hawkins to control . Instead each horse was led and held in check by a groom. The final resting place at an elevated spot on Riverside Park was well chosen, according to one of the pall bearers, William Tecumseh Sherman . It overlooked the river and harbour, Long Island Sound and Forts Lee and Washington . [409] But he might also have added that it lay not a stone's throw from

---

[406] Richard Goldhurst, *Many are the Hearts*. Page 218.

[407] Dr. George Shrady, *General Grant's Last Days*. Page 66.

[408] *New York Times*, July 31st, 1885 . Page 1.

[409] William T. Sherman, "An Address on Grant," in James Grant Wilson and Titus Munson Coan, eds., *Personal Recollections of the War of Rebellion. Addresses Delivered Before the New York Commandery of the Loyal Legion of the United States, 1883-1891* . New York. Published by the Commandery, 1891, Page 112.

Harlem Lane, the scene of those spectacular road duels and brushes of speed that Grant loved so much.

Chapter 25

The Colorado Ranger

It is perhaps not surprising that the involvement of Ulysses Grant's name with the American horse didn't end in Drexel's Cottage at Mount McGregor in 1885. Ten years after his initial experiments, Randolph Huntington was still doggedly pursuing his dream of creating the supreme carriage horse, but he had refined his theories. He believed it necessary to breed the two Grant stallions , but especially "Leopard" , with a desert mare. Three years after Grant's death, Huntington imported a Roger Upton-bred mare of desert pedigree from England called "Naomi ". She turned out to be a prolific breeder, having ten foals by "Leopard" or his progeny. Huntington never bred "Naomi" to "Linden" ,which was perhaps the closest he ever came to admitting that the horse wasn't of Arab blood. [410]

But in 1893, Huntington received two severe blows. Firstly he discovered that he was financially ruined : swindled out of his savings by his long-time secretary, Francis Weeks. Though his hundred-head stud farm at Bloomfield was put into receivership the following year , many eastern horsemen took note of the good prices paid for the stock at the sale by Kellogg Auctioneers. It might well have signaled that the Clayarab had arrived and was now much admired by discerning

---

[410] George Conn, "Randolph Huntington". *Western Horseman*, Apr. 1949.

New York horsemen. Though well into his sixties, Huntington clawed his way back into the business with characteristic toughness, settling this time in Oyster Bay, Long Island.

But the second blow he was to receive in 1893 would prove more insidious and cruel. That year, a noisy gasoline-powered buggy chugged tentatively out of a garage in Huntington's home town of Springfield, Massachusetts. At a cruising speed of five miles an hour, the "Duryea" would have seemed to pose little threat to the fleet roadsters that Huntington had at his barn. But by the end of the decade it had made the coach horse, if not redundant, then at least less fashionable, as the mechanised buggy became the new status symbol. Huntington's grand dream was over. When the Oyster Bay stud was broken up for good in 1906 it showed to what extent things had changed in the intervening years. The pedigree horses fetched prices way below those of the 1894 liquidation sale. The proud, historic "Anazeh", son of "Leopard" and "Naomi", and the first pure-bred Arab to be foaled in America, sold for $320. The other foals were scattered to all parts of the country, like Seward's Arabians three decades before, exerting a significant though undocumented influence on many strands of American horse.

By this time the story of Grant's stallions had taken an unexpected twist. "Leopard" and "Linden", now well on in years, had been acquired by General George Colby of Nebraska in the late 1880s and were moved west. There they were bred to the native mares on the Colby ranch - a mixture of retired U.S. cavalry thoroughbreds and mustangs. As the years passed, their foals acquired a formidable reputation among ranchers. They were versatile, had bottomless stamina and steady temperaments. To use the practical local term, they were "good using horses with a lot of cow". On the strength of their reputation, the horses were introduced into the state of Colorado by rancher A. C. Whipple through the purchase of a stallion and several mares from the Colby ranch. The stallion chosen was a grandson of "Leopard" on both dam and sire side called "Tony", a grey with distinctive black ears, (a medicine hat). The brood mares were all daughters of either "Leopard" or "Linden Tree".

The migration west was an appropriate journey for the descendants of Grant's stallions. The general had been the first president to visit the state in 1873, when the citizens of Central City paved the streets with silver in his honour. He had also gifted his prized trotting stallion, "Claymore", to the breeding stock of Colorado when he presented him to Alexander Hunt in 1875. In the 1890s the great "Leopard" broke a leg and had to be put down. "Linden" proved more resilient, living and breeding until 1900. This meant that "Linden" spent a full twelve years in the west, influencing the native stock for longer. [411]

In the early years of the Twentieth Century, the legendary horseman of the plains, Mike Ruby, came to play a significant part in shaping the future of Leopard's and Linden's colts. He had been attracted by the horses' reputation for cow savvy and saw their potential. Ruby acquired two stallions from the line, called "Patches" (out of "Tony") and "Max" (son of the much admired stallion "Waldron Leopard", a grandson of "Linden Tree".) With these two stallions in his possession, Ruby embarked on a well organised breeding programme keeping meticulous ,hand written records of all his horses and their foals. This was an unusual practice for the time and perhaps reflected that Mike Ruby, like Randolph Huntington, also had a vision of a new breed of American horse.

Acknowledgment of Ruby's long, painstaking work came in 1934 when he was invited to show two stallions of choice at the national western stock show in Denver . The two he chose to display were magnificent descendants of "Leopard" - Leopard#3 and his son Fox#10. With their loud and striking leopard spots and attractive compact conformations, they made a lasting impression on the thousands of visitors who flocked to the showcase event, and at a time well before the foundation of the Appaloosa horse society. Faculty members of Colorado's State University encouraged Ruby to declare his stallions part of a new American breed. It would be called the Colorado Ranger: originating in the state of Colorado - bred under range conditions. A year later Ruby founded the breed's association with his handwritten records serving as the breed's register. [412] In spite of the amazing array of coat patterns and colours within the Ranger stock, it was never a colour breed. It was always bloodlines that counted, with every member having to trace a direct line of descent to the two foundation sires, "Max" or "Patches" .

Mike Ruby now faced a deadly threat to his stock . The dry, merciless winds that swept through his grazing pastures for the last number of years had reduced them relentlessly to a parched, barren wasteland. Drought was threatening to wipe out his whole herd and a lifetime's dedicated work. Many were already dead. In a desperate bid for survival, Ruby trailed the one hundred and thirty strong herd on an epic three hundred mile migration . Their destination was the fertile western slopes

---

[411] Nancy van Orden Botelho, "The Colorado Rangerbred in Canada and the Northwestern United States", *Horse Magazine*. Mar/Apr 1986. Page 11.

[412] Vera Knisley, *A Kingdom for my Horse* . Page 11.

of the Rockies. Ruby's journey made history in Colorado and perhaps in the United States. No other rancher in this period had attempted such an ambitious trail with a herd of such size , let alone one where the survival of a breed was at stake. Accompanied by his son David and cousins Walt and Joe, Ruby set out in the Spring of 1936 from Wray, Colorado across the central plain to Burlington and then on to Strasburg. Several major rivers had to be crossed on the way, adding to the challenge. At this point an enormous storm halted their progress and threatened the entire expedition. The only way forward now was to transport the horses by rail. It was a logistical nightmare, involving the loading of the entire herd onto four railway cars in blizzard conditions . [413] Yet all the horses arrived safely at their new pastures in Grandby, including a nursing mother who started to produce milk for the foal that lay dead three hundred miles away. It says a lot for the trailing skills of the Rubys and the temperaments of their horses, that the task was accomplished so successfully.

In 1939 the rain made a welcome return to the region, making the old pastures viable once more . The herd had been almost three years away from its pastures. Now Mike Ruby once again prepared to trail over a hundred horses all the way back to Burlington . He didn't lose a single individual on the journey. They returned in a strong and robust state.

At the instigation of the breed, the Rangerbred association was strictly limited to fifty members, since only fifty horses could be traced directly to the foundation sires," Max" and "Patches" . This curtailed the number of horses who were eligible for registration and indirectly threatened the extinction of the breed. But in the 1960s the association took the brave decision to open up its register. It was decided that outcrosses would be permitted, selecting the cream of other breeds to strengthen the quality of Rangerbreds. [414] Many thoroughbreds with proven form were chosen to be "admitted stallions", denoted by a star in front of their name. One such was the Irish bred, "the Tetrarch" , dubbed "the Spotted Wonder", and still remembered in his native Kilkenny to this day: his grave marked with a large granite rock and a bronze plaque. Other distinguished thoroughbred guests included "Lord Vanity" , son of the English Derby champion "Hyperion".

Perhaps the most interesting admitted stallion of all was the trick horse "Pavo", famous for his rodeo exhibitions throughout the United States. It was hoped

---

[413] Cheryl Snyder, Letter to author Dec. 22nd , 2002.

[414] Vera Knisley, *A Kingdom for my Horse*. Page 29-30.

that "Pavo" would add unsurpassed intelligence and trainability to the breed. Under his trainer, Will Goulet , and later trick rider, Dick Griffiths , there was no trick "Pavo" couldn't do from rearing ,to wheeling to jumping through fire. His rider was no less of a prodigy - a world champion at nine who rode his pony into the Oval Office to shake hands with President Harding. "Pavo" was a distinctive individual, bearing a spiky mane and a roan coat with white loins dotted with red spots.

A condition of these stallions' admittance to the register was that their progeny must be bred back to horses with clear Rangerbred pedigree, the practice favoured by Randolph Huntington in his breeding of the Clays. This would strengthen and enhance the quality of the breed. [415] A system of grading for breeders was also devised by Mike Ruby, who was to die suddenly at his Lazy J Bar Ranch four years after he made his successful return to his pastures with the herd . With the foundation stallions being assigned the letter "Z", breeders could gauge how closely their foals came to this letter by averaging the grade of the foal's sire and dam. [416]

Now that the register had opened up, the breed could also take in Appaloosas with Rangerbred heritage, numbering one eighth of the Appaloosa population. Outcrosses were permitted and encouraged, mainly with horses associated with the Arab such as thoroughbreds, Clay-Arab, Ara-Appaloosa and Quarter horse. But animals with paint, pinto or pony heritage were excluded . A quick glance at the pedigree of Fox#10 in the ranger stud book reveals the presence of several influences that Ulysses Grant would have recognised, including Hambletonian, Thoroughbred, and Clydesdale .

It is hard to believe that the ultimate cow horse of Colorado had its origins in the royal stables of Constantinople . For all his zeal and single-mindedness , Randolph Huntington failed to create a distinctive American breed from "Leopard" and "Linden Tree" . But the horsemen of the West, like Mike Ruby, did succeed admirably by unhitching the horse from the carriage and letting it adapt to its surroundings - shaping the descendants of Grant's oriental horses into something quintessentially American. Rounding up cattle on western ranches, they turned out to be very different animals in both use and appearance from the flighty carriage horses that Randolph Huntington or indeed Ulysses Grant would have had in mind.

Although bred to work, Rangerbreds are intensely versatile horses and can be trained to do almost anything. For instance Mike Ruby's son, David, taught one of

---

[415] Ibid. Page 30.

[416] Linda Richards, "Looking at Breeds - the Colorado Rangerbred." *Horse Magazine,* Mar/Apr 1986. Page 8.

his own stallions to "one foot", and horses with ranger blood have competed in all equestrian disciplines - dressage, show jumping, endurance and cross-country. Their blood has touched the race track as well. It seems that "Linden Tree" had the last word on his early detractors. It was undoubtedly his Barb influence that gave these horses their unparalleled using qualities and also the varied coat patterns, for which they are so admired.

    As a type, the Rangerbred would have made an ideal battle horse if it been in existence at the time of the Civil War : compact, comfortable, standing on average 15.2 hands, with unrivaled stamina and speed , a wither that could hold a saddle in any terrain, tough and courageous and able to withstand extremes of climate. The Colorado Ranger is proof of one of Randolph Huntington's favourite mottoes: "blood will tell ". But above all it is a testament to the unique horsemanship of Ulysses Grant.

Bibliography

Primary Printed

Ames, Mary Clemmer, *Ten Years in Washington. Life & Scenes in the National Capital*. A. D. Worthington 1873.
Badeau, Adam, - *Grant in Peace.* S. S Scranton & Co. 1887.
 - *Military History of General U. S. Grant.* Vol .1,11,111. D Appleton & Co. 1888.
Burr, Frank. *The Life and Deeds of General Grant*. J. B. Furman and Co. 1885.
Byers, Major S. H. M., *With Fire and Sword.* Neale Publishing Co. New York. 1911.
Cadwallader, Sylvanus, *Three Years with Grant.* Bison Books. Univ. of Nebraska Press. 1996.
Chetlain, Gen. A.L., *Recollections of Seventy Years.* The Gazette Publishing Co. 1899.
Childs, George, *Recollections*. J. B. Lippincott Co. 1890.
Clews, Henry, *Twenty Eight Years in Wall Street*. Irving Publishing Co. 1888.
Coppee, Henry, *The Life of Grant*. Richardson and Co. New York. 1868.
Crook, W. H., *Memories of the White House*. Little, Brown & Co. 1911.
Dana, Charles A., *The Life of General U. S. Grant*. Gurdon Bill & Co. 1868.
Dana, Charles A. *Recollections of the Civil War*. Collier Books. 1963.
Deming, Henry C., *The Life of Ulysses S. Grant*. S. S. Scranton & Co. 1868.
Depew, Chauncey M., *My Memories of Eighty Years*. Charles Scribner's Sons. 1921.
Dodge, Maj. Gen. Grenville M., *Personal Recollections*. The Monarch Printing Co. 1914.

Dunbar, Alexander, *A Treatise on the Diseases Incident to the Horse.* James and Webb. 1871.

Fancher, P. H. P., *American Farrier and Horse Trainer*. O. H. P Fancher. Louisville, Kentucky. 1867.

Fellman, Michael ed., Young, John Russell, *Around the World with General Grant.* Johns Hopkins Univ. Press 2002.

Garland, Hamlin, *Ulysses S. Grant -His Life and Character*. Doubleday & Mcclure Co. 1898.

Gilbert E. Govan, ed., *The Haskell Memoirs. (*Memoirs of John Haskell*)* .G. P. Putnam's Sons. 1960.

Grant, Jesse R., *In The Days of my Father.* Harper & Bros. 1925.

Grant, Ulysses S.,*Personal Memoirs*. Penguin Classics. 1999.

Hamlin, Capt. Percy: ed.,*The Making of a Soldier. Letters of General R. S. Ewell* . Whittet and Shepperson. 1935.

Hershberger, H. R.,*The Horseman: A Work on Horsemanship.* Henry G. Langley . NY. 1844.

Howe, Henry, *Historical Collections of Ohio: an encyclopedia of the state ; history both general and local, geography ... sketches of eminent and interesting characters, etc., with notes of a tour over it in 1886* . Henry Howe & Son. 1891.

Huntington,Randolph., *General Grant's Arabian horses, Leopard and Linden tree, and their sons Beale and Hegira.* J. B. Lippincott Co. 1885.

Jo Davis's County Republican Central Committee, *Portrait and biographical album of Jo Daviess County, Illinois:containing full page portraits and biographical sketches of prominent and representative citizens of the county*. 1889.

Marcy, Capt. Randolph B., *The Prairie Traveller*. Perigree Books. 1994.

Maury, General Dabney H., *Recollections of a Virginian*. Charles Scribner's Sons. 1894.

McDonald, General John, *Secrets of the Great Whiskey Ring.* Belford, Clark & Co.1880.

McLellan, Charles Arthur, *The Art of Shoeing and Balancing the Trotter.* The Trotter & Pacer 1927.

Palmer, Gen. Friend, *Early Days in Detroit.* Hunt & June. 1906.

Pendel, Thomas F., *Thirty Six Years in the White House.* Neale Publishing Co. 1902.

Porter, Horace, *Campaigning with Grant*. Nebraska University Press. 2000.

Pratt, Prof. O. S., *The Horse's Friend* . Self published.1876.

Rhodes, Robert Hunt, *All for the Union. The Civil War Diary and Letters of Elisha Hunt Rhodes.* Orion Books 1985.
Richardson, Albert D. *A Personal History of Ulysses S. Grant.* American Publishing Co. 1868.
Roberge, David, *The Foot of the Horse.* Lessiter Books. 2001.
Shrady, George, *General Grant's Last Days.* Self Published. 1908.
Simon, John Y. ed., - *The Papers of Ulysses S. Grant.* Vol. 1 - 26. Southern Illinois Univ. Press.
   - *The Personal Memoirs of Julia Dent Grant.* Southern Illinois Univ. Press 1975.
Smith, Matthew Hale, - *Twenty Years on Wall Street.* American Book Co. 1871.
   - *Sunshine and Shadow in New York.* 1880. J. B. Burr Publishing Co.
Splan, John, *Life with the Trotters.* H. T. White Chicago. 1889
Stevens, Walter, *Grant in St. Louis.* The Franklin Club. 1916. Repub. Applewood Books. 2008.
Sumner, Merlin ed., *The Diary of Cyrus B. Comstock.* Morningside House. 1987.
Taylor and Crooks, *Sketchbook of St. Louis.* G. Knapp & Co. 1858.
Townsend, George Alfred, *Historic Sketches at Washington.* James Betts & Co. 1877.
Tripler, Eunice, *Some Notes of her Personal Recollections.* Grafton Press. 1910.
Wallace, W. H. *Wallace's American Trotting Register.* Vol. 1, 3 and 5. Published at the Offices of Wallace's Monthly.
Wilson, James Grant, *General Grant's letters to a Friend. 1861-1880.* T. Y. Crowell & Co. 1897.
Wilson, James Grant, *General Grant.* D. Appleton and Co. 1897.
Wilson, James Grant & Coan, Titus Munson, ed.s., *Personal Recollections of the War of Rebellion. Addresses Delivered Before the New York Commandery of the Loyal Legion of the United States, 1883-1891.* New York. Published by the Commandery, 1891.
Wilson, James Harrison, - *The Life of John A. Rawlins.* Neale Publishing Co. 1916.
   - *Under the Old Flag.* Vol. i and ii. D. Appleton & Co. 1912.
Withers, William T., *High Bred Trotting Stock at Fairlawn Stock Farm.* Seventh Catalogue, 1881. Fifteenth catalogue 1889.
Wood, Lieut. Oliver E., *The West Point Scrap Book: a Collection of Stories, Songs and Legends.* D. Van Nostrund. 1871.
Woodruff, Hiram, *The Trotting Horse of America.* J. B. Ford. 1869.

Young, John Russell, *Men and Memories*. F. Tennyson Neely. 1901.

Secondary

Ambrose, Stephen E., *Duty, Honour, Country. A History of West Point*. Johns Hopkins Univ. Press. 1999.
Armstrong, William H., *Warrior in Two Camps. Ely S. Parker*. Syracuse Univ. Press. 1978.
Arnold, James R., *Jeff Davis's own. Cavalry, Comanches, and the battle for the Texas Frontier*. John Wiley & Sons Inc. 2000.
Bauer, K. Jack, *Zachary Taylor*. Louisiana State University Press. 1985.
Bowker, Nancy, *John Rarey: Horse Tamer*. J. A. Allen & Co. 1996.
Bradford, Gamaliel, *Lee the American*. Dover Publications. 2004.
Bradley, John, *Modern Trotting Sire Lines*. Russell Meerdink Co. 1997.
Catton, Bruce, - *Grant moves South. 1861-1863*. Little, Brown and Co. 1960
  - *Grant takes Command. 1863-1865*. Castle Books. 2000.
Chartrand, Rene, *Santa Anna's Mexican Army 1821- 48*. Osprey Books. 2004.
Christensen, Lawrence O., *Dictionary of Missouri Biography*. University of Missouri Press. 1999.
Cowley, Robert & Guinzburg, Thomas, *West Point. Two Centuries of Honor and Tradition*. Warner Books 2002.
Davenport, Homer, *My Quest of the Arabian Horse*. B.W. Dodge and Co. 1908.
Edwards, Elwyn Hartley, *The Saddle. In Theory and Practice*. J. A. Allen. London. 1990.
Ellington, Charles G., *The Trial of U. S. Grant*. Arthur H. Clark Co. 1987.
Essin, Emmett M., *Shavetails & Bell Sharps*. The History of the U. S. Army Mule. Univ. of Nebrasa Press. 1997.
Foote, Shelby, *The Civil War. A Narrative in Three Volumes*. Pimlico.
  - *Fort Sumter to Perryville*. 2000.
  - *Fredericksburg to Meridian*. 1994.
  - *Red River to Appomattox*. 1999.
Frost, Lawrence A., *U. S. Grant Album*. Bonanza Books. 1966.

Furman, Bess, *White House Profile*. Bobbs- Merrill Co. 1951.
Goldhurst, Richard, *Many are the Hearts*. Reader's Digest Press. 1975.
Grabau, Warren E., *Ninety-Eight Days. A Geographer's View of the Vicksburg Campaign*. Univ. of Tennessee Press. 2000.

Grant III, Ulysses S., *Ulysses S. Grant. Warrior and Statesman*. William Morrow & Co. 1969.
Haslip, Joan, *The Sultan*. Holt, Rinehart & Wilson 1958.
Hatch, Thom, *Clashes of Cavalry*. Stackpole Books. 2001.
Hervey, John, *The American Trotter*. Coward- McCann Inc. 1947.
Hoag, Maury, *Stagecoaching on the California Coast. The Coast line Stage*. Fithian Press. 2001.
Hollandsworth Jr., James G., *Pretence of Glory. The Life of Gen. Nathaniel P. Banks*. Louisiana State Univ. 1998.
Honigsbaum, Mark, *The Fever Trail. In Search of the Cure for Malaria*. Pan Books. 2001.
Howard, Robert West, *The Horse in America*. Follett Publishing Co. Chicago. 1965.
Humphreys, Margaret, *Malaria*. Johns Hopkins Univ. Press. 2001.
Hunt, Frazier and Robert, *Horses and Heroes*. Charles Scribner's & Sons. 1949.
Hurst, Jack, *Nathan Bedford Forrest*. Vintage Books. 1994.
Johnson, Carl H., *The Building of Galena. An Architectural Legacy*. Johnson Creative Inc. 1997.
Johnson, James Ralph & Hoyt, Alfred Bill, *Horsemen Blue and Gray*. Oxford Univ. Press 1960.
Johnson, Robert Underwood, *Remembered Yesterdays*. Little, Brown & Co. 1923.
Johnston, Col William Preston, *The Life of Albert Sidney Johnston*. Da Capo Press. 1997.
Jones, George R. *Joseph Russell Jones*. Privately published. 1964.
Jones, James Pickett, *Yankee Blitzkrieg*. The University Press of Kentucky. 2000.
Josephson, Matthew, *The Robber Barons*. Harvest/ Harcourt Brace & Co 1995.
Kadzis, Peter, *Blood - Stories of Life & Death from the Civil War*. Thunder's Mouth Press & Balliett Fitzgerald Inc. 2000.
Kemble, J. H., *The Panama Route*. Univ. California Press. 1943.
Kinsley, Vera, *A Kingdom for my Horse*. Vera Knisley 1988.
Knopp, Ken R., *Confederate Saddles & Horse Equipment*. Publisher's Press Inc. 2001.

Krick, Robert K., *The American Civil War. The War in the East 1863-1865.* Essential Histories. Osprey Publishing 2001.

Katcher, Philip, *Union Cavalryman 1861-1865.* Osprey.1995.

Kollbaum, Marc E., *Gateway to the West. The History of Jefferson Barracks from 1826-1894.* Vol.1. Friends of Jefferson Barracks. 2002.

Lewis, Lloyd, *Captain Sam Grant.* Little, Brown and Co. 1950.

Lipsey, Julia, *Governor Hunt of Colorado Territory. His life and his Family.* 1960.

Longacre, Edward G., *Lincoln's Cavalrymen.* Stackpole Books. 2000.

Marshall ,Charles, *Lee's Aide-de-Camp.* Univ. of Nebraska Press. 2000.

Mauck, Jeffrey, *U. S. Grant in the War with Mexico.* American Kestrel Books. 1996.

McCarr, Ken, *The Kentucky Harness Horse.* University Press of Kentucky. 1978.

McFeeley, William S. & McFeeley ,Mary Drake, *Grant. Memoirs and Selected Letters.* The Library of America 1990.

Meed, Douglas V., *The Mexican War 1846-1848.* Essential Histories. Osprey 2002.

Morris Jr., Roy, *Sheridan.* Vintage Books 1993.

Morrison, James L., *The Best School. West Point ,1833-1866.* Kent State Univ. Press. 1998.

Nester ,William R., *From Mountain Man to Millionaire. The Life of Robert Campbell.* Univ. of Missouri Press 1999.

O'Bright, Alan W. and Marolf, Kirsten R., *The Farm on the Gravois .Historic Structures Report.* Ulysses S .Grant National Hist .Site. 1999.

Owens, Kenneth N., *Galena, Grant and the Fortunes of War*. Pick & Gad Publications, 1963.

Perry, Mark, *Grant and Twain.* Random House. 2004.

Pines ,Philip, *The Complete Book of Harness Racing.* Arco Publishing. 1982.

Pritzker, Barry, *Mathew Brady* . Bison Books. 1992.

Repp ,Steve, *Ulysses S. Grant. The Galena Years.* Steve Repp. 1985,1994.

Roberts, David, *A Newer World. Kit Carson, John C. Fremont and the Claiming of the American West.* Touchstone Books. 2000.

Rodenbough ,Theo F., *The Photographic History of the Civil War: the Cavalry.* Fairfax Press. 1983.

Ross ,Ishbel, *The General's Wife*. Dodd, Mead and Co.1959.

Rottenberg ,Dan, *The Man who made Wall Street. Anthony J. Drexel and the Rise of Modern Finance*. Univ. of Pennsylvania Press. 2001.

Sarnoff, Paul, *Russell Sage: the Money King*. Ivan Oblensky. 1965.

Sanfilippo, Pamela K., *Agriculture in Antebellum St. Louis*. Ulysses S. Grant National Hist. Site. 2000.

Sears, Stephen W.,*George B. McClellan. The Young Napoleon*. Da Capo Press. 1999.
Simon, John Y. ed., - *Grant and Halleck: Contrasts in Command*. Marquette University Press. 1996.
- *General Grant, with a rejoinder by Mark Twain*. Mathew Arnold. Kent State Univ. Press 1995.
Simpson, Brook D., *Ulysses S. Grant. Triumph over Adversity, 1822-1865*. Houghton Mifflin Co. 2000.
Smith, Jean Edward. *Grant*. Simon & Schuster 2001.
Smith, Col. Nicholas, *Grant, the Man of Mystery*. The Young Churchman Co. 1909.
Steffen, Randy, *United States Military Saddles, 1812-1943*. Univ. of Oklahoma Press. 1973.
Thompson, Gerald, *Edward F. Beale and the American West*. Univ. of New Mexico Press, 1983.
Truman, Margaret, *White House Pets*. David McKay Co. 1969.
Vanderbilt, Arthur T., *Fortune's Children. The Fall of the House of Vanderbilt*. William Morrow. 1989.
Vandiver, Frank E., *Mighty Stonewall*. Texas A & M Univ. Press. 1995.
Ward, Geoffrey C. et al, *The Civil War*. Bodley Head. 1991.
Waugh, John C., *The Class of 1846*. Ballantine Books New York. 1999.
Wert, Jeffrey D.,*General James Longstreet*.Touchstone Books. 1994.
Williams, Kenneth P., *Lincoln finds a General*. Vol. 3 and 5. MacMillan Co.1952 and 1959.
Woodward, W. E., *Meet General Grant*. Garden City Publishing Co. 1928.
Woodworth, Steven E. .ed., *Grant's Lieutenants from Cairo to Vicksburg*. Univ. Press of Kansas, 2001.

General Reference

Bonneville, Captain L.E., *The Adventures of Captain Bonneville*. ed. Washington Irving .The Narrative Press California. 2001.
Carter, Samuel, *Cyrus Field: Man of Two Worlds*. G. P. Putnam's Sons. 1968.
Chestnut, Mary, *A Diary from Dixie*. Gramercy Books. 1997.

Dickens, Charles, *American Notes for General Circulation*. Penguin Classics. 2000.
Hamilton, Jill, *Marengo. The Myth of Napoleon's Horse.* 4th Estate. 2000.
Kaltman, Al, *Cigars, Whiskey & Winning. Leadership Lessons from General Ulysses S. Grant.* PrenticeHall. 1998.
Kehoe, Elizabeth, *Fortune's Daughters.* Atlantic Books. 2004.
Krick, Robert E.L., *Staff Officers in Gray.* Univ. of North Carolina Press. 2003.
Livermore, Mary A., *My Story of the War*. Da Capo Press. 1995.
McPherson, James M., general ed., *To the Best of My Ability . The American Presidents.* DK Publishing. 2004.
Ransom, John, *Andersonville Diary.* Berkley Books.1994.
Seifert, Shirley, *Captain Grant . A Novel.* J. B. Lippincott Co. 1946.
Sheridan, P. H., *Personal Memoirs*. Vol. 1 & 2. Charles L. Webster & Co. 1888.
Sherman, William Tecumseh, *Memoirs*. Penguin. 2000.
Stevens, Peter F., *The Rogue's March: John Riley and the St. Patrick's Battalion.* Brassey's .1999.
Stiles, T. J. *Jesse James :Last Rebel of the Civil War*. Pimlico. 2002.
Twain, Mark, *Autobiography* Vol. 11. Harper & Bros. 1924.

Magazines . Periodicals . Newspapers

American Saddlebred Magazine: Nov /Dec 1998
Arabian Horse World, July 1979.
Atlantic Monthly, Vol. 38. Issue 225.
Bulletin of the Missouri Historical Society, XXXV, 4 (July 1979), pages 191-201. "Grant at Hardscrabble," by John Y. Simon.
Century Magazine. Vol. 30, May 1885.
Chicago Tribune, Sep 24th 1866 , Aug 9th 1885
Colman's Rural World. Nov 19th 1870.
Daily Democratic Times, Mar 9th 1885.
Daily Northwestern, Aug 15th 1903.
Daily Republican. Apr 14th 1897.

Decatur Republican ,Dec 19th 1889.
Eventing. June 2002. Page 20-22.
Fort Wayne Gazette ,May 28th 1881
Granite Monthly Vol. 34 1903, page 95, Alice Bartlett Stevens.
Grant's Forum .(Ulysses S. Grant National Historic Site.) Vol. 1 xii .no. 3. Winter 2003.
Harper's New Monthly Magazine, April 1898, Sept 1876, Vol. LIII.
*Herald and Torchligh*t ,Oct 18th, 1865, 27th Mar 1884. Pg 2.
Horse Magazine Mar/April 1986. "Looking at Breeds - the Colorado Rangerbred." Page 7-8.
"The Colorado Rangerbred in Canada and the Northwestern United States". Page 11-12.
Illinois Historical Journal, lxxix 245-56. "Ulysses S. Grant One Hundred Years Later", Prof. John Y. Simon.
Irish Times, Jan 4th , 1879.
Journal of the House of Representatives 1868-1869, Library of Congress.
Journal of Sport History. Vol. 8. No. 1. Spring 1981. "The First Modern Sport in America: Harness *Racing in New York City*, 1825-1870. by Melvin A. Adelman .
McClure's Magazine , II, 6 (May 1894), pages 532-35. "Some Reminiscences of Grant". *McClure's Magazine* Jan 1896.
McClure's Magazine April 1897.
Midland Monthly, VI, 5 (Nov 1896), pages 387-99.
Mountain Democrat 19th July 1879.
New York Herald ,Dec 19th ,1909
New York Times, June 17th 1885,June 17th 1869,Oct 7th 1872, Dec 27th 1879,June 12th 1881,Feb 7th 1885. Mar 15th 1885.
North American Review, Vol. CXLI, No. 347. (Oct 1885), Pages 361-373.
North American Review, Vol. CXLI, No. 348.(Nov 1885), Pages 421-30.
*Ohio Democra*t, June 26th 1868.
Ohio History, the Scholarly Journal of Ohio historical Soc. Vol. 31.
Paxton Weekly Record, July 4th 1872.
St. Louis Dispatch ,Oct 1st 1875.
St. Louis Globe Democrat, Oct 1st 1875.
Southern Historical Society Papers. Vol. XVIII . Jan-Dec 1890. Vol. XIX.
Spirit of the Times , Sat June 17th 1876.
Steven's Point Gazette, Sept 5th 1885
Sun Herald, May 12th 1927.

Syracuse Herald, Sept 1,1911.
Western Horseman. May/June 1947. April 1949, "Randolph Huntington American Horse Breeder."

CD ROM

Harper's Weekly Vol. 3:Jan 1863- Dec 1863.
Harper's Weekly Vol. 4:Jan 2,1864-Dec 31 1864.
Harper's Weekly Vol. 5:Jan 7 1865- Nov 11,1865.

Internet

http://www.unz.org/
Googlebooks,http://books.google.ie
Internet Archive, http://www.archive.org/
Jstor, www.jstor.org/
http://www.rameltontidytowns.com/robert-bonner/
Library of Congress, http://www.loc.gov/index.html
The Making of America, Cornell University Library,http://digital.library.cornell.edu
Ulysses S. Grant National Historic Site, http://www.nps.gov/ulsg/
Ulysses S. Grant Association. Mississippi State University, http://library.msstate.edu/usgrant

Index

"Abdallah" (trotting sire) 169,184

"Addie", (horse of USG) 140,146,164,165,167

Ammen, Admiral Daniel (friend of USG) 6,101,105,122,123,136,148,176,193

Babcock, Orville (staff officer of USG) 102,130,132

Backman, Charles (horse breeder) 140,157,158,162,173,186,194

Badeau, Adam (staff officer of USG) 78,122,148

Banks, Gen. Nathaniel P. 89,90

Barnes, Bill (USG groom) 118,121

Barrington, Sir John (mayor of Dublin) viii

Beale, General Ned 55,59,172,175,181,187-9,191,193

Bethel (Ohio) 19,45

Bonner, Robert 138,149-52,154-8,164,166,170,188-9,196

Bonneville, Col. Benjamin 50

Borie, Adolph 154,164,170,191

Bowers, Col. Theodore (staff officer of USG) 79

Buchanan, Col. Robert 26,53

Buckner, Gen. Simon Bolivar 54,73

Burnside, Gen. Ambrose 129

"Butcher Boy" (horse of USG) 135,140-2,174

Cadwallader, Sylvanus 79,80,86,87

Carlin, Nat 168,171-2

"Charlie" (horse of Gen. N.P. Banks) 89-91

Childs, George 143,152,154,192,196

"Cicotte Mare" (horse of USG) 45-9

Cincinnati (city) 2,10,24,103,160,165

"Cincinnati" (horse of USG) 68,69,88,97,98,101-7,110,112-4,120,121,125, 128,131,132,135,146,147,152,156,175,176

Colorado Ranger (horse breed) vii,xi,xii, 201-5

Comanche, The 31,32,37,197

Comstock, Col. Cyrus (aide de camp of USG) 16,17,18,97,102,112,119,122

Cox, Edmund 187

Curtin, Richard 160

Dana, Charles A. 78,82,87

"Dave" (horse of USG) 9,13

Davis, Jefferson (president of Confederacy) 81,113

Dent, Ellen Wrenshall (mother-in-law of USG) 28

Dent, Frederick (brother-in-law of USG) 25,43

Dent, "Col." Frederick (father-in-law of USG) 25-7,45,60,143

Detroit 46-8,144

"Dexter" (horse of Robert Bonner) 138,139,149-51,153-7,159,162,163,165,185

Doble, Budd 149,150,163,185

Drexel, Anthony 154

Drexel's Cottage 200

Dunbar, Alexander (farrier) 156,157,161,162

"Eclipse" (horse of USG) 52,53

Elrod, Sarah (Simpson) 136

Elrod, William 136,137,142,165-8,170

"Egypt" (horse of USG) 96-9,101,118,120,121,125,143,146,147

"Ethan Allen" (trotting stallion) x,151,161,163,165,168

Ewell, Capt. Richard 26-7

"Farmer Ralston's Colt" (horse of USG) 1,4

"Fashion" (horse of USG) 24,25

Ford, Charles W. 46,57,65,127,142,143,160,161,164,167,168, 170,171

Fort Humboldt (California) 52,53

Fort Vancouver 50,51,53

Foster, Stephen 47,138

Galena (Illinois) 61-6,72,77,78,79,88,142

"General Blair" (horse of John Rawlins) 77

Georgetown(Ohio) 2,3,4,6,11,13,16,19

Goldsmith, Alden 157,158,169,185,196

Gould, Jay 152,154,157,160,193

Grant, Ellen (Nellie) (daughter of USG) 128,146

Grant, Frederick (son of USG) 49,57,58,64,69,71,84,103,113,114,124,127,128, 170,178,196,198

Grant, Hannah (mother of USG) 1,3,45

Grant, Jesse Root (father of USG) 1-6,9,10,13,19,45,59,61,63,143,154

Grant, Jesse Root (son of USG) 98,99,124-6,128,140,141,143,146-8,170,172,178,180,190

Grant, Julia Boggs Dent (wife of USG) ix,25-8,33,40,43,45-50, 52,56,59-62, 64,67, 68, 70,72,85,88,91,97,99,103,121,127,136,138,140, 143,144,145,159,172,177-9,185-7,192,193,196

Grant, Simpson (brother of USG) 61,103

Grant, Ulysses S.
    boyhood 1-12
    bushwhacking abilities 115
    business acumen 4,48,193
    carriage driving x,46,47,138-44, 146,150-2,164,174, 175, 186,187,194
    circus triumphs 2,7,19,20,33
    Civil War career 63-134
    cure for headaches 6,87,132
    desire for cavalry post xi, 24, 63, 101-2
    dislike of bullfighting 42-3
    dislike of military dress 24-5,63,116
    dislike of tanning business 3,7
    eating habits 58,110
    fearlessness in saddle ix, xii,3,12, 37, 72,178,182
    fondness for cigars 73,84,104,111,121,157,196

fondness for jumping hurdles
  7,18-19,51,83
illness 2, 51,53,60,67,86,140
legendary rides
  27,37,53,82,83,186-7,195
letter-writing x,xii,28,31, 34,43,
  49,58,67,91,97,127,135,136,
  140,142,157,158,159,161,170
liking for horses as gifts
  85,96, 97,99,103-4, 108,
  140,154-5,163,165,166,
  170,173,174,180-1,188,201
love of farming x,xi,3,51,55-6,60,
  79,118-9,136,160,172
love of travel xii,4,9,10,
  12,32, 61,140,177-8,197
loyalty ix,102,134,141,158,172-3
presidency viii,x,141,143-5,
  147,149,150,159,160,164
reconnoitering during Civil War
  69,74,85,93,95,111,114,
  115,118,125,129,135
riding accidents 3,70,89-92,102
riding triumphs at West Point
  ix, 13-22
and trotting culture x,49,138,
  149-60, 165,169,184,
  185,186,192,197

Grant Jun., Ulysses (Buck) (son of USG) 124,128,146,194

Grimsley, Thornton (St. Louis saddler) 36,49,60,65,66,87

Halleck, Gen. Henry 76,79

Hamer, Congressman Thomas 14

Hamid II, Abdul (Sultan of Turkey) xi, 179,180,188,190,191

Hancock, Gen. Winfield Scott 110,198
Hardscrabble Farm xii,56,133

Hawkins, Albert (USG coachman) 146,147,160,198

Hays, Alexander 28,110

Henry Clay horses 163-5,169,188,189,191,204

Hershberger, Henry (riding instructor at West Point) 16-19,21,22,183

Hickok, Orrin 185

Hillyer, William (staff officer of USG) 671,75

Hoey, John 143

Hunt, Alexander Cameron (Gov. Colorado) 174,201

Huntington, Randolph 188,189,190,191,197,200,201,202,204,205

Ingalls, Rufus 18,28,50,119,124

Isthmus of Panana 50,52,193

"Jack" (horse of USG) 68-75,79,80,92-4,96,174

Jackson, Gen. Thomas J. (Stonewall) 17

"Jeff Davis" (horse of USG)
88,92,98,105,108,113-5,118,120,123-6,130,143,
146,147

Jefferson Barracks (St. Louis) vii,
25,26,45,63,161,172

Jenifer, Walter (confederate saddle designer) 109

"Jennie", (horse of USG)
128,146,162,170,173

Jerome, Leonard 139,152

Johnson, President Andrew 139,140

Jones, J. Russell 70,142,174

"Kangaroo" (horse of USG)
64,81,82,85,86,87,88,114

Kiernan, John (farrier) 161

Kitteridge, Herbert 189

Lagow, Clark (staff officer of USG)
78,85,88

Lee, Gen. Robert E.
38,40,100,105-12,115-7,119,121,122,129-34

"Leopard" (horse of USG)
177,181,188-91,197,200,210,202,204

"Lexington" (racing sire) x,
103,106,131,134,166,186,194

Lincoln, Abraham
63,98,105,125,131,136,139

"Linden Tree" (horse of USG)
177,181,188-91,197,200-02,204,205

"Little Rebel" (horse of Grant children)
125,126-8,143,146,148

"Logan" (horse of USG) 146,169,170-2

Long, Fent (Judge) 173

Long Branch (Grant Summer cottage)
143,144,152,154,170,194,196

Longstreet, Gen. James 18,33,45,94,112

Markland, Absolom H. 135

"Maud S." (horse of W. Vanderbilt)
155,156,194,195

McClellan saddle 65,66,109

McDonald, Gen. John 164-5

Meade, Gen. George
38,100,101,105,110,111,118,130,131,139

Mexican War ix,30-44,45,52, 53, 54,
62,66,73,88,93,100,110,134

Mississippi River
25,26,60,71,72,76,81,82,84,90

Missouri
25,26,45,55,56,65,69,71,121,160,164

Monroe, George 186

Morgan (horse bloodline)
49,163,164,165,167,188

Nellie Bly (carriage horse of USG)
47,144

Nelly (horse of USG) 30,37

New York
13,22,54,79,91,138,139,150,152,154,157,184,
185,188,192,194,195,197,198,201

"Old Whitey" (horse of Gen. Z. Taylor)
30

Parker, Ely (staff officer of USG)
59,62,78

Porter, Horace (staff officer of USG)
26,65,98,102,105,110,112,115,120,123

"Psyche" (horse of Julia Dent Grant)
24,26,179

Rawlins, John A. (USG aide-de-camp)
62,71,77,78,87,92,118,128,147,148

Roberge, David (farrier) 156,157

Romero, Mattias 196

"Rondy" (horse of USG) 63,64,79

Rowley, William (staff officer of USG)
62,79

Ruby, Mike vii, 202-5

"Rysdyk's Hambletonian" (trotting sire)
x,138,140,158,162,184

Sackets Harbour 45,46,48,49,57

Sage, Russell 153,154,193

San Patricio Regiment (Mexico) 41

Santa Anna (Mexican leader) 38,39,40

Scott, General Winfield
24,36,38,39,40,41,44

Sheridan, Gen. Philip Sheridan
94,131,132,140,187

"St Julien" (trotting horse) 184,185

St Louis (city) vii,x,xii,25,36,43, 45,48,49,
57,60,61,65,66,71,78,99,103,119,127,128,136,1
37,142,143,160,162,163,164,166,167,172,173,1
74,175,188,196

Sherman, Gen. William T. ix,xi,
14,75,77,84,93,94,113,128,187,198

Shrady, Henry 147

"Silver" (horse of USG) 193-4,196

Splan, John 185

Stanford, Leland 175,186

Stuart, Gen. Jeb 23,109

Taylor, Gen. Zachary
30,31,33,34,37,38,63,124

Tom & Bill (farms horses of USG) 55-60

"Topsey" (horse of USG) 140,163,173

"Traveller" (horse of R.E.Lee) 107-10,115,116,122,130-4,176

Twain, Mark 10,197,198

Tyrrell, Harrison 198

Vanderbilt, William 155,194,195,198

Wallace, John 158,184

Ward, Ferdinand xii,194,195

Washburne, Elihu 65,175

Washington
79,99,101,124,134,136,138,140-5,147,148,160, 163,164,167,175,177,187,188

West Point Military Academy ix,xi, 13-25,28,32,50,60,82,101,102,110,128,139,155, 183,198

White Haven, (St Louis farm and plantation) xii,26,27,49,58, 60,127, 136,162-8,170-3,175,197

White House x, 48,57,128,136,143-8,154,161,165,167,171,172, 175,197

White Mountains 189

Wilson, Col. James Harrison (staff officer of USG) 72,83,94,96,97,117

Woodruff, Hiram 149,151

"York"(West Point horse) 13,20,21,22,28

"Young Hambletonian" (horse of USG) 140,159,162-5,167,169,170,172,173,175